The Chicks' Guide Series

the
chicks
guide to
football

A complete guide to tight ends

by Carol A. Stout

All Rights Reserved. Copyright © 2001 Carol A. Stout

No part of this book may be reproduced or transmitted in any form or by any means,
graphic, electronic, or mechanical, including photocopying, recording, taping or by
any information storage or retrieval system, without the permission in writing from the publisher.

Published by
Millennium Marketing and Publishing

Information in this guide is based on authoritative data available at the time of printing.
Every effort has been made to provide correct information.

Stout, Carol A.
    The chicks guide to football : a complete guide to
tight ends / by Carol A. Stout -- 1st ed.
    p. cm. -- (The chick's guide series)
    Includes index.
    LCCN: 00-093155
    ISBN: 1-886161-07-0

1. Football. I. Title.

GV950.6.S76 2001   796.332'02'024
                                    QBI01-201003

Printed in the United States of America

ACKNOWLEDGMENTS

A special thanks to my family, who kept me focused and fed and my friends for putting up with me and my schedule. Thanks to Jeanie Hambright for her trivia contributions and her dad, Richard "Chief" Hambright. Thank you Mike Waters for your great football pool contribution. A special thanks to the football lover who inspired me to start this project.

Cover Design	Shelly Wells
Book Design and Layout	Shelly Wells and Julie Dhondt
Author Photos	Dana Wright-Wiggens
Illustrations:	Ed Robinson
Edited by	Christa Dickey; Greg Hallaman, Richard Meek

Culinary Contributor: Jennifer Wittman, Art Institute of Los Angeles, Culinary Program

Dallas Cowboys quarterback Troy Aikman and Indianapolis Colts quarterback Peyton Manning. Photo courtesy of *The Indianapolis Star News* via www.Merlin-Net.com.

Indianapolis Colts Edgerrin James and Dallas Cowboys Deion Sanders. Photo courtesy of *The Indianapolis Star News* via www.Merlin-Net.com.

Indianapolis Colts Peyton Manning and his offensive line. Photo courtesy of *The Indianapolis Star News* via www.Merlin-Net.com.

Indianapolis Colts running back Edgerrin James. Photo courtesy of *The Indianapolis Star News* via www.Merlin-Net.com.

Green Bay Packers quarterback Brett Favre. Photo courtesy of *The Dallas Morning News* via www.Merlin-Net.com.

Buffalo Bills quarterback Rob Johnson. Photo courtesy of *The Indianapolis Star News* via www.Merlin-Net.com.

St Louis Rams quarterback Kurt Warner. Photo courtesy of *The St. Louis Post-Dispatch* via www.Merlin-Net.com.

Rams running back Marshall Faulk. Photo courtesy of *The St. Louis Post-Dispatch* via www.Merlin-Net.com.

Patriots quarterback Drew Bledsoe. Photo courtesy of *The Boston Globe* via www.Merlin-Net.com.

Dallas Cowboys quarterback Troy Aikman. Photo courtesy of Ron St. Angelo via www. Merlin-Net.com.

Indianapolis Colts Peyton Manning. Photo courtesy of *The Indianapolis Star News* via www.Merlin-Net.com.

Photos courtesy of the Miami Dolphins, the Arizona Cardinals, the Cincinnati Bengals, the Minnesota Vikings and the Denver Broncos.

NFL and the NFL shield design are registered trademarks of the National Football League. The team names, logos and uniform designs are registered trademarks of the teams indicated.

The AFL League and AFL team insignias depicted herein are trademarks owned by the Arena Football League, LLC and licensed by the AFL and may not be reproduced without its written consent.

Portions of the Official Arena Football League 2001 Record and Fact Book have been reprinted herein through permission granted by the Arena Football League LLC. The AFL retains all rights in these reprinted portions.

Football uniform and equipment for author photographs courtesy of Galyan's Sporting Goods, Castleton Mall, Indianapolis, Indiana.

Referee uniform and equipment for author photographs and official signals courtesy of Galyan's Sporting Goods.

To all those who love the game or love those who love the game.

table of
contents

Miami Dolphins WR Ward Dedric.

Offense

RUNNING BACK

RUNNING BACK

QUARTERBACK

WIDE RECEIVER

WIDE RECEIVER

TACKLE

GUARD

GUARD

CENTER

TACKLE

TIGHT END

TACKLE

END

END

TACKLE

Defense

OUTSIDE LINEBACKER

MIDDLE LINEBACKER

OUTSIDE LINEBACKER

CORNERBACK

CORNERBACK

SAFETY

SAFETY

abbreviations and positions

QB - Quarterback: The leader of the team. Calls the plays, receives the ball from the center. Hands it off to a running back or throws it to a receiver.

C - Center: The guy in the middle who hands off the ball to the quarterback and also blocks for the offensive play.

RB - Running Back: A player who runs with the football. Running backs also are referred to as tailbacks, halfbacks, and wingbacks.

FB - Fullback: A player who is responsible for blocking for the running back and also for pass-blocking to protect the quarterback.

WR - Wide Receiver: A player who uses his speed and quickness to elude defenders and catch the football. Teams use as many as two to five wide receivers on every play.

TE - Tight End: A player who serves as a receiver and also a blocker. This player lines up beside the offensive tackle to the right or the left of the quarterback.

LG - Left Guard: The inner member of the offensive line that lines up left of the quarterback, whose job is to block for and protect the quarterback and ball carriers.

RG - Right Guard: The inner member of the offensive line that lines up right of the quarterback, whose job is to block for and protect the quarterback and ball carriers.

LT - Left Tackle: One of the outer two members of the offensive line

RT - Right Tackle: One of the outer members of the offensive line.

DT - Defensive Tackle: The inner two members of the defensive line, whose job is to maintain their position in order to stop a running play or to run through a gap in the offensive line to pressure the quarterback or disrupt the backfield formation.

DE - Defensive End: The outer two members of the defensive line. Generally, their job is to overcome offensive blocking and meet in the backfield, where they combine to tackle the quarterback or ball carrier. On running plays

St. Louis Rams quarterback Kurt Warner talks on a headset during first-half action at Veterans Stadium in Philadelphia, Pennsylvania.

to the outside, their job is to force the ball carrier either out-of-bounds or toward the pursuit of their defensive teammates.

LB - Linebacker: The players who line up behind the defensive linemen and generally are regarded as the team's best tacklers. Depending on the formation, most teams employ either three or four linebackers on every play. Linebackers often have the dual role of defending the run and the pass.

CB - Cornerback: The players who line up on the wide parts of the field, generally opposite the offensive receivers.

K - Kicker: Special team players who kick extra points (field goals).

S - Safety: The players who line up the deepest in the secondary: the last line of defense. There are free safeties and strong safeties, and must defend the deep pass and also the run. *Free Safety* - The deep guy who rotates into double coverage or roams into centerfield. *Strong Safety* - Lines up near the line to cover the TE (tight end) and provide run support.

Chapter 1
Football Jumpstart

Introduction

Ladies, you know the adage, "if you can't beat 'em, join 'em," right? Well, if you know a football lover, or you love a football lover, then you understand the time demands of watching a sport that starts a pre-season in August with a final sha-bang game at the end of January. Want to talk to your football lover during those months? Then learn this game!

So, the object of the game is for a bunch of men to run headlong into each other, or throw their bodies into the path of a large man running at full speed to stop the opposing team from scoring points. The men, or team as they like to be referred to, scoring the most points wins. Pretty simple? Not on your life!

This book is your guide to the excruciating detail that is the game of football. A complicated game at first, football can be easily "decoded" to a quick study learning the terms and mastering the play strategy behind the sport. You now have access to the mysterious addiction of football followers who file into the stadium on a Sunday afternoon, or camp in front of the television on Monday night. Let's get started!

The first thing to determine is which team is the "good guys" and which are the "bad guys." In this book, we refer to the home team as the good guys, simply because I would hate to be in your shoes rooting for the other team on the "home" turf.

Time

Every football game is divided into quarters. In college and pro football, each quarter lasts 15 minutes; high school quarters last 12 minutes. Halftime is after the second quarter, a 12-minute break that gives players time to rest. Do the math, and the game should only last about 75 real minutes. But, chicks, this is a game played primarily by men and we know how they operate, so expect the game to last two-and-a-half to three hours. College halftimes are often longer, therefore it is not unusal for a game to last 3 1/2 hours.

Miami Dolphins runningback, Autry Denson.

The Kick Off

You will hear the start of a football game referred to as "kick-off." Prior to this, you might see a bunch of over-padded men doing aerobics on the field. These are warm-ups: pre-game stretching and loosening of those very powerful muscles. After this, non-starting players and cheerleaders line up in two rows, and the announcer introduces the starting players and the head coach to the crowd. The National Anthem is played, or performed.

Field Advantage

A coin toss decides which team kicks off. Team captains meet with the officials (referees in black and white) at the center of the field, the 50-yard line. The captain of the visiting team (Bad Guys) calls "heads" or "tails" when the coin is in the air. The team that wins the toss will choose between kicking or receiving. More specifically, the captains will select receiving the opening kickoff or selecting which end zone to defend.

Strategically, a team will want to receive the kickoff, because they will have an opportunity to score by moving the ball first. However, if the wind is blowing strongly toward one end zone, a team may forfeit first rights to the ball, and decide to kick off. When the second half of the game begins, the team that lost the coin toss now has the choice of receiving the third quarter kickoff or selecting the end zone. Remember, the defense is trying to "defend" their own goal. They do not want the other guys crossing their goal line.

A kickoff starts each half of a football game. In pro football, the kickoff takes place from the kicking team's 30-yard line. In college 35-yard line and high school, the kickoff is made from the 40-yard line. The ball is placed on the kicking tee, which is 1" high in the NFL and 2" high in college and high school. The kickoff team, consisting of 11 non-starting players, is known as the special teams unit. You will find a handful of regulars on kicking teams, though usually not many.

The Kick Off Return

The kicking team arranges itself in a semi-straight line behind the line of scrimmage. The kicker stands in the middle of the field near where the football is to be placed for kickoff. Five players line up between the kicker and the sideline on the right side, and five players line up on the kicker's left.

The return team will line up in a variety of formations. There are one or two runners (receivers) near the goal line at the end zone they are defending. They will try to receive the kickoff and run the ball down the field, toward the other end zone.

An official must handle the ball before it is put into play. When the official gives the defensive place kicker the football, the player will signal with an upraised arm that he is ready to kick. The kicker and the other players on the kicking team, lined up about 10 yards behind the ball, begin running forward. They must stay behind the kicker until the ball is kicked. Once the ball is kicked, the game is underway.

The Tackle

Now, this is where tackle football gets its name. Once the ball travels 10 yards downfield, it is a free ball, meaning any player on any team may recover it. When the ball comes down, especially when it's caught, the game takes on a more competitive and fiercer feel. The player in possession of the ball becomes the target! In order to stop the play, and keep the runner from gaining crucial yardage, the defense must bring down or tackle the runner. Once the runner is down, the ball is down. The official places the ball at the point where the tackle took place.

When a kickoff goes out-of-bounds between the goal lines without being touched by the receiving team, the ball belongs to the receivers 30 yards from the spot of the kick.

Know the Downs

Once the kickoff play is over, the offensive and defensive players take the field as the special teams leave. The offense now must move the ball down the field within four plays, called downs. The ball must be moved at least 10 yards in four attempts.

When the offense gains 10 or more yards, it earns another four downs to move the ball another 10 yards. The ball is temporarily out of play after every down and cannot be returned, kicked or advanced. To keep track of the offense's progress toward a first down the situation is known as a "first-and-10," because the offense has 10 yards to go to gain a first down. If your offense ran a play on first down in which you advanced the ball three yards, your status would be "second-and-7," and second down is played with the goal to advance the seven yards to secure a first down.

Play Ball

Before each play begins, the offensive team huddles. The quarterback announces the team's next play, the formation the team is to use and the signal on which the center is to snap the ball. The quarterback crouches behind the center, places his hand under the center's legs and calls the signal. Once the ball is snapped, the quarterback then hands the ball to a running back, or will drop back and throw a pass to one of his open receivers downfield. The quarterback may also keep the ball and "scramble" by running with it. The passer must throw from behind the line of scrimmage, and only the ends and running backs are allowed to catch the pass, unless it is deflected.

The tackles, guards and center from the offensive team must remain behind the line of scrimmage until the quarterback gets rid of the ball. As the quarterback is getting set to throw, the defensive players will cover the receivers and backs. They then can race downfield and block the receiver from catching the ball by knocking it out of the air or trying to intercept the pass. Presuming the ball is caught and moving toward the end zone, the defense will try to tackle the receiver. If successful, the play stops, and the next play starts from the line where the referee determines the previous play ended.

Point Structure

The receiver either carries the ball into the end zone, or receives a pass there, and SIX points are awarded for the touchdown. (TOUCHDOWN: fair ball into the end zone of the opposing team by way of a player.) After a touchdown, the scoring team has a chance for one or two extra points. The options are to kick the ball through the goal posts for a PAT, or point after touchdown or to attempt to run or pass the ball across the goal line for a TWO POINT CONVERSION.

TYPE OF SCORE	POINT
Touchdown	6
Field Goal	3
Safety	2
2-point conversion	2
Point-After-Touchdown	1

A PAT equals ONE extra point. The two-point conversion is a play with one down, and equals, obviously, TWO points. But, say the touchdown is not made. If the team has driven far enough downfield (usually within 30 to 40 yards from the end zone) and they have at least one down remaining, the team in possession of the ball may attempt a THREE-point field goal.

Punt Option

A team will punt when it has tried, unsuccessfully, to move the ball down the field on its first three attempts to make a first down. Say they now have the ball on their own 28-yard line with eight yards to go for a first down. If a team tries for a first down and fails, the other team (defensive team) takes control of the ball. If this happens, the ball is now being played too close to the defensive team's end zone and a touchdown or a field goal is likely.

To avoid this risky situation, the team punts the ball down the field to the defensive team, who runs the ball back down the field in the opposite direction. After the ball is punted, the receiver may raise his hand to signal a fair catch. Making the catch ends the play. The ball now belongs to the defensive team.

Now, the ball has changed possession. The teams move from offense to defense, respectively. Or, in other words, the team that was trying to score is now defending the opposite end zone. A whole new set of players run on field, but the rules don't change! The defense will still fiercely protect their territory (end zone), and the offense will continue to out-maneuver and out-smart its opponents to gain yards down the field. Until time runs out, both teams struggle to put points on their side from strategically moving the ball up and down the field. But, at any time, one team might TURNOVER possession of the ball. Actually, it would be unusual if the ball didn't turnover during a game.

CONGRATULATIONS! You have made it through the fundamentals of the sport! But, there's much more to learn ...

May we suggest a movie?

Rudy (1993)
Sean Astin, Vince Vaughn, Jon Favreau
Astin portrays Daniel "Rudy" Ruettiger, a young man obsessed with the legendary Notre Dame football program. In pursuit of his dream to play for the Fighting Irish, a story develops that shows a stifled relationship between a father and son and the kind of raw determination we all wished we had. Early performances by Vaughn and Favreau (Swingers) round out a great cast. Look forward to a great goosebumps ending.

Any Given Sunday (1999)
Directed by Oliver Stone
Al Pacino, Cameron Diaz, Dennis Quaid, Jamie Foxx, James Woods
An edgy movie, as directed by Stone, shows professional football as big business. Pacino portrays the head coach of a struggling pro team, challenged along the way by the team young and headstrong owner (Diaz), a cocky quarterback (Foxx) impressed more with his new-found fame than his talent and a fading star quarterback (Quaid) fighting to end his career with dignity.

Brian's Song (1971)
James Caan, Billy Dee Williams
Originally made-for-TV, this movie is based on the life and story of Chicago Bears teammates Gale Sayers and Brian Piccolo. A healthy rivalry on-the-field turns into an inspirational friendship when Piccolo is diagnosed with cancer. This movie tugs at your heartstrings, so be prepared to reach for the Kleenex.

The Program (1993)
James Caan, Halle Berry, Omar Epps, Craig Sheffer
Sheffer plays a star quarterback of an esteemed college football program, who participates and succumbs to the intense pressure of his coach and team. Combined with the antics of other players, this movie is a journey through the danger and the glory of college sports. Guys particularly like this movie!

Jerry Maguire (1996)
Tom Cruise, Cuba Gooding, Jr., Renee Zellweger
The movie that made "Show me the money" a common phrase is an excellent behind-the-scenes football flick. The story follows Tom Cruise as Jerry Maguire, super-agent who crashes to reality when his firm fires him and his clients deflect to his rival representative. As he rebuilds his career, he finds a new love and a new reason to live. Watch for cameos from professional players and owners, such as Troy Aikman, Drew Beldsoe and Cowboy's Owner, Jerry Jones.

Remember the Titans (2000)
Denzel Washington, Based on a true story, this movie is inspirational, uplifting and has great football. Back in 1971, when high school football was everything to the residents of Alexandria, Virginia, local officials were forced to integrate the schools and hire a black man, Herman Boone, as head coach of the T.C. Williams Titans. First, he and the older, beloved white coach with more seniority, Bill Yoast, had to learn to work together. Then they were faced with molding a group of rebellious teenage boys into a winning team while teaching them valuable lessons about becoming men. Their respect, friendship and determination healed a town torn by fear, ignorance and prejudice.

Continued on page 65.

chapter 2
In the Beginning

... Man created football. It took more than 200 years to evolve into today's modern version of football. The uniforms are different, the ball is different, and the players have gradually morphed into quicker, bigger and better athletes. This sport's history is quite interesting, as intriguing, you might say, as watching a bunch of guys pat each other on the butt, a seemingly perfectly acceptable gesture under the disguise of a uniform.

History of Football

Many historians place the origin of football in the sport of rugby, which began entirely by chance in 1823 at the famous Rudger's boys' school in England. At the time, American students at Princeton University were already playing a game they called "balloon," in which they used their fists, and later their feet, to advance the ball. The freshman and sophomore classes at Harvard competed in a type of football game on the first Monday of each school year—called Bloody Monday because the game was so rough. Organized football began earlier in high schools than in colleges, with games on the Boston Common starting in about 1860. A 17-year-old student organized the Oneida Football Club of Boston, which played between 1862 and 1865.

Colleges began to organize football games after the American Civil War ended in 1865. The so-called Princeton Rules were established in 1867, with 25 players on each team. The first football was patented that year. Rutgers College also established football rules in 1867, and its location a short distance from Princeton led the two schools into what has been called the first intercollegiate football game. It was played on November 6, 1869, at Rutgers, but the game was actually more like soccer. Rutgers won that historic game, six goals to four. For the next few years some colleges continued to play the soccer-type game.

In 1871, Harvard students began playing the "Boston Game," which included elements of rugby (the player could pick up the ball and, if pursued, run with it) and soccer (kicking a round ball was still essential). Two years later, representatives of Columbia, Princeton, Rutgers, and Yale met in New York City to formulate the first intercollegiate football rules for the soccer-style game. (Harvard chose not to attend because its playing rules were different.)

Next McGill University of Montreal challenged Harvard to a series of games. The schools played two games at Harvard in the spring of 1874: the first with Harvard rules, and the second with Canadian rugby rules, using the egg-shaped ball. After the McGill games, Harvard challenged Yale to a football game that was played under mixed soccer and rugby rules in November 1875. In 1876, Yale, Princeton, Harvard, and Columbia established the Intercollegiate Football Association, which set the size of the field at 140 by 70 yards and the number of players on a team at 15.

The evolution from the rugby-style game to what became the modern game of American football began under the direction of Walter Camp, the Yale coach who is known as the Father of American Football. Yale had not officially joined the association until 1879 because it was holding out for 11-man teams. Led by Camp, the rules committee soon cut the number of players per side from 15 to 11. The committee also cut the size of the field to 110 by 53 yards. In addition, Camp instituted a type of scrimmage in which a player snapped the ball back by kicking it to the quarterback. In 1882, Camp also introduced the system of downs. (At first, a team had three downs to advance the ball 5 yards or give up possession; the number of yards was changed to 10 in 1906, and the fourth down was added in 1912.) Tackling below the waist was legalized in 1888. Professional football began in 1895, in Latrobe, Pa., after the Intercollegiate Football Association was disbanded in shambles.

Within a decade, concern about the increasing brutality of the game led some colleges to ban football. Mass plays, involving such formations as the flying wedge, had seriously injured nearly 180 players, including 18 who were killed. In 1905, President Theodore Roosevelt called on Harvard, Princeton, and Yale to help save the sport. Representatives of 13 Eastern schools met at year-end and agreed on reforms. At a second meeting, attended by more than 60 schools, the group appointed a seven-member Football Rules Committee and set up the Intercollegiate Athletic Association, which became the NCAA five years later.

The new rules makers revolutionized football by legalizing the forward pass, which resulted in a more open style of play. They also prohibited all the rough mass plays, and teammates were prohibited from locking arms to clear a path for their ballcarrier. To further minimize mayhem, they reduced the length of the game from 70 to 60 minutes and established the neutral zone, which separates the teams by the length of the ball before each play begins.

Chronological History of the National Football League from the Pro-football Hall of Fame

1869

- Rutgers and Princeton play the first ever college soccer football game on November 6 using modified London Football Association rules. This leads to the proliferation of rugby, which sparks the development of modern Football.

1876

- The first rules are written for American football at the Massosoit Convention.
- Walter Camp becomes involved with the game. He will later be known as the Father of American football.

1892

- Former Yale All-America guard William (Pudge) Heffelfinger becomes the first professional football player on November 12. He is paid $500 to play for the Allegheny Athletic Association (AAA) in a game against the Pittsburgh Athletic Club (PAC). The AAA won the game 4-0 on Heffelfinger 's 25-yard fumble return for a touchdown.

1893

- The PAC becomes the first team to sign a player to a professional contract. The player is probably halfback Grant Dilbert, and the contract covers all of the PAC 's games for the year.

1895

- John Brallier is the first player to openly turn pro, being paid $10 plus expenses to play for the Latrobe YMCA against the Jeanette Athletic Club.

1896

- The AAA becomes the first team to field a completely professional team. All of their players are paid for their two-game schedule.

1897

- The Latrobe Athletic Association follows the AAA 's lead by fielding an entirely professional team for its full season of play.

1898

- The touchdown is changed from four points to five.

1899

- Chris O 'Brien forms a neighborhood team on the south side of Chicago known as the Morgan Athletic Club. The team will later be known as the Normals, then the Racine (for a street in Chicago) Cardinals, the Chicago Cardinals, the St. Louis Cardinals, the Phoenix Cardinals, and finally, in 1994, the Arizona Cardinals. The Cardinals remain the oldest continuing operation in professional football.

1900

- Taking over the team payments for the Duquesne Country and Athletic Club, William C. Temple becomes the first known individual club owner.

1902

- Major League Baseball 's Philadelphia Athletics and Philadelphia Phillies form professional football teams. They join with the Pittsburgh Stars in the first attempt at a pro football league. The league is known as the National Football League.

- The Athletics win the first football game played at night, 39-0 over Kanaweola AC in Elmira, New York, on November 21.

- All three teams claim the first pro football championship, but the league president, Dave Berry, gives the Stars the title.

- A five-team tournament is played at New York's original Madison Square Garden. Dubbed the World Series of pro football, it consists of the Orange (New Jersey) AC, the Warlow AC, the Syracuse AC, the New York Knickerbockers, and a team made up of players from Philadelphia's Athletics and Phillies, but simply named New York.

- In the World Series, New York and Syracuse play the first indoor football game in front of 3,000 people on December 28. Syracuse wins 6-0 and goes on to win the tournament with Glen (Pop) Warner at guard.

1903

- The Franklin (Pennsylvania) Athletic Club wins the second, and last, World Series. They beat out the Oreos AC of Asbury Park, New Jersey, the Watertown Red and Blacks, and the Orange AC.

- Pro football becomes popular in Ohio when the Massillon Tigers, an accomplished amateur team, hires four pros from Pittsburgh to play against Akron in their season finale.

- Pro football declines in Pennsylvania and the emphasis in the sport shifts to Ohio.

1904

- The field goal is changed from five points to four.

- There are at least seven pro teams in Ohio. The Massillon Tigers win the Ohio Independent championship, which is equivalent to the pro title.

- There is some talk of forming a state-wide league. Such a move would be intended to end spiraling salaries brought on by constant bidding for players, and to write universal rules for the game. The talk goes nowhere and the attempt to create a formal league fails.

- Halfback Charles Follis signs a contract with the Shelby (Ohio) AC. He is the first known black pro football player.

1905

- The Canton AC, later to become the Canton Bulldogs, turns professional.

- Massillon again wins the Ohio League championship.

1906

- The forward pass is legalized. The first pass completion occurred on October 27 when George (Peggy) Parratt of Massillon threw to Dan (Bullett) Riley in a victory over a combined Benwood-Moundsville team.

- Heated rivals Canton and Massillon play twice, with Canton winning the first game but Massillon winning the second game and the Ohio League championship.

- A betting scandal, coupled with financial difficulties brought about by paying huge salaries, causes a temporary decline in interest in Canton, Massillon, and the state of Ohio.

1909

- The field goal is dropped from four points to three.

1912

- The touchdown is increased from five points to six.

- Jack Cusack revives a strong professional team in Canton.

1913

- Jim Thorpe plays for the Pine Village Pros in Indiana. He is a former football and track star at Carlisle Indian School (Pa.). He is also a double gold medal winner at the 1912 Olympics in Stockholm.

1915

- Massillon fields a major team and revives its old rivalry with Canton.

- Cusack signs Thorpe to play for Canton for $250 a game.

1916

- Canton goes 9-0-1 behind the play of Thorpe and Pete Calac to win the Ohio League championship.

1917

- Canton again wins the Ohio League championship despite an upset loss to Massillon.

1919

- The Canton team is turned over from Cusack to Ralph Hay and wins another Ohio League championship.

- Earl (Curly) Lambeau and George Calhoun organize the Green Bay Packers. Lambeau 's employer, the Indian Packing Company, provides $500 for equipment and allows the team to use the company 's field for practices. The Packers go 10-1.

1920

- Pro football is plagued by three major problems — dramatically rising salaries, players jumping from one team to another chasing the highest offer, and the use of college players still enrolled in school.

- An organizational meeting is held to discuss the possibility of a league in which all the members would follow the same rules. The Akron Pros, Canton Bulldogs, Cleveland Indians, and Dayton Triangles are represented at this meeting. It is held at the Jordan and Hupmobile Auto Showroom in Canton, Ohio on August 20. The American Professional Football Conference is born as a result of this meeting.

- A second meeting is held with representation from four states - Akron, Canton, Cleveland, and Dayton from Ohio, the Hammond Pros and Muncie Flyers from Indiana, the Rochester Jeffersons from New York, and the Rock Island Independents, Decatur Staleys, and Racine Cardinals from Illinois. At this meeting the name of the league is changed to the American Professional Football Association. Jim Thorpe is elected president and Stanley Cofall of Cleveland is elected vice president. A membership fee of $100 is charged to each club but no team ever pays it. Scheduling is left to the teams. This leads to wide variations in the overall number of games played and in the number of games played against APFA member teams.

- Sometime during the year, the Buffalo All-Americans, Chicago Tigers, Columbus Panhandles, and Detroit Heralds join the league.

- The first game featuring an APFA team is played at Rock Island 's Douglas Park on September 26. The Independents defeat St. Paul Ideals 48-0 in front of 800 spectators.

- On October 3, the first game between APFA teams is held. At Triangle Park in Dayton, Ohio, the Triangles defeat Columbus 14-0. Lou Partlow of Dayton scores the first touchdown in a game between Association teams. On the same day, Rock Island defeats Muncie 45-0.

- A series of late-season games between championship contenders Akron, Buffalo, Canton, and Decatur leaves Akron as the only undefeated team in the Association. Some of the teams, including the Chicago Tigers and Detroit Heralds, finish their seasons, disband, and have their franchises canceled by the Association.

- At one game, Akron sells tackle Bob Nash to Buffalo for $300 and five percent of the gate receipts. This is the first APFA player deal.

1921

- At the league meeting in Akron on April 30, the previous season's title is granted to the Akron Pros. The APFA is reorganized. Joe Carr of the Columbus Panhandles is named president and Carl Storck of Dayton is the secretary-treasurer.

- Carr moves the Association's headquarters to Columbus, gives teams territorial rights, restricts player movement, develops membership criteria for franchises, drafts a league constitution and by-laws, and issues standings for the first time with the intention of giving the APFA a clear champion.

- The Association grows to 22 teams, including the Green Bay Packers who are awarded to John Clair of the Acme Packing Company.

- Thorpe moves from Canton to the Cleveland Indians, but is hurt early in the season and sees very little action.

- A.E. Staley turns the Decatur Staleys over to player — coach George Halas. Halas moves the team to Cubs Park in Chicago. Staley pays Halas $5,000 to keep the name Staleys for one more year. Halas is partnered with Ed (Dutch) Sternaman.

- The Staleys claim the APFA championship with a 9-1-1 record, as does Buffalo with a 9-1-2 record. Carr rules in favor of the Staleys, giving Halas his first championship.

1922

- Clair and the rest of the Green Bay management withdraw from the APFA after admitting the use of players who had college eligibility remaining during the 1921 season. Curly Lambeau promises to obey league rules and buys back the franchise with $50 of his own money. Bad weather and low attendance cause Lambeau to go broke but he receives a $2,500 loan from local merchants to keep the team running. A public non-profit corporation is set up to operate the team, with Lambeau as head coach and manager. This setup remains in place today.

- The Association changes its name to the National Football League on June 24.

- The Chicago Staleys become the Chicago Bears.

- The league fields 18 teams, including the Oorang Indians of Marion, Ohio. Oorang is an all-Indian team featuring Thorpe, Joe Guyon, and Pete Calac, sponsored by the Oorang dog kennels.

- Led by player-coach Guy Chamberlin and tackles Link Lyman and Wilber (Pete) Henry, Canton emerges as a powerhouse, going 10-0-2.

1923

- For the first time, all of the franchises considered part of the NFL field teams.

- Thorpe plays first for Oorang, then for the Toledo Maroons. Against the Bears, Thorpe fumbles and Halas returns it 98 yards for a touchdown. This record lasts until 1972.

- Canton goes undefeated for the second year in a row with an 11-0-1 record, earning the NFL title.

1924

- The league fields 18 teams with new franchises in Kansas City, Kenosha, and Frankford, a section of Philadelphia.

- Although Canton was successful on the field they were unsuccessful at the box office and the owner of the Cleveland franchise purchases them. He keeps the Canton franchise inactive while using the best players for his Cleveland team, which he renames the Bulldogs.

- Cleveland wins the title with a 7-1-1 record.

1925

- The NFL awards five new franchises - the New York Giants to Tim Mara and Billy Gibson for $500, the Detroit Panthers, featuring Jimmy Conzelman as owner, coach, and tailback, the Providence Steam Rollers, a new Canton Bulldogs team, and the Pottsville Maroons. Pottsville had probably been the most successful independent pro team.

- The first player limit is established at 16.

- After the University of Illinois' season ends, the Chicago Bears sign All-America halfback Harold (Red) Grange. A crowd of 36,000 - the largest in pro football history - witness the Bears battle to a scoreless tie against the Chicago Cardinals on Thanksgiving Day. In December, the Bears conduct a barnstorming tour, playing eight games in 12 days in St. Louis, Philadelphia, New York, Washington, Boston, Pittsburgh, Detroit, and Chicago. Seventy-three thousand attend the game against the Giants at the Polo Grounds, which serves as a needed boost in the arm for the troubled New York franchise. The Bears go on to play nine more games in the South and West, including a game against the Los Angeles Tigers in front of 75,000 fans.

- League-leading Pottsville schedules a game against a team of former Notre Dame players to be played in Shibe Park in Philadelphia on December 12. Frankford protests on the grounds that the game is in Frankford's protected territory, and it is to be played the same day as a Yellow Jackets home game. Carr decides to forbid the game and gives three separate notices to Pottsville informing them of this. Pottsville played the game anyway. The day of the game, Carr fines the club, suspends it from all rights and privileges (including the right to play for the NFL championship), and returns its franchise to the league.

- The Cardinals, with the best record in the league, are named the 1925 champions.

1926

- C.C. Pyle, Red Grange's manager, demands that the Bears pay Grange a five-figure salary and give him one-third ownership of the team. The Bears refuse. Pyle leases Yankee Stadium in New York and petitions the league for a franchise. The league refuses. He then starts the first American Football League. The league lasts one season and includes Grange's New York Yankees as well as eight other teams. The Philadelphia Quakers win the AFL championship and play a December game against the New York Giants, the seventh-place team in the NFL. The Giants win the game 31-0 and the AFL folds.

- Halas pushes through a rule prohibiting any team from signing a player whose college class has not graduated.

- The league grows to 22 teams. One of these teams is the Duluth Eskimos, who sign All-America fullback Ernie Nevers of Stanford. Nevers gives the league a gate attraction to rival Grange. Dubbed the Iron Men of the North, the Eskimos play 29 exhibition and league games, 28 of which are on the road. Nevers plays in all but 29 minutes of the games.

- In December, Frankford scores in the final two minutes against the Bears to take the game 7-6 and move ahead of the Bears in the standings. Frankford goes on to win the championship.

1927

- A special meeting is held in Cleveland on April 23. Carr decides to solidify the league's future by eliminating the financially weaker franchises and consolidating the quality players onto a limited number of teams. The NFL now consists of 12 teams and the league 's epicenter shifts to the east coast.

- Grange's New York Yankees are one of the remaining 12 franchises but he suffers a knee injury and the Yankees finish in the middle of the pack. The Yankees were later absorbed into the NFL.

- The New York Giants win the championship, posting 10 shutouts in 13 games.

1928

- Red Grange and Ernie Nevers retire from pro football.

- Duluth disbands as the NFL falls to only 10 teams.

- The Providence Steam Rollers win the championship. Providence plays its home games in the Cycledrome, a 10,000 seat oval built for bicycle races.

1929

- Chris O 'Brien sells the Chicago Cardinals to David Jones on July 27.

- A fourth official, the field judge, is added on July 28.

- Grange and Nevers return from retirement. Nevers scores six rushing touchdowns and four extra points as the Cardinals beat Grange's Bears 40-6. The 40 points scored by Nevers sets the record, which remains the oldest in the NFL.

- Providence hosts the Cardinals on November 3, becoming the first NFL team to host a game at night under floodlights.

- The Packers edge the Giants and quarterback Benny Friedman to win their first NFL championship with the help of back Johnny Blood McNally, tackle Cal Hubbard, and guard Mike Michalske.

1930

- The Dayton Triangles, the last of the NFL's original franchises, are purchased by William B. Dwyer and John C. Depler. They move the team to Brooklyn and change the name to the Dodgers.

- The Spartans of Portsmouth, Ohio, enter the league.

- The Packers edge the Giants for the championship.

- The Bears are the league's most improved team with All-America rookie fullback-tackle Bronko Nagurski. Halas retires as a player and replaces himself as a coach with Ralph Jones. Jones refines the T-formation, introducing wide ends and a halfback in motion.

- The Giants play an exhibition against a team of former Notre Dame players coached by Knute Rockne, winning 22-0 before 55,000 fans at the Polo Grounds. Proceeds go to the New York Unemployment Fund to help those suffering in the Great Depression. The convincing victory brings credibility to the NFL in the eyes of the press and the public.

1931

- The NFL shrinks to 10 teams and Frankford folds halfway through the season.

- Carr fines the Bears, Packers, and Spartans $1,000 each for using players that had not graduated college.

- The Packers become the first team to win three consecutive NFL championships, beating out the Spartans who were led by rookie backs Earl (Dutch) Clark and Glenn Presnell.

1932

- A franchise is awarded in Boston to George Preston Marshall, Vincent Bendix, Jay O'Brien, and M. Dorland Doyle. The team is called the Braves and loses money in its first year. Due to financial losses, Marshall is left as the sole owner at the end of the year.

- NFL membership drops to eight teams — the lowest in NFL history.

- Official statistics are kept for the first time.

- The First Playoff Game.
  From the start of the National Football League in 1920, every league championship was determined based on the regular season standings. Then in 1932, the Portsmouth Spartans and the Chicago Bears finished their regularly scheduled games tied for first place. So, for the first time in NFL history, a one-game playoff was staged to determine the 1932 championship. However, a blizzard with deep snow and sub-zero wind chill blew into Chicago and made it impossible to play the game at Wrigley Field. So, the game was moved indoors at Chicago Stadium and played on a modified field — only 60 yards long and 30 feet narrower. The end zones were not regulation size and the sidelines butted up against the stands. The Bears proceeded to shutout the Spartans, (who in 1934 moved to Detroit and became the Lions) 9-0. The lone touchdown of the game was a disputed pass play from Bronko Nagurski to Red Grange. Rules at the time stipulated that a forward pass had to be thrown from at least five yards behind the line of scrimmage.
  The Spartans contested that Nagurski did not drop back five yards before firing the jump pass to Grange. The play stood and the Bears later added a safety to put the final touches on their victory. The game became a benchmark for a new era in pro football. Because of the cramped quarters of the unusual venue, several NFL rules changes were employed for the following season.

1933

- The NFL makes its first departure from the college game, adopting a number of significant rule changes to suit its preferred style of play. Hash marks and goal posts placed on the goal lines are adopted — direct innovations of the 1932 title game. On February 25, the forward pass was legalized from anywhere behind the line of scrimmage.

- On July 8, Marshall and Halas sponsor a proposal dividing the NFL into two divisions, with the winners to meet in an annual championship game.

- Three new franchises are awarded — the Pittsburgh Pirates to Art Rooney, the Philadelphia Eagles to Bert Bell and Lud Wray, and the Cincinnati Reds.

- The Staten Island Stapletons suspend operations for a year, never returning to the league.

- Halas buys out Sternaman, becoming sole owner of the Bears, and reinstates himself as head coach.

- Marshall changes the names of the Boston team from the Braves to the Redskins.

- David Jones sells the Chicago Cardinals to Charles W. Bidwell.

- In the first NFL championship game to be scheduled before the season, the Western Division champion Bears defeat the Eastern Division champion Giants 23-21 at Wrigley Field on December 17.

1934

- G.A. (Dick) Richards purchases the Portsmouth Spartans, moves them to Detroit, and renames them the Lions.

- The Bears play to a scoreless tie against a team consisting of the best college football players in the country on August 31. The game is played before 79,432 fans at Soldier Field and the Bears' impressive showing brings new prestige to the league.

- The Reds lose their first eight games before being suspended from the league for defaulting on payments. The St. Louis Gunners, an independent team, join the NFL by buying the Reds and go 1-2 over the final three weeks.

- Rookie Beattie Feathers becomes the league's first 1,000-yard rusher. He gains 1,004 yards on 101 carries.

- The Giants trail the Bears 13-3 in the championship game before deciding to switch to basketball shoes. Their improved footing in the extremely cold and icy atmosphere of the Polo Grounds helps them to come back for a 30-13 win on December 9. The game has since been known as the Sneakers Game.

- The player waiver rule is adopted on December 10.

1935

- The NFL adopts Bert Bell's proposal to hold an annual draft of college players. The draft will begin on May 19, 1936, with teams selecting in an inverse order of finish.

- The hash marks are moved nearer the center of the field, 15 yards from the sidelines.

- All-American end Don Hutson of Alabama joins the Packers.

- The Lions defeat the Giants 26-7 for the title on December 15.

1936

- For the first time in league history, there are no franchise transactions. It is also the first year in which all teams play the same number of games.

- University of Chicago halfback and Heisman Trophy winner Jay Berwanger becomes the first player ever selected in the NFL draft. On February 8, he goes to the Philadelphia Eagles. The Eagles trade his rights to the Bears, but Berwanger never plays pro football.

- The first drafted player to actually sign a contract was the No. 2 pick, Riley Smith of Alabama, who was selected by Boston.

- A rival league is formed, the second to call itself the American Football League. The Boston Shamrocks win the AFL title.

- The NFL championship is won by Green Bay, 21-6, over the Redskins. Although the Redskins were supposed to host the game in Boston, it was moved to the Polo Grounds in New York because of poor attendance.

1937

- A franchise in Cleveland is awarded to Homer Marshman on February 12. They are known as the Rams.

- Marshall moves the Redskins to Washington, D.C. on February 13.

- The Redskins sign TCU All-America tailback Sammy Baugh, who leads them to a 28-21 victory over the Bears in the championship game on December 12.

- The Los Angeles Bulldogs win the AFL's second title before the fledgling league folds.

1938

- With Halas 's backing, Hugh (Shorty) Ray becomes a technical advisor on rules and officiating.

- A new rule provides for a 15-yard penalty for roughing the passer.

- The Giants defeat the Packers 23-17 in the championship game on December 11.

- Marshall, Los Angeles Times sports editor Bill Henry, and promoter Tom Gallery establish the Pro Bowl. It is to be played between the NFL champion and a team of professional all-stars.

1939

- The New York Giants win the first Pro Bowl game 13-10 on January 15 at Wrigley Field.

- Carr dies in Columbus on May 20. He has been NFL president since 1921. Carl Storck is named acting president on May 25.

- The first televised NFL game occurs when the Brooklyn Dodgers play the Philadelphia Eagles at Ebbets Field. NBC broadcasts the game to approximately 1,000 TV sets in New York.

- Green Bay defeats New York 27-0 in the title game held at Milwaukee.

- NFL attendance exceeds 1 million in a season for the first time.

1940

- The third rival league to call itself the American Football League is formed. The Columbus Bullies win the AFL championship.

- Halas' Bears defeat Washington 73-0 for the title in the most decisive game in NFL history on December 8. The game popularizes the Bears' T-formation with a man in motion. It is the first championship game carried on net-work radio. The game, broadcast by Red Barber, is transmitted to 120 stations of the Mutual Broadcasting System, which paid $2,500 for the rights.

- Art Rooney sells the Pittsburgh Pirates to Alexis Thompson on December 9. He then buys a part interest in the Philadelphia Eagles

1941

- Elmer Layden becomes the NFL's first com-missioner on March 1. Acting president Carl Storck resigns on April 5.

- NFL headquarters are moved to Chicago.

- Bell and Rooney trade the Eagles to Thompson for the Pirates. They then re-name the team the Steelers.

- Homer Marshman sells the Rams to Daniel F. Reeves and Fred Levy, Jr.

- League by-laws are revised so ties in division races will be decided by playoffs and ties in playoff games will be decided in sudden death overtime.

- The official NFL Record Manual is published for the first time.

- Columbus again wins the AFL championship but the two-year-old league folds.

- The first divisional playoff game in league his-tory is made necessary when the Bears and Packers finish tied for the Western Division title. The Bears win the divisional playoff game 33-14, then defeat the Giants 27-9 for the NFL title on December 21.

1942

- Players departing for World War II service deplete NFL rosters. Halas leaves his team in midseason to join the Navy and Luke Johnson and Heartley (Hunk) Anderson serve as co-coaches for the Bears.

- After going 11-0 in the regular season, the Bears lose to the Redskins, 14-6, in the championship game on December 13.

1943

- With co-owners Reeves and Levy in military service, the Rams are granted permission to suspend operations for one season on April 6. Levy transfers his stock in the team to Reeves on April 16.

- The NFL adopts free substitution on April 7.

- The wearing of helmets is made mandatory.

- A 10-game schedule is approved for all teams.

- Philadelphia and Pittsburgh receive permission to merge for one season on June 19. The team is known as Phil-Pitt, but is referred to as the Steagles by its fans. They divide home games between the two cities and Earl (Greasy) Neale of Philadelphia and Walt Kiesling of Pittsburgh serve as co-coaches. The merger automatically dissolves on the last day of the season, December 5.

- Ted Collins is awarded a franchise for Boston. It becomes active in 1944.

- Sammy Baugh leads the league in passing, punting, and interceptions. The Redskins beat the Giants 28-0 in a divisional playoff for the Eastern Division title, then lose 41-21 to the Bears for the league title on December 26.

1944

- Unable to have a franchise in Yankee Stadium in New York, Collins names his new team in Boston the Yanks.

- The Brooklyn Dodgers change their name to the Tigers.

- Coaching from the bench is legalized on April 20.

- The Cardinals and Steelers receive permission to merge for one season on April 21. They are known as Card-Pitt and are coached by Phil Handler of the Cardinals and Walt Kiesling of the Steelers. The merger automatically dissolves on the last day of the season, December 3.

- In the championship game on December 17, Green Bay beats the New York Giants 14-7.

1945

- The hash marks are moved in to 20 yards from the sidelines.

- Brooklyn and Boston merge. They play home games in both cities and are simply known as the Yanks. They are coached by former Boston head coach, Herb Kopf.

- The Brooklyn franchise withdraws from the league and joins the new All-America Football Conference. All players on its active and reserve lists are assigned to the Yanks, who once again become the Boston Yanks.

- Returning from Navy service, Halas rejoins the Bears late in the season. While Halas takes over much of the team's control, Anderson and Johnson remain the coaches of record throughout the season.

- Philadelphia's Steve Van Buren leads the NFL in rushing, kickoff returns, and scoring.

- At the end of World War II, 638 former or active NFL players have served in the war, with 21 of them dying in action.

- Cleveland beats the Redskins 15-14 for the NFL championship behind rookie quarterback Bob Waterfield on December 16.

1946

- The contract of Commissioner Layden is not renewed. He is replaced by Bert Bell, co-owner of the Steelers, on January 11.

- Bell moves the league headquarters to Bala-Cynwyd, a suburb of Philadelphia.

- Free substitution is withdrawn. Substitutions are limited to no more than three men at a time.

- Forward passes are made immediately incomplete upon contact with the goal post on January 11.

- Reeves receives permission to move the NFL-champion Rams to Los Angeles.

- Halfback Kenny Washington and End Woody Strode sign with the Rams on March 21 and May 7, respectively. They become the first African-Americans to play in the NFL in the modern era.

- The rival All-America Football Conference begins play with eight teams. The Cleveland Browns defeat the New York Yankees 14-9 for the first AAFC title behind the coaching of Paul Brown.

- Steeler Bill Dudley leads the NFL in rushing, interceptions, and punt returns, winning the Most Valuable Player award.

- Backs Frank Filchock and Merle Hapes of the Giants are questioned regarding a New York man's attempt to fix the championship game against the Bears. Bell suspends Hapes, but allows Filchock to play.

- Filchock plays well for the Giants but they still lose the championship game to the Bears, 24-14, on December 15.

1947

- A fifth official, the back judge, is added.

- For the first time, a bonus choice is created for the NFL draft. One team each year will make the special selection before the first round begins. The Chicago Bears win a lottery and the rights to the first choice. With this choice they select Bob Fenimore of Oklahoma A&M.

- The New York Yankees lose to the Cleveland Browns, 14-3, in the second AAFC title game.

- Charles Bidwell, Sr., owner of the Cardinals, dies on April 19. His wife and sons retain ownership.

- The Cardinals win the NFL championship game 28-21 over the Philadelphia Eagles on December 28. The Eagles reach the championship by defeating Pittsburgh 21-0 in a divisional playoff.

1948

- Plastic helmets are prohibited.

- A flexible, artificial tee is permitted at the kickoff.

- Officials other than the referee are equipped with whistles, rather than horns, on January 14.

- Fred Mandel sells the Detroit Lions to a syndicate headed by D. Lyle Fife on January 15.

- Los Angeles' Fred Gehrke paints horns on the Rams' helmets. These are the first modern helmet emblems in pro football.

- The Cleveland Browns win their third straight AAFC championship. They go 14-0 in the regular season and then defeat the Buffalo Bills 49-7.

- The Eagles take the NFL championship 7-0 over the Cardinals in a blizzard on December 19.

1949

- Alexis Thompson sells the champion Eagles to a syndicate headed by James P. Clark on January 15.

- The Boston Yanks become the New York Bulldogs, sharing the Polo Grounds with the Giants.

- Free substitution is adopted for one year on January 20.

- There are two 1,000-yard rushers in the NFL for the first time. Steve Van Buren of Philadelphia and Tony Canadeo of Green Bay both achieve the mark.

- The AAFC plays with a one-division, seven-team format. Bell announces a merger agreement on December 9. Three AAFC franchises - Cleveland, San Francisco, and Baltimore - will join the NFL in 1950.

- The Browns win the fourth and final AAFC title over the 49ers, 21-7, on December 11.

- The Eagles beat the Rams in a driving rain, 14-0 for the NFL title on December 18.

1950

- Unlimited free substitution is restored, paving the way for two platoons and specialization in the pro game on January 20.

- Curly Lambeau, Green Bay 's founder and coach since 1921, resigns under fire on February 1.

- After three months as the National-American Football League, the National Football League name is restored.

- The American and National conferences are created, replacing the Eastern and Western divisions on March 3.

- The New York Bulldogs become the Yanks, dividing the players of the AAFC 's Yankees with the Giants.

- A special allocation draft is held. The 13 teams draft the remaining AAFC players, with special consideration given to Baltimore, which receives 15 choices compared to 10 for everyone else.

- The Los Angeles Rams are the first team to have all of their games - home and away - televised. The Redskins soon follow suit. Other teams arrange to put selected games on television.

- Former AAFC champion Cleveland defeats defending NFL champion Philadelphia 35-10 in the first game of the season.

- Deadlocks occur in both conferences for the first time, forcing dual divisional playoffs. The Browns defeat the Giants in the American

Conference and the Rams defeat the Bears in the National Conference.

- Cleveland takes the NFL championship by defeating Los Angeles 30-28 on December 24.

1951

- Dormant since 1942, the Pro Bowl game is revived under a new format. All-Stars from each conference are matched at the Los Angeles Memorial Coliseum. The American Conference defeats the National Conference, 28-27, on January 14.

- Abraham Watner returns the Baltimore franchise and its player contracts to the league for $50,000. Baltimore 's former players are made available for drafting along with college players on January 18.

- A rule is passed on January 18 prohibiting tackles, guards, or centers from catching a forward pass.

- The Rams reverse their television policy and televise only road games.

- The first coast-to-coast NFL championship game telecast sees the Rams defeat the Browns 24-17 on December 23. The DuMont Network pays $75,000 for the rights to the game.

1952

- Ted Collins sells the New York Yanks franchise back to the league on January 19. A new franchise is awarded to a group in Dallas after it purchases the assets of the Yanks on January 24. The new team, the Texans, goes 1-11. The owners turn the franchise back to the league in midseason. The team is operated by the commissioner's office for the last five games of the season. The franchise is canceled at the end of the season. This is the last time that an NFL franchise failed.

- The Steelers are the last team to abandon the Single-Wing for the T-formation.

- The Lions win their first NFL title in 17 years, defeating the Browns 17-7 on December 28.

1953

- A Baltimore group headed by Carroll Rosenbloom is granted a franchise and is awarded the holdings of the defunct Dallas organization on January 23. The team will be known as the Colts.

- The Colts put together the largest trade in league history, acquiring 10 players from Cleveland in exchange for five.

- The American and National conferences are changed to the Eastern and Western conferences on January 24.

- Jim Thorpe dies on March 28.
- The founder of the Cleveland Browns, Mickey McBride, sells the franchise to a syndicate headed by Dave R. Jones on June 10.
- U.S. District Court Judge Allan K. Grim upholds the NFL's "TV" policy of blacking out home games on November 12 in Philadelphia.
- The Lions defeat the Browns again for the NFL championship, 17-16, on December 27.

1954

- The Canadian Football League begins a series of raids on NFL teams. They sign quarterback Eddie LeBaron and defensive end Gene Brito of Washington and defensive tackle Arnie Weinmeister of the Giants, among others.
- 49ers fullback Joe Perry becomes the first player in league history to rush for 1,000 yards in consecutive seasons.
- Cleveland defeats Detroit 56-10 for the NFL championship on December 26.

1955

- The Rams beat the Giants 23-17 in sudden death overtime in a preseason game in Portland, Oregon. It is the first use of the sudden death overtime rule in a preseason game.
- A new rule declares the ball dead immediately if the ball carrier touches the ground with any part of his body except his hands or feet while in the grasp of an opponent.
- The Baltimore Colts sign Johnny Unitas as a free agent.
- Otto Graham plays his last game as the Browns defeat the Rams 38-14 in the NFL championship game on December 26. Graham quarterbacked the Browns to 10 championship game appearances in 10 years.
- NBC replaces DuMont as the network for the title game, paying $100,000 for the rights.

1956

- The NFL Players Association is founded.
- Grabbing an opponent 's face mask (other than the ball carrier) is made illegal.
- Using radio receivers to communicate with players on the field is prohibited.
- A natural leather ball with white end stripes replaces the white ball with black end stripes for night games.
- The Giants move from the Polo Grounds to Yankee Stadium.
- Halas retires as coach of the Bears, and is replaced by Paddy Driscoll.

- CBS becomes the first network to broadcast some NFL regular-season games to selected television markets across the nation.
- The Giants blow out the Bears, 47-7, in the championship game on December 30.

1957

- Pete Rozelle is named General Manager of the Rams.
- Anthony J. Morabito, founder and co-owner of the 49ers, dies of a heart attack during a game against the Bears at Kezar Stadium on October 28.
- An NFL-record crowd of 102,368 watches the 49ers-Rams game at the Los Angeles Memorial Coliseum on November 10.
- Detroit overcomes a 20-point deficit for a 31-27 playoff victory over the 49ers. The Lions go on to defeat Cleveland 59-14 for the title on December 29.

1958

- The bonus selection in the draft is eliminated on January 29. Quarterback King Hill of Rice is the last bonus selection made by the Chicago Cardinals.
- Halas reinstates himself as coach of the Bears.
- Cleveland's Jim Brown gains an NFL-record 1,527 yards rushing.
- In a divisional playoff game, the Giants hold Brown to eight yards and defeat Cleveland 10-0.
- Led by coach Weeb Ewbank, Baltimore beats the Giants 23-17 in the first sudden death overtime NFL championship game on December 28. Colts fullback Alan Ameche wins the game on a one-yard touchdown run after 8:15 of overtime.

1959

- Vince Lombardi is named head coach of the Green Bay Packers on January 28.
- Tim Mara, the co-founder of the Giants, dies on February 17.
- Lamar Hunt of Dallas announces his intention to launch a second pro football league. A meeting is held in Chicago on August 14 consisting of Hunt representing Dallas, Bob Howsam of Denver, K.S. (Bud) Adams of Houston, Barron Hilton of Los Angeles, Max Winter and Bill Boyer of Minneapolis, and Harry Wismer of New York City. The make plans to begin play in 1960.
- The new league becomes the fourth to be known as the American Football League on August 22.

- Buffalo, owned by Ralph Wilson, becomes the seventh franchise on October 28. Boston, owned by William H. Sullivan, becomes the eighth team on November 22.

- Joe Foss is named AFL Commissioner on November 30.

- An additional draft of 20 rounds is held by the AFL on December 2.

- NFL Commissioner Bert Bell suffers a heart attack and dies at Franklin Field in Philadelphia during the last two minutes of a game between the Eagles and the Steelers on October 11. Treasurer Austin Gunsel is named president in the office of the commissioner on October 14.

- The Colts defeat the Giants again for the NFL championship, 31-16, on December 27.

1960

- Pete Rozelle is elected NFL Commissioner as a compromise choice on the twenty-third ballot on January 26.

- Rozelle moves the league offices to New York City.

- Hunt is elected AFL president for 1960 on January 26.

- Minneapolis withdraws from the AFL on January 27. The same ownership is given an NFL franchise for Minnesota on January 28 to start in 1961.

- An NFL franchise is awarded on January 28 to Dallas to begin play in 1960.

- Oakland receives an AFL franchise on January 30.

- The AFL adopts the two-point option on PAT attempts on January 28.

- A no-tampering verbal pact, relative to players' contracts, was agreed to between the NFL and AFL on February 9.

- The Chicago Cardinals move to St. Louis on March 13.

- The AFL signs a five-year television contract with ABC on June 9.

- The Boston Patriots beat the Buffalo Bills in front of 16,000 fans in Buffalo on July 30. It is the AFL's first preseason game.

- The Denver Broncos defeat the Patriots 13-10 before a crowd of 21,597 in Boston in the AFL's first regular season game on September 9.

- Philadephia defeats the Packers 17-13 in the NFL championship game on December 26.

1961

- In the first AFL championship game, the Houston Oilers defeat the Los Angeles Chargers 24-16 before 32,183 fans on January 1.

- Bears end Willard Dewveall plays out his option and then joins the AFL 's Oilers on January 14. He becomes the first player to deliberately jump from one league to the other.

- Ed McGah, Wayne Valley, and Robert Osborne buy out their partners in the Oakland Raiders on January 17.

- The Chargers move to San Diego on February 10.

- David R. Jones sells the Browns to a group headed by Arthur B. Modell on March 22.

- The Howsam Brothers sell the Broncos to a group headed by Calvin Kunz and Gerry Phipps on May 26.

- NBC is awarded a two-year deal for the radio and television rights to the NFL championship game for $615,000 on April 5. Three-hundred thousand dollars of that sum goes directly into the NFL Player Benefit Plan.

- Canton, Ohio, home to the NFL 's formation in 1920, is chosen as the site of the Pro Football Hall of Fame on April 27. Former Redskins executive Dick Cann is named Executive Director.

- Representative Emanuel Celler sponsors a bill in Congress to legalize single-network television contracts by professional sports leagues. It passes the House and Senate and is signed into law by President John F. Kennedy on September 30.

- Houston defeats San Diego 10-3 for the AFL championship on December 24.

- Green Bay wins its first NFL championship since 1944, defeating the New York Giants 37-0 on December 31.

1962

- The Western Division defeats the Eastern Division, 47-27, in the first AFL All-Star Game, played before 20,973 in San Diego on January 7.

- Both leagues prohibit grabbing any player's face mask.

- The AFL makes the scoreboard clock the official timer of the game.

- The NFL agrees to a $4.65 million annual contract with CBS for telecasting rights to all regular season games on January 10.

- Judge Roszel Thompson of the U.S. District Court in Baltimore ends a two-and-a-half year antitrust lawsuit by ruling in favor of the NFL against the AFL on May 21. The AFL had charged the NFL with monopoly and conspiracy in the areas of expansion, television, and player signings. The trial lasted two months.

- McGah and Valley acquire controlling interest in the Raiders on May 24.

- The AFL assumes financial responsibility for the New York Titans on November 8.

- Daniel F. Reeves regains the ownership of the Rams. With Commissioner Rozelle as referee, Reeves outbids his partners in sealed-envelope bidding for the team on November 27.

- The Dallas Texans defeat the Oilers, 20-17, for the AFL championship in a game lasting a record 77 minutes and 54 seconds on December 23. Tommy Brooker kicks a 25-yard field goal to end the sudden death overtime and win the game.

- Judge Edward Weinfeld of the U.S. District Court in New York City upholds the legality of the NFL's television blackout within a 75-mile radius of home games, and denies an injunction that would force the championship game to be televised in New York City.

- The Packers beat the Giants, 16-7, for the NFL title on December 30.

1963

- The Dallas Texans move to Kansas City and change their name to the Chiefs on February 8.

- The New York Titans are sold to a five-man syndicate headed by David (Sonny) Werblin on March 28.

- The Titans are renamed the Jets and Weeb Ewbank is hired as the team's new coach on April 15. The team begins play in Shea Stadium.

- NFL Properties, Inc. is founded to serve as the NFL's licensing arm.

- Commissioer Rozelle suspends Green Bay halfback Paul Hornung and Detroit defensive tackle Alex Karras for placing bets on their own teams and on other NFL games. Five other Detroit players are fined $2,000 each for betting on a game in which they did not participate. The Lions are also fined $2,000 on each of two counts for failure to report information promptly and for lack of sideline supervision.

- Paul Brown, the only coach Cleveland has ever had, is fired and replaced by Blanton Collier.

- Don Shula replaces Weeb Ewbank as coach of the Colts.

- The AFL allows the Jets and Raiders to select players from other teams in an effort to create greater competitive balance on May 11.

- NBC is granted exclusive broadcasting rights for the 1963 AFL Championship Game for $926,000 on May 23.

- The Pro Football Hall of Fame is dedicated in Canton, Ohio on September 7.

- The U.S. Fourth Circuit Court of Appeals reaffirms the lower court 's finding for the NFL in the $10 million suit brought by the AFL, ending three-and-a-half years of litigation on November 21.

- Jim Brown sets the NFL rushing record with 1,863 yards for the Browns.

- Boston wins the first AFL divisional playoff game 26-8 over Buffalo on December 28.

- The Bears win the NFL championship over the Giants, 14-10, on December 29. The title is Halas' sixth, a record, and will be his last in his 36 years as coach of the Bears.

1964

- The Chargers beat the Patriots 51-10 in the AFL championship game on January 5.

- William Clay Ford purchases the Lions on January 10. Ford has been the team's president since 1961.

- A group representing the late James P. Clark sells the Eagles to a group headed by Jerry Wolman on January 21.

- Carroll Rosenbloom, the majority owner of the Colts since 1953, acquires complete ownership of the team on January 23.

- The AFL signs a five-year, $36 million television contract with NBC to begin with the 1965 season on January 29.

- Rozelle negotiates an agreement on behalf of the NFL teams to purchase Ed Sabol 's Blair Motion Pictures on March 5. It is renamed NFL Films.

- Hornung and Karras are reinstated by Rozelle on March 16.

- CBS submits the winning bid of $14.1 million per year for the 1964-65 regular season television rights on January 24.

- CBS acquires the rights to the 1964-65 NFL championship games for $1.8 million per game on April 17.

- Pete Gogolak of Cornell signs with the Buffalo Bills. He is the first soccer-style kicker in pro football.

- Buffalo defeats San Diego 20-7 for the AFL title on December 26.

- Cleveland wins the NFL title 27-0 over Baltimore on December 27.

- Joe Namath signs with the Jets for a stunning $400,000.

1965

- All NFL teams pledge not to sign any college seniors until they have completed all of their games, including bowl games on February 15. The Commissioner is empowered to punish violating clubs as severely as the loss of an entire draft.

- A sixth official, the line judge, is added on February 19.

- The color of the officials' penalty flags is changed from white to bright gold on April 5.

- A new NFL franchise is awarded to Rankin Smith, Sr., on June 30 to begin play in 1966. The team will be known as the Atlanta Falcons.

- Miami is awarded a new AFL franchise on August 16 to begin play in 1966. They will be known as the Dolphins, owned by Joe Robbie and Danny Thomas.

- Field Judge Burl Toler becomes the first African-American official in the NFL on September 19.

- Professional football is named as the fans' favorite sport in a Harris survey in October. Fans choose pro football (41 percent) over baseball (38 percent).

- Green Bay defeats Baltimore 13-10 in a sudden-death divisional playoff game, and goes on to beat the Browns 23-12 in the NFL championship game on January 2.

- The Bills again defeat the Chargers, 23-0, for the AFL championship on December 26.

- CBS acquires the rights to the NFL regular-season games in 1966 and 1967, with an option for 1968, for $18.8 million per year on December 29.

1966

- The AFL and NFL spend a combined $7 million to sign their draft picks. The NFL signs 75 percent of its 232 draftees, the AFL 46 percent of its 181.

- Rozelle names Buddy Young Director of Player Relations on February 1. Young is the first African-American to work in the league office.

- The rights to the 1966 and 1967 NFL championship games are purchased by CBS for $2 million per game on February 14.

- Foss resigns as AFL Commissioner on April 7. Raiders head coach and general manager Al Davis is named to replace him on April 8.

- The NFL standardizes goal posts as being offset from the goal line, painted bright yellow, and with uprights 20 feet above the cross-bar on May 16.

- A series of secret meetings are held with Hunt of Kansas City and Tex Schramm of Dallas regarding a possible AFL-NFL merger in the spring.

- On June 8, Rozelle announces an AFL-NFL merger. The two leagues will combine to form a 24-team league. The new league will be increased to 26 in 1968 and to 28 in 1970, or soon thereafter. All existing franchises will be retained and none will be transferred outside their existing metropolitan areas. The leagues will maintain separate schedules through 1969, but an annual AFL-NFL World Championship Game will be played, beginning in January 1967. A combined draft will also begin in 1967. Official regular-season play will begin in 1970 when the two leagues have merged to form a single entity with two conferences. Rozelle is named commissioner of the expanded setup.

- Davis returns to the Raiders and Milt Woodard is named president of the AFL on July 25.

- The Cardinals move into newly constructed Busch Stadium.

- Barron Hilton sells the Chargers to a group headed by Eugene Klein and Sam Schulman on August 25.

- Congress approves the AFL-NFL merger and passes legislation to exempt the agreement from antitrust action on October 21.

- New Orleans is awarded an NFL franchise to begin play in 1967 on November 1. They will be known as the Saints and John Mecom, Jr., of Houston is designated majority stockholder and president of the franchise on December 15.

- The NFL is realigned for the 1967-69 seasons on December 2. There will be a Capitol and a Century Division in the Eastern Conference and a Central and a Coastal Division in the Western Conference.

- New Orleans and the Giants agree to switch divisions in 1968 and return to the 1967 alignment in 1969.

- CBS and NBC purchase the rights to televise the Super Bowl for four years for $9.5 million on December 13.

1967

- Green Bay defeats Dallas 34-27 on January 1 to win the NFL championship and the right to represent the league in the first AFL-NFL World Championship Game. On the same day, the Chiefs defeat Buffalo 31-7 to represent the AFL.

- The Packers defeat the Chiefs 35-10 before 61,946 fans at the Los Angeles Memorial Coliseum on January 15. It is the first game ever played between AFL and NFL teams. The Packers earn $15,000 each for the win, and the Chiefs each receive $7,500. The game is televised both by CBS and NBC.

- The "sling-shot" goal post and a six-foot-wide border around the field are made standard in the NFL on February 22.

- Baltimore makes Michigan State defensive lineman Bubba Smith the first choice in the first combined AFL-NFL draft on March 14.

- The AFL designates a new franchise on May 24 to begin play in 1968 in Cincinnati. The franchise is awarded to a group with Paul Brown as part owner, general manager, and head coach on September 27.

- Cleveland Browns president Arthur B. Modell is elected president of the NFL on May 28.

- Defensive back Emlen Tunnell of the New York Giants becomes the first African-American player to enter the Pro Football Hall of Fame on August 5.

- Denver beats Detroit in a 13-7 preseason game on August 5. It is the first victory by an AFL team over an NFL team.

- Green Bay again beats Dallas for the NFL championship 21-17 on a last-minute, 1-yard quarterback sneak by Bart Starr in 13-below-zero weather in Green Bay on December 31. The game becomes known as the "Ice Bowl." Oakland defeats Houston 40-7 for the AFL title on the same day.

1968

- Green Bay wins Super Bowl II, 33-14 over Oakland in Miami on January 14. The game has the first $3 million gate in pro football history.

- Vince Lombardi resigns as head coach of the Packers on January 28, remaining as general manager.

- Werblin sells his shares in the Jets to his partners Don Lillis, Leon Hess, Townsend Martin, and Phil Iselin on May 21. Lillis assumes the presidency of the club. He dies on July 23. Iselin is appointed president on August 6.

- Halas retires for the fourth, and last, time as coach of the Bears on May 27.

- The Oilers move from Rice Stadium to the Astrodome, becoming the first NFL team to play in a domed stadium.

- On November 17, the Raiders score two touchdowns in the last 42 seconds to beat the Jets 43-32. Millions of television fans fail to see the final 1:05 of the game and the ensuing comeback because NBC cuts away so it can broadcast the movie *Heidi* on time. After dealing with thousands of irate fans, unwritten television rules dictate that all games carried on television will be broadcast through their conclusion. The game becomes known as the "Heidi Bowl."

- Ewbank becomes the first coach to win titles in both the AFL and NFL when the Jets defeat the Raiders 27-23 for the AFL championship on December 29. Baltimore defeats the Browns 34-0 for the NFL title on the same day.

1969

- A playoff format is established for the AFL's 1969 season on January 11. The winner in one division will play the runner-up in the other.

- An AFL team wins the Super Bowl for the first time when the Jets defeat the Colts 16-7 in Miami on January 12 in Super Bowl III. The title Super Bowl is recognized in the NFL for the first time. The Jets' victory also brings creditibility to the AFL.

- Vince Lombardi becomes part owner, executive vice-president, and head coach of the Washington Redskins on February 7.

- Wolman sells the Eagles to Leonard Tose on May 1.

- Baltimore, Cleveland, and Pittsburgh join the AFL teams to form the 13-team American Football Conference of the NFL in 1970 on May 17.

- The NFL creates a playoff format which includes one "wild card" team per conference, that team being the second-place team with the best record.

- *Monday Night Football* is created. ABC acquires the rights to televise 13 NFL regular-season Monday night games in 1970, 1971, and 1972.

- Redskins president emeritus George Preston Marshall dies on August 9 at 72.

- The NFL marks its 50th year by wearing a special patch by each of the 16 teams.

1970

- Kansas City defeats Minnesota 23-7 in Super Bowl IV in New Orleans on January 11. The gross receipts of approximately $3.8 million are the largest ever for a one-day sporting event.

- Four-year television contracts are announced January 26. CBS will televise all the NFC games and NBC will televise all the AFC games (excluding Monday night games). The two networks will divide the Super Bowl and Pro Bowl games.

- Art Modell resigns as NFL president on March 12. Milt Woodard follows suit by resigning as AFL president on March 13. Lamar Hunt is elected AFC president and George Halas is elected NFC president on March 19.

- The newly-merged league makes several rule changes, putting names on the backs of players' jerseys, making a point after touchdown worth only one point, and making the scoreboard clock the official timing device of the game on March 18.

- The Pittsburgh Steelers move into Three Rivers Stadium.

- The Cincinnati Bengals move into Riverfront Stadium.

- Lombardi dies of cancer on September 3 at age 57.

- Tom Dempsey of New Orleans kicks a game-winning, NFL-record 63-yard field goal against Detroit on November 8.

1971

- Jim O'Brien's 32-yard field goal with five seconds remaining lifts Baltimore over Dallas 16-13 in Super Bowl V at Miami on January 17. The NBC telecast is viewed in an estimated 23,980,000 homes, the largest audience ever for a one-day sporting event.

- The NFC defeats the AFC 27-6 in the first AFC-NFC Pro Bowl in Los Angeles on January 24.

- The Boston Patriots change their name to the New England Patriots on March 25. They christen their new home, Shaefer Stadium, with a 20-14 preseason victory over the Giants.

- The Philadelphia Eagles leave Franklin Field for the new Veterans Stadium.

- The San Francisco 49ers leave Kezar Stadium for Candlestick Park.

- Rams President and GM Daniel F. Reeves dies at 58 on April 15.

- The Dallas Cowboys move from the Cotton Bowl to Texas Stadium on October 24.

- Miami defeats Kansas City 27-24 in the longest game in NFL history. Garo Yepremian's 37-yard field goal wins the AFC divisional playoff game after 82 minutes and 40 seconds of play on December 25.

1972

- Dallas beats Miami 24-3 in Super Bowl VI in New Orleans on January 16. CBS's telecast is viewed in an estimated 27,450,000 homes, the top-rated one-day telecast ever.

- On March 23 the hash marks are moved nearer to the center of the field: 23 yards, one foot, nine inches from the sidelines.

- The method is changed by which ties effects win-lose percentages on May 24. Tie games previously were not counted in the standings. Now, they are made equal to a half-game won and a half-game lost.

- Robert Irsay buys the Los Angeles Rams on July 13. He then transfers ownership of the club to Carroll Rosenbloom in exchange for the Baltimore Colts.

- William V. Bidwill buys out his brother's, Charles (Stormy) Bidwill, stock in the Cardinals to become sole owner on September 2.

- The National District Attorneys Association endorse the position of professional leagues in opposing proposed legalization of gambling on professional team sports on September 28.

- The Steelers gain their first postseason win ever, 13-7, over the Raiders, on Franco Harris' "Immaculate Reception" on December 23.

1973

- Rozelle announces on January 3 that all Super Bowl VII tickets have been sold and that the game will be telecast in Los Angeles, the site of the game, on an experimental basis.

- Miami completes the first perfect season by beating Washington 14-7 in Super Bowl VII on January 14 to finish the year 17-0. The NBC telecast is watched by 75 million people.

- A jersey numbering system is adopted on April 5: 1-19 for quarterbacks and specialists, 20-49 for running backs and defensive backs, 50-59 for centers and linebackers, 60-79 for defensive linemen and interior offensive linemen other than centers, and 80-89 for wide receivers and tight ends. Players who have been in the league prior to 1973 are allowed to keep their old numbers.

- Congress adopts experimental legislation (for three years) requiring any NFL game which has been declared a sellout 72 hours prior to kickoff to be made available for local television on September 14. The legislation provides for an annual review to be made by the Federal Communications Commission.

- The Buffalo Bills move from War Memorial Stadium to Rich Stadium in nearby Orchard Park.

- The Giants' final game in Yankee Stadium ends in a 23-23 tie against the Eagles on September 23. The Giants finish the rest of the season at the Yale Bowl in New Haven, Connecticut.

- The rival World Football League is formed on October 2. It plans to begin play in 1974.

- O.J. Simpson of Buffalo sets the NFL single-season rushing mark with 2,003 yards.

1974

- Miami defeats Minnesota 24-7 in Super Bowl VIII in Houston on January 13. The CBS telecast is viewed by approximately 75 million people.

- Rozelle signs a 10-year contract on February 27, effective January 1, 1973.

- Tampa Bay is awarded a franchise on April 24. The team will be known as the Buccaneers, which will begin play in 1976.

- A series of rule changes are implemented to increase the action and tempo of the game on April 25.
  - One sudden-death overtime period is added for preseason and regular-season games.
  - Goal posts are moved from the goal line to the end lines.
  - Kickoffs are moved from the 40- to the 35-yard line.
  - After missed field goals from beyond the 20-yard line, the ball is to be returned to the line of scrimmage.
  - Restrictions are placed on members of the punting team to open up return possibilities.
  - Roll-blocking and cutting of wide receivers is eliminated.
  - Downfield contact between a defender and an eligible receiver is restricted.
  - Penalties for offensive holding, illegal use of the hands, and tripping are reduced from 15 to 10 yards.
  - Wide receivers blocking back toward the ball within three yards of the line of scrimmage are prohibited from blocking below the waist.

- Larry Csonka, Jim Kiick, and Paul Warfield of the Miami Dolphins all sign with the Toronto Northmen of the WFL on March 31.

- Seattle is awarded a franchise on June 4 to begin play in 1976. The team will be known as the Seahawks.

- Seahawks president Lloyd W. Nordstrom and Buccaneers president Hugh Culverhouse sign franchise agreements on December 5.

- The Birmingham Americans defeat the Florida Blazers 22-21 in December in the WFL 's World Bowl for the league title.

1975

- Pittsburgh wins Super Bowl IX 16-6 over Minnesota in New Orleans. It is the Steelers ' first championship since joining the league in 1933. The NBC telecast is viewed by approximately 78 million people.

- The divisional winners with the highest won-loss percentage are made the home team for the divisional playoffs, and the surviving winners with the highest percentage made home teams for the championship games on June 26.

- Referees are equipped with wireless microphones for all preseason, regular-season, and playoff games.

- Detroit moves into the Pontiac Silverdome.

- The Giants move into Shea Stadium.

- The Saints move into the Louisiana Superdome.

- The World Football League folds on October 22.

1976

- Pittsburgh defeats Dallas 21-17 in Super Bowl X in Miami. The Cowboys become the first wild card team to play in the Super Bowl. An estimated 80 million people view the CBS telecast.

- Seahawks president Lloyd Nordstrom dies at 66 on January 20. He is succeeded by his brother Elmer as the majority representative of the team.

- The use of two 30-second clocks is adopted for all games on March 16. The clocks are to be visible to both players and fans to note the official time between the ready-for-play signal and the snap of the ball.

- An expansion draft is held to stock Seattle and Tampa Bay with 39 players each on March 30-31. Seattle and Tampa Bay each receive eight extra choices in the college draft on April 8-9.

- The Giants move into Giants Stadium in East Rutherford, New Jersey.

- St. Louis beats San Diego 20-10 in a preseason game before 38,000 in Korakuen Stadium in Tokyo on August 16. It is the first NFL game played outside North America.

1977

- Oakland defeats Minnesota 32-14 in Super Bowl XI in Pasadena on January 9, marking the fifth consecutive Super Bowl victory by the AFC. The paid attendance sets a professional record at 103,438. The NBC telecast is viewed by 81.9 million.

- The NFL Players Association and the NFL Management Council ratify a new collective bargaining agreement which extends until 1982.

- The San Francisco 49ers are bought by Edward J. DeBartolo, Jr., on March 28.

- A 16-game regular season and 4-game pre-season is adopted on March 29.

- A second wild card team is adopted for the playoffs beginning in 1978, creating a first-round "Wild Card Game."

- The Seahawks are permanently aligned in the AFC Western Division and the Buccaneers in the NFC Central Division on March 31.

- Rule changes are made to open up the passing game and cut down on injuries. Defenders are permitted to make contact with eligible receivers only once. The head slap is outlawed. Offensive linemen are prohibited from thrusting their hands to an opponent 's neck, face, or head. Wide receivers are prohibited from clipping, even in the legal clipping zone.

- Rozelle negotiates what industry sources consider to be the largest single television package ever negotiated on October 12. All three networks will divide all NFL regular-season and postseason games, along with selected preseason games for the next four years.

- Chicago Bear Walter Payton sets the single-game rushing record with 275 yards on 40 carries against Minnesota on November 20.

1978

- Dallas wins Super Bowl XII by defeating Denver 27-10 in the Louisiana Superdome in New Orleans on January 15. More than 102 million people view the CBS telecast. This makes it the most watched show of any kind in the history of television.

- Seventy percent of the nation's sports fans say they follow football according to a Louis Harris Sports Survey on January 19. This is in comparison to 54 percent for baseball.

- A seventh official, the side judge, is added to the officiating crew on March 14.

- More rules are implemented to open up the game on March 17. Defenders are permitted to maintain contact with a receiver within five yards of the line of scrimmage, but contact is restricted beyond that point. The pass-blocking rule is interpreted to permit the extending of arms and open hands.

- A study is done during seven nationally televised preseason games on the use of instant replay as an officiating aid.

- The NFL plays its first game in Mexico City when the Saints defeat the Eagles 14-7 in a preseason game on August 5.

- NFL paid attendance exceeds 12 million (12,772,800) for the first time, bolstered by the regular-season expansion from 14 to 16 games. The per-game attendance of 57,017 is the third highest in NFL history and the most since 1973.

1979

- Pittsburgh wins Super Bowl XIII by beating Dallas 35-31 in Miami on January 21. The NBC telecast is viewed in more than 35 million homes, by an estimated 96.6 million fans.

- More rule changes are made to enhance player safety on March 16. Players on the receiving team are prohibited from blocking below the waist during kickoffs, punts, and field-goal attempts. The wearing of torn or altered equipment and exposed pads is prohibited. The zone in which there can be no crackback blocks is extended. Officials are instructed to quickly whistle a play dead when a quarterback is clearly in the grasp of a tackler.

- Rams president Rosenbloom drowns at 72 on April 2. His widow, Georgia, assumes control of the club.

1980

- Pittsburgh wins its fourth Super Bowl by defeating the Rams 31-19 in Super Bowl XIV in Pasadena on January 20. The game is watched in a record 35.3 million homes.

- Rule changes place greater restrictions on contact in the area of the head, neck, and face. Under the heading of "personal foul," players are prohibited from directly striking, swinging, or clubbing on the head, neck, or face. Starting in 1980, a penalty can be called for such contact whether or not the initial contact was made below the neck area.

- CBS wins the national radio rights to 26 regular-season games, including *Monday Night Football*, and all 10 postseason games for the 1980-82 seasons for $12 million.

- The Los Angeles Rams move to Anaheim Stadium in nearby Orange County, California.

- The Raiders join the Los Angeles Coliseum Commission's antitrust suit against the NFL. The suit contends the league violated antitrust laws when they failed to approve a proposed move by the Raiders from Oakland to Los Angeles.

- NFL regular-season attendance sets a record for the third year in a row with 13.4 million attendees. The average paid attendance for the 224-game regular season is 59,787, the highest in the league's 61-year history. NFL games in 1980 are played before 92.4 percent of total stadium capacity.

- Television ratings are the second best in NFL history, trailing only 1976. All three networks post gains and NBC 's 15.0 rating is its best ever. CBS and ABC enjoy their best ratings since 1977, with 15.3 and 20.8 respectively. CBS radio reports a record audience of 7 million for Monday night and special games.

1981

- Oakland wins Super Bowl XV by defeating Philadelphia 27-10 at the Louisiana Superdome in New Orleans on January 25. Oakland becomes the first wild-card team to win a Super Bowl.

- Gerald and Allan Phipps sell the Denver Broncos to Edgar F. Kaiser, Jr., on February 26.

- Owners adopt a disaster plan on March 20 for re-stocking a team in the event a club is involved in a fatal accident.

- A CBS-New York Times poll shows that 48 percent of sports fans prefer football to 31 percent for baseball.

- NFL regular-season attendance sets a record for the fourth year in a row. Fans numbering 13.6 million attend games at an average of 60,745 per game. Games are played before 93.8 percent capacity crowds and NFL average attendance exceeds 60,000 for the first time.

- ABC and CBS both experience all-time rating highs. ABC finishes with a 21.7 rating and CBS with a 17.5 rating. NBC is down slightly to 13.9.

1982

- San Francisco wins its first Super Bowl by defeating Cincinnati 26-21 in the Pontiac Silverdome on January 24. CBS achieves the highest rating of any televised sporting event ever, 49.1 with a 73.0 share. A record 110.2 million fans watch the game. CBS Radio reports a record 14-million listeners for the game.

- A new five-year contract is signed with ABC, CBS, and NBC to televise all regular-season and postseason games starting with the 1982 season.

- A jury rules against the NFL in the antitrust trial brought by the Los Angeles Coliseum Commission and the Oakland Raiders on May 7. This victory clears the path for the Raiders ' move to Los Angeles.

- At midnight on Monday, September 20, the NFLPA calls a players' strike, which lasts for 57 days. The 1982 season is reduced from a 16-game schedule to nine. Play resumes on

November 21-22 following the ratification of a new Collective Bargaining Agreement by the NFL owners on November 17 in New York.

- The new Collective Bargaining Agreement runs through 1986 and affords for the NFL draft to be extended through 1992, the veteran free-agent system to be basically left in tact, the establishment of a minimum salary schedule for years of experience, the increasing of training camp and postseason pay, the increase of players' medical insurance and retirement benefits, and the introduction of a severance pay system to aid in career transition.

1983

- Due to the 57-day player strike, a 16-team Super Bowl Tournament format is adopted for the playoffs. Washington, the No. 1 seed from the NFC, defeats Miami, the No. 2 seed from the AFC, 27-17 in Super Bowl XVII in the Rose Bowl at Pasadena on January 30.

- Super Bowl XVII is the second highest rated live television program of all time, giving the NFL a sweep of the top 10 live programs in television history. The game was viewed in more than 40 million homes.

- Bears owner Halas dies at 88 on October 31. He was the last surviving member of the NFL's second organizational meeting.

1984

- The Los Angeles Raiders win Super Bowl XVIII by defeating Washington 38-9 in Tampa Stadium on January 22. The game records a 46.4 rating and a 71.0 share.

- Dallas owner Clint Murchison, Jr., sells the Cowboys to an 11-man group headed by H. R. (Bum) Bright on March 20. Club president Tex Schramm is designated as Managing General Partner.

- Edgar Kaiser, Jr., sells a majority interest in the Broncos to Patrick Bowlen on March 21.

- The Colts relocate to Indianapolis on March 28.

- The New York Jets move their home games to Giants Stadium in East Rutherford, New Jersey.

- Eugene V. Klein sells a majority interest in the San Diego Chargers to Alex G. Spanos on August 28.

- The 100th overtime game since its inception in 1974 is played when Houston beats Pittsburgh 23-20 on December 2.

- A number of significant records are set as Miami's Dan Marino passes for 5,084 yards and 48 touchdowns, Rams' running back Eric

Dickerson rushes for 2,105 yards, Washington's Art Monk catches 106 passes, and Walter Payton of the Bears breaks Jim Brown's career rushing mark with 13,309 yards.

1985

- San Francisco defeats Miami 38-16 in Super Bowl XIX in Stanford Stadium in Stanford, California, on January 20. President Ronald Reagan takes his second oath of office before tossing the coin for the game and joining the other 115,936,000 viewers. The game draws a 46.4 rating and a 63.0 share. Six million people watch the game in the United Kingdom and Italy.

- NBC Radio acquires the rights to a 37-game package in each of the 1985-86 seasons on March 6. The package includes 27 regular-season games and 10 postseason games.

- Norman Braman and his partner Edward Leibowitz buy the Philadelphia Eagles from Leonard Tose on April 29.

- Virginia Tech defensive lineman Bruce Smith is the first player chosen in the 50th NFL draft on April 30.

- Tom Benson, Jr., is approved to purchase the New Orleans Saints from John W. Mecom, Jr., on June 3.

- The NFL owners adopt a plan on May 23 to hold a series of overseas preseason games, beginning in 1986, with one to be played in England/Europe and/or one game in Japan each year.

- A single-weekend paid attendance record is set on the weekend of October 27-28, as 902,657 tickets are sold.

- The Chicago-Miami Monday Night game receives the highest rating, 29.6, and a share of 46.0, of any prime-time game in NFL history on December 2. The game is seen in more than 25 million homes.

- The NFL shows ratings increase on all three networks for the season, with NBC gaining 4 percent, CBS gaining 10 percent, and ABC gaining 16 percent.

1986

- Chicago defeats New England 46-10 in Super Bowl XX at the Louisiana Superdome on January 26. The NBC telecast replaces the final episode of M*A*S*H as the most viewed television program in history with an audience of 127 million viewers. Aside from gaining a 48.3 rating and a 70 percent share in the United States, the game is televised in 59 foreign countries. An estimated 300 million Chinese view a tape-delay broadcast of the game in March. NBC Radio reports an audience of 10 million.

- A limited use of instant replay is adopted as an officiating aid on March 11. Players are prohibited from wearing or otherwise displaying equipment, apparel, or other items that carry commercial names, names of organizations, or personal messages of any type.

- Following an 11-week trial, a jury in U.S. District Court in New York award the United States Football League one dollar in its $1.7 billion antitrust suit against the NFL on July 29.

- *Monday Night Football* becomes the longest-running prime-time series in the history of the ABC network.

- Instant replay is used to reverse two plays in 31 preseason games. Thirty-eight plays are reversed in 224 regular-season games, during which 374 total plays are closely reviewed via instant replay. Eighteen plays are closely reviewed in 10 postseason games resulting in three reversals.

1987

- The New York Giants defeat the Broncos 39-20 in Super Bowl XXI in Pasadena's Rose Bowl, winning their first NFL title since 1956. The CBS broadcast is viewed by 122.64 million people in the U.S. The game is watched live or tape-delayed in 55 foreign countries and NBC Radio's broadcast of the game is heard by a record 10.1 million people.

- An all-time paid attendance record of 17,304,463 is set for all games including pre-season, regular-season, and postseason.

- The owners vote to continue the instant replay system for one year.

- The regular-season is reduced from 16 to 15 games following a 24-day player strike. The strike is called on September 22 following the New England-New York Jets game. Games to be played on the season 's third weekend are canceled, but games for the fourth, fifth, and sixth weeks are played with replacement players. The striking players returned for the seventh week of the season on October 25.

- Instant replay is used to reverse eight plays in 52 preseason games. Nearly 500 regular-season plays are closely reviewed with instant replay, leading to 57 reversals. Eighteen postseason reviews lead to three reversals.

1988

- Washington defeats the Broncos 42-10 in Super Bowl XXII in San Diego's Jack Murphy Stadium. The ABC broadcast is viewed in the U.S. by 115,000,000 people. The game is seen live or on tape in 60 foreign countries, including China. The CBS radio broadcast is heard by 13.7 million people.

- In a unanimous 3-0 decision, the 2nd District Circuit Court of Appeals in New York upholds the jury's verdict in July of 1986 when the United States Football League was awarded one dollar in its $1.7 billion antitrust suit against the NFL.

- Instant replay is approved for a third consecutive season by a 23-5 owners' vote. An Instant Replay Official is assigned to the regular seven man on-the-field crew.

- A 45-second play clock is approved to replace the 30-second clock between plays.

- The Cardinals' transfer from St. Louis to Phoenix is approved.

- Two supplemental drafts are implemented - one prior to training camp and one prior to the regular season.

- Steelers founder and owner Art Rooney dies at 87 on August 25.

- Johnny Grier becomes the first African-American referee in the NFL on September 4.

- Paid and average attendance of 934,271 and 66,734 at 14 games on October 16-17 set single weekend records.

- Buffalo sets an NFL team single-season, in-house attendance mark of 622,793.

1989

- San Francisco defeats Cincinnati 20-16 in Super Bowl XXIII in Miami's Joe Robbie Stadium. The game is viewed by 110,780,000 people in the U.S. and is broadcast live or tape-delayed in 60 foreign countries.

- Rozelle announces his retirement from the office of Commissioner, pending the naming of a successor, on March 22.

- Instant replay is continued for a fourth straight season by a 24-4 owners' vote.

- Rozelle announces a strengthened policy against anabolic steroids and masking agents.

- Unconditional free agents numbering 229 sign with new teams under management's Plan B system on April 1.

- H. R. (Bum) Bright sells a majority interest in the Dallas Cowboys to Jerry Jones on April 18.

- Tex Schramm is named president of the new World League of American Football to work with a six-man committee of Dan Rooney, chairman; Norman Braman, Lamar Hunt, Victor Kiam, Mike Lynn, and Bill Walsh on April 18.

- Art Shell becomes the new coach of the Raiders on October 3, making him the NFL's first African-American head coach since Fritz Pollard coached the Akron Pros in 1921.

- Paul Tagliabue becomes the NFL's seventh chief executive on October 26. He is chosen on the sixth ballot of a three-day meeting in Cleveland, Ohio. The transfer from Commissioner Rozelle to Commissioner Tagliabue takes place at 12:01 A.M. on Sunday, November 5.

- The NFL's paid attendance of 17,399,538 is the highest total in league history.

1990

- San Francisco defeats Denver 55-10 in Super Bowl XXIV at the Louisiana Superdome on January 28.

- Changes are made in the league's draft eligibility rules on February 16. College juniors become eligible but must renounce their collegiate football eligibility before applying for the NFL Draft.

- NFL teams will play their 16-game schedule over 17 weeks in 1990 and 1991. They will play the same 16-game schedule over 18 weeks in 1992 and 1993.

- The playoff format is revised to include two additional wild-card teams (one from each conference).

- The owners vote to continue a limited system of instant replay, 21-7, on March 12. Beginning in 1990, the replay official will have a two-minute time limit to make a decision.

- One hundred eighty-four plan B unconditional free agents sign with new teams by April 2.

- NFL total paid attendance of 17,665,671 is the highest total in league history.

1991

- The New York Giants defeat Buffalo 20-19 in Super Bowl XXV in Tampa Stadium on January 26. The ABC broadcast is seen by 112 million people in the United States and is seen live or taped in 60 other countries.

- Robert Tisch buys a 50 percent share of the New York Giants from Mrs. Helen Mara Nugent and her children, Tim Mara, and Maura Mara Concannon on Februrary 2.

- Owners vote 21-7 on March 19 to continue a limited system of instant replay.

- The World League of American Football is launched on March 23. The league becomes the first sports league to operate on a weekly basis on two separate continents.

- A recommendation is approved from the Expansion and Realignment Committee on May 25 to add two teams for the 1994 season, resulting in six divisions of five teams each.

- Cleveland Browns and Cincinnati Bengals founder Paul Brown dies at the age of 82 on August 5.

1992

- The Washington Redskins take Super Bowl XXVI by defeating the Bills 37-24 at the Hubert H. Humphrey Metrodome on January 26. The CBS broadcast is seen by more than 123 million people in the United States.

- NFL total paid attendance sets a new record for the third consecutive season. Nearly 18 million people attend 296 preseason, regular-season, and postseason games.

- Instant replay fails to be approved for a seventh season on March 18. The owners vote 17-11 in favor of continuing instant replay but 21 votes are needed.

- Victor Kiam sells a controlling interest in the New England Patriots to James Orthwein on May 11.

- The Expansion Committee recommends five cities as finalists for the two expansion teams on May 19: Baltimore, Charlotte, Jacksonville, Memphis, and St. Louis.

1993

- The Cowboys beat Buffalo 52-17 in Super Bowl XXVII in Pasadena's Rose Bowl on January 31. The NBC broadcast becomes the most watched program in television history and is seen by 133,400,000 people nationally. The game is also seen live or taped in 101 foreign countries. The game receives a 45.1 rating.

- NFL attendance sets records for the fourth consecutive season at 17,784,354 through 296 preseason, regular-season, and postseason games.

- The NFL and NFL Players Association officially sign a new seven-year Collective Bargaining Agreement on June 29, the first such agreement since the 1982 agreement expired in 1987.

- Plans are announced to allow fans to join players and coaches in selecting the annual AFC and NFC Pro Bowl teams for the first time on October 12.

- The league's twenty-ninth franchise is unanimously awarded to the Carolina Panthers on October 26.

- Don Shula overtakes George Halas as the winningest coach in NFL history when Miami beats Philadelphia for Shula's 325th win on November 14.

- The Jacksonville Jaguars are awarded the league's 30th franchise on November 30.

1994

- A regular-season paid attendance record was set in 1993, with an average of 62,354 fans attending every game.

- The Buffalo Bills become the first team to lose four consecutive Super Bowls when they lose 30-13 to the Cowboys in Super Bowl XXVIII on January 30. The game is viewed by 134.8 million people, the largest U.S. audience in television history.

- The New England Patriots are transferred from James Orthwein to Robert Kraft on February 22.

- Trying to encourage offensive production, a series of rule changes are made on March 22. There are modifications in line play, chucking rules, and the roughing-the-passer rule. The two-point conversion is adopted and the spot of the kickoff is moved back to the 30-yard line.

- A majority interest in the Dolphins is transferred from the Robbie family to H. Wayne Huizenga on March 23.

- A total paid attendance record is achieved for the fifth consecutive year, with 17,951,831 attendees at all 1993 games.

- The Philadelphia Eagles are transferred from Norman Braman to Jeffrey Lurie on May 6.

- The league reaches agreement on a new seven-year contract with the game officials on September 22.

- Commissioner Tagliabue assigns the two new expansion teams into the AFC Central (Jacksonville) and the NFC West (Carolina) for the 1995 season only on November 2. A special committee on realignment is appointed to make recommendations on the 1996 season and beyond.

- The NFL sets a regular-season paid attendance record for the second consecutive season, topping 14 million for the first time with 14,034,977 attendees.

1995

- The 49ers win their record fifth Super Bowl by defeating the Chargers 49-26 in Super Bowl XXIX at Joe Robbie Stadium in Miami on January 29.

- Carolina and Jacksonville begin to build their teams by selecting 66 players from other NFL teams in a veteran player allocation draft in New York on February 16.

- Total paid attendance breaks a record for the sixth consecutive year, exceeding 18 million for the first time (18,010,262).

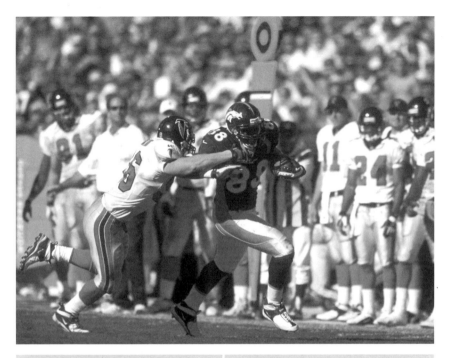

- The Tampa Buccaneers are transferred from the estate of the late Hugh Culverhouse to Malcolm Glazer on March 13.

- The Los Angeles Rams move to St. Louis on April 12.

- The Raiders move back to Oakland on July 22.

- NFL paid attendance totals 963,521 for 15 games in Week 12, the highest weekend total in the league's 76-year history, on November 19-20.

- A number of significant marks are achieved on the field:
  - Miami's Dan Marino surpasses Hall of Famer Fran Tarkenton in four major passing categories — attempts, completions, yards, and touchdowns — to become the NFL's all-time career leader.
  - San Francisco's Jerry Rice becomes the all-time reception and receiving-yardage leader with career totals of 942 catches and 15,123 yards.
  - Dallas' Emmitt Smith scores 25 touchdowns, breaking the season record of 24 set by Washington's John Riggins in 1983.

1996

- The Dallas Cowboys defeat Pittsburgh 27-17 in Super Bowl XXX in Sun Devil Stadium in Tempe, Arizona on January 28. The largest television audience in U.S. history, 138.5 million people, watches the game.

- Art Modell receives approval to move the Browns to Baltimore and renames them the Ravens.

- An agreement is reached between the city of Cleveland and the NFL on February 9. Under the agreement, the city of Cleveland retains the Browns' heritage and records, including the name, logo, colors, history, playing records, trophies and memorabilia. In return, the city commits to build a new 72,000-seat stadium for a re-activated Browns' franchise to begin play there no later than 1999.

- Total paid attendance again sets a record, eclipsing 19 million for the first time at 19,202,757.

- The Oilers move from Houston to Nashville on April 20. Home games are played for this one year in Memphis.

- Points scored total 762 and NFL paid attendance totals 964,079 for 15 games in Week 11, the highest weekend totals in either category in the league's 77-year history on November 10-11.

- Former NFL Commissioner Pete Rozelle dies at his home in Rancho Santa Fe, California on December 6. He led the league from 1960-1989.

1997

- Indianapolis Colts owner Robert Irsay dies on January 14 from complications related to a stroke suffered in 1995.

- The Packers win their first Super Bowl in 29 years by defeating the Patriots 35-21 in Super Bowl XXXI at the Louisiana Superdome in New Orleans on January 26.

- Washington Redskins owner Jack Kent Cooke dies in his home in Washington, D.C., on April 6.

- Jack Kent Cooke stadium opens in Raljon, Maryland. A crowd of 78,270 witnesses a Redskins victory over the Cardinals 19-13 on September 14.

- The Seattle Seahawks defeat the Tennessee Oilers 16-13 in the Kingdome on October 5 in the NFL 's 10,000th regular-season game.

- Atlanta Falcons owner Rankin Smith dies of heart failure three days prior to his seventy-third birthday on October 26.

- NFL paid attendance totaled 999,778 for 15 games in Week 12, the highest weekend total in league history on November 16-17.

1998

- The Denver Broncos win their first NFL champi-onship by defeating Green Bay 31-24 in Super Bowl XXXII at Qualcomm Stadium in San Diego on January 25.

- The league approves a six-year extension of the Collective Bargaining Agreement through 2003.

- An expansion team is unanimously approved for Cleveland on March 23 to fulfill the commit-ment to return the Browns to the field in 1999.

1999

- The Denver Broncos defeat the Falcons 34-19 in Super Bowl XXXIII at Miami 's Joe Robbie Stadium.

- Instant replay is reinstated for the 1999 season.

- The new Cleveland Browns franchise makes Kentucky quarterback Tim Couch its first over-all selection in the 1999 college draft.

- Denver quarterback John Elway retires on May 2.

2000

- The St. Louis Rams defeat the Tennessee Titans 23-16 in Super Bowl XXXIV at Atlanta's Georgia Stadium.

- Quarterback Steve Young retires from the San Francisco 49ers. Legendary Miami quarterback Dan Marino retires as well.

- Corey Dillon of Cincinnati sets new single-game rushing mark with 278 yards on 22 carries against Denver on October 22.

2001

- The Baltimore Ravens defeat the New York Giants 34-7 in Superbowl XXXV at Tampa's James Raymond Stadium

- Legendary great Troy Aikman announces his retirement.

Minnesota Vikng punter,
Brian Morton.

Chapter 3
Football Basics

The Field

It's important to know the size and specs of a regulation football field because invariably, men will compare the size of it to something else, as in a piece of land or a parking lot is the size of two football fields. (Who knew? Size really does matter to men!) In any case, the standard field is marked in excruciating detail for player and spectator visibility in downs and yards gained and lost.

The rectangular playing field is 120 yards long and 53-1/3 yards wide (300 feet by 160 feet). The end lines and sidelines are 4 inches wide and rimmed by a solid white border a minimum of 6 feet wide. The goal lines are 10 yards inside at each end of the field.

The distance of the field between the two lines is 100 yards. Extending beyond each goal line is an end zone that is 10 yards deep. To make all these white lines, teams use paint or marking chalk. All boundary lines, goal lines, and marked yard lines are continuous lines until they intersect with one another. When players are in possession of the ball inside these white lines, they're considered to be in play, and the ball is live.

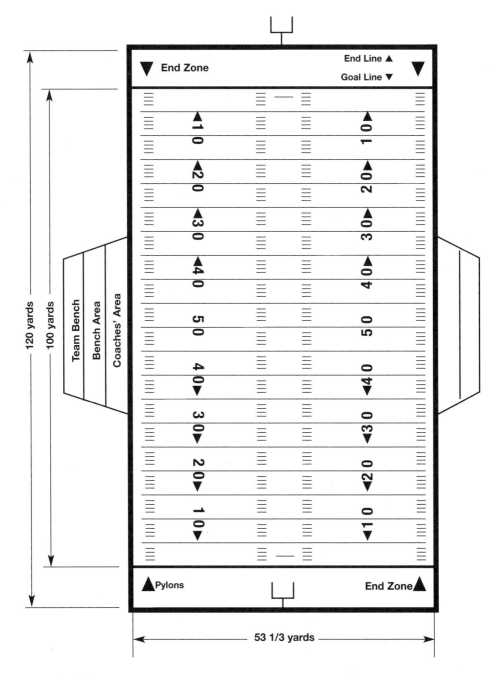

Yard Line

Yard lines run parallel to the goal lines at intervals of five yards and are marked across the field from sideline to sideline. These lines stop eight inches short of the six-foot solid border in the NFL. Yard lines are necessary to give players and fans an idea of how far a team must advance the ball in order to obtain a first down.

Since an offensive team must gain 10 yards in order to post a first down, the field is numbered in multiples of 10, every 10 yards, starting from the goal lines. In the NFL, the bottoms of these numbers are placed 12 yards from each sideline. The numbers 10, 20, 30, 40, and one 50-yard line are two yards in length. A white directional arrow is next to the top portion of each number (except the 50) and points toward the goal line in that half of the field. All these lines and numbers are white.

There are a series of lines running all the way across the field in between each of the five-yard markers. There are two sets of four short lines, with each pair designating a one-yard increment on the field these are hash marks. Two yards before each goal line and in the middle of it, there is a one-yard long line that is parallel to the goal line. This is the line on which the ball is placed for an extra point or a two-point conversion after a touchdown.

In the middle of the field is the 50-yard line. It is a distance of 50 yards from each end zone to the middle of the field. So, when you are 40 yards from one end zone, you are on the opponents 40-yard line going towards the 30, 20 and 10 yard lines, each of which you will reach before the end zone. But if you are 60 yards from one end zone, you are on your own 40-yard line, and you must cross the 50-yard line first when heading toward the end zone.

The Line of Scrimmage

The line of scrimmage is two invisible lines, each one beginning at the end-tip of the ball and running parallel to the goal lines. The ball is placed on this line to begin the next play. The offensive and defensive teams face each other along these lines of scrimmage. The area between the two scrimmage lines — which is the length of the ball —- is called the neutral zone. No player other than the center is permitted to have any part of his body inside the neutral zone as the ball is being snapped, otherwise the offending team will be penalized.

Hash Marks

Midfield is the 50-yard line. From there, hash marks mark each yard line 70 feet, nine inches from the sidelines in the NFL and 53 feet, four inches from each sideline in high school and college play. Two sets of hash marks (each hash is one yard in length) run parallel to each other down the length of the field and are approximately 18 1/2 feet apart.

When the ball carrier is either tackled or pushed out-of- bounds, or the ball is punted out of bounds, the officials return the ball in-bounds to the closest hash mark. The hash marks are used for ball placement prior to most offensive plays so that more of the game can be played in the middle of the field, making play more wide open. But, when teams run the ball and the ball carrier is tackled between the hash marks, the ball is declared dead at that spot and is generally placed where the ball carrier was stopped.

An important thing to remember is that an incomplete pass is returned to the spot of the preceding play, not where it actually goes out-of-bounds or where the quarterback was standing when he threw it.

Red Zone

Twenty yards before the end zone is the "red zone." This is an "invisible" zone where the opportunity to score looms before the players, hence the naming "red," as in red flag. When both teams are in this zone, remember that one team is defending the end zone, and the other is expecting to penetrate it for points on the board. Expect the sense of urgency to heighten when teams near the red zone.

Dallas Cowboys quarterback Troy Aikman (now retired) congratulates Indianapolis Colts quarterback Peyton Manning after their game at the RCA DOME.

The End Zone and Goal Posts

In the NFL, end zones are 10 yards deep at each end of the field. The end zone boundaries are the goal line, end line and sidelines. The goal lines separate the playing field from the end zone, and are eight inches wide in the NFL and four inches wide at the high school and college levels. The four intersections of goal lines and sidelines and end lines and sidelines are marked at the inside corners of the white lines with florescent orange pylons mounted on flexible shafts. (You may see a ball carrier diving into these fixtures in a frenzied attempt to score.)

Rising from the back of each end zone are the goalposts. All eyes focus on these structures after the ball carrier reaches the end zone and scores a touchdown (a.k.a. six points).

The goalposts are the squared, U-shaped structures. The ball will be kicked for an extra point or three-point play through these structures. The two goalpost uprights are connected by a crossbar 10 feet above the ground and hold the uprights, which are 18 1/2 feet apart in the NFL. In high school and college, the uprights are 23 feet, four inches apart.

The goalposts, which are usually painted white or neon yellow, are a single standard type, known as the sling-shot design. A sling-shot goalpost has one post in the ground and a curved extension that sweeps the crossbar into place. This post is fully padded to protect players who might collide with it in the back of the end zone.

The uprights, the two poles extending up from both ends of the crossbar, rise 30 feet (20 feet in college and

A little history ...

The goalposts used to be located on the goal line, and then inside the goal line, and finally they were moved permanently from the goal line to the end zone's end line in 1974.

high school) and are three to four inches in diameter. A four by 42-inch ribbon is attached to the top of each goalpost to help the kicker get an idea of the wind speed and direction and to aid the officials in determining the exact top of the upright when judging whether a kick is good.

Player Benches

The area directly around the field is the sideshow to the action on the field. Here, coaches, non-starting players, assistants and other crews are found working, watching and strategizing during the game. This takes place six feet outside the border of the field, or six feet from the sidelines, where a broken white line defines where only coaches and substitute players may stand.

Players and coaches on the sidelines are only allowed to stand between the 32-yard lines. Within this area, off-limits to fans and media, much of the "behind-the-scenes" activity occurs; players rest and watch the game, team doctors and trainers examine injured players, and quarterbacks and other players talk by telephone to coaches and coordinators that are located in team boxes above the field.

Team officials will also call from the sideline telephones to inform the team's public relations staff of player injuries. This information is then relayed to members of the media (newspaper reporters, magazine writers, radio & TV broadcasters) so announcers can inform the audience.

All NFL bench areas are a minimum of 30-feet deep, and they extend to each 32-yard line. High school and college fields aren't as restrictive as NFL fields, although some adhere to the same dimensions, particularly the 32-yard line limit.

Field Surfaces

There is quite a controversy over artificial or natural turf. Which is better? What shoes perform best on the respective turfs? Players usually have strong opinions on the matter, either advocating the natural grass on Green Bay 's Lambeau Field or the well-groomed artificial stuff on an indoor stadium like Indianapolis' RCA Dome.

In the NFL, 21 teams currently play on natural grass for home games, while 11 still play on artificial surfaces, but those numbers are continually changing. The natural grass surface depends on the region's temperature and the stadium's drainage system. Similar to a lawn, artificial grass has been perfected to withstand heavy wear and destructive cleats (spikes on shoes). Weather conditions and the composition of the field on real grass often results in players and uniforms becoming so dirty and muddy that the fans can barely read their numbers. As you can imagine, artificial turf is much cleaner and easier to maintain.

The original intent of artificial turf was to allow a game to be played indoors at the Astrodome — the first domed stadium. Without natural sunlight, no grass would grow. So, the first artificial surface was developed in the 1950s and installed on a Providence, RI high school field.

Later, in 1965, it was installed in Houston's Astrodome. From the "Astro" dome, the first surface was dubbed Astroturf. After Astroturf was developed, companies consistently improved the product, prompting outdoor stadiums to install artificial surfaces because they are cheaper to maintain than natural grass, which needs to be watered, mowed and replaced.

In many cities where the stadiums are used for both baseball and football, artificial turf is more economical. Additionally, many stadiums are also used for outdoor concerts, rallies, and other sports such as baseball and soccer. With these events, some areas of the grass inevitably become trampled and destroyed by throngs of people walking on it, so the artificial surface quickly became advantageous.

Artificial surfaces are made from synthetic nylon fibers that resemble very short blades of grass. Traditionally, artificial surfaces are harder than natural grass because they often lay over cement, blacktop, or dirt. There are drawbacks to man-made turf, many of which cause extra preparation on game day.

Extremely hot days cause artificial surfaces to retain heat, increasing the temperature of the field by 5 to 10 degrees. Increased injuries and uncertain traction are also causes for team concern. On artificial turf, the game is faster, and the footing is more precise, which allows players the ability to turn on a dime and stop and start with incredible agility. But, because artificial turf is often laid over asphalt, more injuries and wear-and-tear on the players can occur. Most players (except kickers, who appreciate the surer-footing artificial turf delivers) complain about their shoes sticking or getting caught, potentially leading to serious knee injuries. With the game being faster, a player making a quick move or stop runs the risk of an easy knee or ankle twist. "Raspberries" or turf burn are also a common injury resulting from aggressive tackles or sliding or diving for a catch.

The Ball

In football jargon, the ball is the pigskin.

When men want to "toss around the pigskin" with their buddies, they simply mean "play catch" with a football. Calling it a pigskin is strangely ironic, because it is not composed of pig skin, but rather of traditional cow leather. In any case, someone around the turn of the century decided the ball resembled a chubby pig, and the name stuck.

The official NFL football was once a round rugby ball and has evolved to the now-traditional elongated shape through the years. The ball is approximately 11 inches long and about 28 to 28 1/2 inches around. The official ball is a Wilson™ brand, and weighs 14 to 15 ounces. It is inflated to an air pressure of 12 1/2 to 13 /12 pounds per square inch (psi) and bears the signature of NFL Commissioner Paul Tagliabue. College balls are the same size as NFL balls, although you will find a white stripe encircling the tip area at both ends of the college and high school ball. The white stripe is designed to help receivers see the ball better during night games.

The ball specs include an inflated rubber bladder encased in pebble-grained leather. It has grooves or ridges, which makes it easy to grab and catch in dry conditions. To make it easier to grip and throw, the ball has eight raised white laces in its center. A quarterback can wrap his hand around the ball with some of his fingers between the laces and the thumb on the back of the ball for a tight grip. The ball is aerodynamically designed to spin after it is thrown.

In the NFL, the home club supplies 36 footballs in an open-air stadium or 24 footballs in a domed stadium. More balls are required for outdoors in case of inclement weather, such as rain, sleet, or snow. The referee is the sole judge as to whether the balls comply with league specifications and will test each football with a pressure gauge approximately 90 minutes prior to kickoff. As recent as 1999, the kicking ball regulations have changed. Kickers are no longer able to manipulate the ball before kickoff. Twelve new footballs, sealed in a special box and shipped by the manufacturer, are opened in the officials' locker room two hours prior to the starting time of the game. These balls are specially marked by the referee and used exclusively for the kicking game. These are known as "K" balls.

All Wilson™ footballs are hand made at the Wilson™ Football Factory in Ada, Ohio. At the Ada facility, Wilson™

Indianapolis Colts Edgerrin James, right, and retired Deion Sanders greet after the Colts/Cowboys game.

manufactures more than one million footballs per year (about 5,000 per day), making it the largest producer of game footballs in the world. The manufacturing process involves approximately 50 steps from start to finish.

Equipment

Suiting up for football is an intricate process. While a player is dressing, he is preparing his body for a possible series of blows, hits and collisions. Fortunately, modern football equipment is designed for that purpose, without spoiling any visibility or movement in the game with overly bulky pads or cushions.

Players wear jerseys and pants that fit snugly and come just below the knee. Keep in mind, the snugness of the uniform isn't designed for the purposes of showing off muscles, legs and tight ends, but for making it difficult to grab clothing when trying to tackle.

Girls, could you imagine getting fined thousands of dollars for showing a little skin?

NFL uniform codes

The NFL strictly enforces uniform codes. Any violations of the code can lead to player or team fines. The following is a list of uniform regulations for the game:

- The NFL shield or logo must be visible on pants, jerseys, and helmets.
- Tear-away jerseys are prohibited.
- All jerseys must remain tucked into the uniform pants.
- Stockings must cover the entire leg area from the shoe to the bottom of the pants and meet the pants below the knee. Uniform stockings may not be altered, and they must be white from the top of the shoe to about mid-calf.
- Size and locations of shoe logos must be approved by NFL Properties.
- Players are not allowed to wear shoes from companies not approved by the league.
- Sleeves cannot be torn or cut.
- All tape used on shoes or socks or pants must be transparent or of a matching color to the team uniform.
- Towels can be only eight inches long and six inches wide and must be tucked into the front waist of the pants.

Jerseys and Padding

The jersey is the team and player identity. It must be large enough to cover the shoulder pads and accommodate the variety of pads that protect the players under their uniforms. Next to the helmet, the shoulder pads are the number-one piece of protection that players wear. Every player wears shoulder pads to protect the shoulders and sternum area, and some cover the top of the arm and the rotator cuff, plus hip pads, thigh pads, and knee pads. The thigh pads and knee pads slip into special pockets sewn into the pants. Most quarterbacks wear special pads to prevent specific injuries to the upper torso, and a flak-like jacket to cushion the ribs.

Jersey numbers sewn on the front and back for player identification did not become a general practice until the 1920s. Today, the numerals are eight inches high and four inches wide. Most high school and college teams have the same specifications, and some of them also place the number on the jersey's sleeve. Under NFL rules, specific positions wear certain numerals: professional quarterbacks and kickers are assigned numbers 1-19; running backs and defensive backs, 20-49; centers and linebackers, 50-59; linemen, 60-79; wide receivers and tight ends, 80-89. Centers may also be assigned numbers up to 79 and defensive linemen and linebackers, 90-99. On the back of each NFL jersey is the player's last name.

Team jerseys' colors and logos further distinguish one team from another. Designs have changed over the years, but the team colors have stayed the same virtually since the inception of the team. In the NFL, the visiting team traditionally wears a white jersey. The colors for visiting teams vary on the high school and level. In college, home teams wear dark jerseys, although an agreement can be reached between the competing teams.

Helmets and face masks

The helmet and face mask are designed to protect a player's face and head from serious injury. Players must also wear a mouth guard to protect their teeth and prevent themselves from biting their tongues. To prevent serious concussions, many helmets have air-filled pockets inside them. The helmet must be a comfortable and fit snug.

All helmets are equipped with face masks. The rounded metal material of the face mask cannot be more than 5/8 inch in diameter. Most linemen wear a face mask called a cage that has a bar extending down from the middle and top of the helmet to below the nose area, protecting him from his eyebrows to his chin. This bar joins two or three bars that extend from both sides, completely preventative of an opponent's hands reaching inside the face area and under the chin.

Shoes and Cleats

To ensure the best footing for quick stops and turns and the ability to dig in and gain traction, each player's shoes have cleats of hard rubber or plastic that screw into the shoe bottom. Cleats are often cone-shaped, but their size and shape vary according to the surface on which the game is being played.

The shortest cleat (1/2 inch) is worn on natural, dry firm fields. This cleat makes a player less prone to injury and provides ideal traction. A little longer 5/8 inch cleat is worn for an average natural field. For slippery grass fields, a 3/4 or 1 inch cleat is used. This helps linemen legs. dig deep and gain traction. Receivers and running backs often wear shoes with fewer cleats than the larger, more physical players do. Most teams are equipped with all sizes and types of shoes in case the weather changes during the course of a game. You may see players changing shoes or cleaning their cleats on a rubber-stemmed mat on the sidelines. In the NFL, players test the playing surface an hour prior to the game and, if necessary, the equipment manager changes the cleats with a power drill.

Scoring

When a team has possession of the football, there are many options to put points on the board. Primarily, a team will want to drive the ball down the field in a series of plays (remember the downs?) that will result in a touchdown. Because that secures the highest level of points, plus an option for at least one extra point, the offense focuses on the TD.
- Six points for a touchdown (carrying or passing the ball across the opposition goal line).
- Three points for a field goal (kicking the ball over the crossbar and through the goalposts).
- Two points for a safety (forcing the other team to down the ball behind its own goal line).
- Two points for the extra points allowed after scoring a touchdown. (Pro teams can kick, run, or pass for the extra points. College and high school rules give two points if the points are made on a run, pass or play or one point if kicked for the extra point.)

Touchdowns

A touchdown is worth six points. A team scores a touchdown when an offensive player carrying the ball advances from anywhere on the field and breaks the plane of his opponents' goal line with the ball. In other words, the goal line is the end zone and it must be penetrated in a fair play to get the points.

Even if the offensive player is hit in mid-air and lands back on the one-yard line, his efforts count for a touchdown, as long as the ball crosses the plane.

Extra Point - Point Conversion

A try for an extra point, also known as a point-after-touchdown (or PAT), is attempted during the scrimmage down that's awarded after a touchdown. The extra point is successful when the kicker kicks the ball between the uprights of the goalpost and above the crossbar, provided that the ball was snapped two yards away (or three yards away in high school or college) from the opponent's goal line. Another post-TD strategy to gain extra points is a two-point conversion.

Two-point conversions have always been a part of high school and college football and were added to the NFL in the 1994 season. This play consists of the offense possessing the

Miami Dolphins runningback, Rob Conrad.

ball on the two-yard line and they must advance the ball across the goal line, or break the plane, as if scoring a touchdown. The try (called a conversion attempt) is over when the officials rule the ball dead or if a change of possession occurs (the defense intercepts a pass or recovers a fumble).

Field Goals

A field goal is worth three points. A team scores a field goal when the kicker boots the ball entirely through the uprights and above the crossbar of the goalpost without touching either the ground or any of his teammates on the offensive team. You get the distance of a field goal by adding 10 yards (the distance from the goal line to where the goalposts are placed) to the spot (yard line) from which the ball is kicked. Or simply add 17 to the number of yards that the offense would have to advance to cross the goal line. For example, if the offense is on its opponents' 23-yard line, a field goal attempt would be 40 yards. This is because kicks are attempted for seven yards behind the line of scrimmage so they will not be blocked.

Safeties

A safety is worth two points. The important factor in a safety is impetus, which is the action a player expends to give the ball momentum. For example, if a ball carrier retreats from the field of play into his own end zone and is downed there, the ball carrier provided the impetus. A defensive player can never push a ball carrier a yard back into the end zone and then be awarded a safety. Only the ball carrier can provide the impetus.

A safety is awarded to the opposing team if the offensive team sends the ball into its own end zone and the ball becomes dead in its possession. This occurs when a quarterback, running back, or receiver is tackled with the ball in his own end zone or goes out-of-bounds behind the goal line.

A safety can occur when the offensive team commits a penalty (say, holding a defensive player who is preparing to tackle the ball carrier in the end zone) that would otherwise require it to have the ball marked in its own end zone.

A safety is also awarded when a blocked punt goes out of the kicking team's end zone. And when the receiver of a punt muffs the ball *(Muff: A failed attempt to catch a punt or kick during which the receiver touches the ball but never gains possession.)* and then, when trying to retrieve the ball, forces or illegally kicks it into the end zone (creating new impetus) and it goes out of the end zone, the defensive team is given a safety, worth two points. If a muffed ball is kicked or forced into the end zone and then recovered there by a member of the receiving team, the defensive team is awarded a safety.

Sudden Death

The sudden death system of determining the winner occurs when the score is tied at the end of the regulation playing time of all NFL games. The team scoring first during overtime play will win, and the game automatically ends upon any score (by safety, field goal, or touchdown) or when points are awarded by a referee for a palpably unfair act.

1. At the end of regulation time, the referee will immediately toss a coin at the center of the field in accordance with rules pertaining to the usual pregame toss. The captain of the visiting team will call the toss.

2. Following a three-minute intermission after the end of the regulation game, play will continue in 15-minute periods or until there is a score. Regular season games are declaired a tie if neither team scores in 15 minutes. Playoff games continue until a team scores. There is a two-minute intermission between subsequent periods. The teams change goals at the start of each period. Each team has three time outs per half and all general timing provisions apply as during a regular game. Disqualified players are not allowed to return.

Time

Football is a game that is played within time limits. In college and professional football, a game lasts 60 minutes. The playing time of a high school game is 48 minutes. The game is divided into halves. Each half is made up of two quarters, often called periods.

An intermission between halves, called half time, lasts fifteen minutes.

There are also two-minute intermissions between the first two and last two quarters. Following each quarter, teams change goals. In pro football, once the official places the ball for the next play, the offensive team has 30 seconds (25 seconds in college and high school football) to begin their first play. That's the amount of time the offensive team has to huddle, call the play, line up at the line of scrimmage, call signals, and snap the ball.

Stopping the Clock

A pro or college game lasts 60 minutes, the time in which the ball is "in play." The official clock that registers those 60 minutes can be stopped for any for the following reasons:

- Either team calls a time-out. Each team is allowed three time-outs per half. Consecutive team time-outs can be taken, but the second time-out is reduced from a full minute to 40 seconds.
- A quarter ends. The time lapse enables teams to change which goal they will defend (they change sides at the ends of the first and third quarters).
- The quarterback throws an incomplete pass.

The Heidi Game

ONE SUNDAY EVENING IN 1968, Jennifer Edwards (the daughter of film director Blake Edwards and stepmother Julie Andrews) became the most hated actress in America. A nationally televised AFL game between the Oakland Raiders and the New York Jets had only 1:05 minutes left to play with the Jets ahead 32 to 29. During a commercial break, an NBC executive made the decision to cut from the football field to the Swiss Alps and air *Heidi,* a made-for-TV movie. Oakland scored two touchdowns after the switch to *Heidi* to win 43-32. After the thousands of protesting phone calls, it was decided that all games would be aired in their entirety.

- The ball carrier goes out-of-bounds.
- A player from either team is injured during a play.
- An official signals a penalty by throwing a yellow flag.
- The officials need to measure whether the offense has gained a first down or need to take time to spot the ball correctly.
- Either team scores a touchdown, field goal, or safety.
- The ball changes possession via a punt, a turnover, or a team failing to have advanced the ball 10 yards in four downs.

With the exception of the last two minutes of the first half and the last five minutes of the second half of an NFL game, the game clock is restarted following a kickoff return, a player going out-of-bounds on a play, or after a declined penalty.

Timing in the Final Minutes of Each Half

On kickoff, the clock does not start until the ball has been legally touched by player of either team in the field of play. A team cannot buy an excess time out for a penalty. However, a fourth time out is allowed without penalty for an injured player, who must be removed immediately. A fifth time out or more is allowed for an injury and a five-yard penalty is assessed if the clock was running. Additionally, if the clock was running and the score is tied or the team in possession is losing, the ball cannot be put in play for at least 10 seconds on the fourth or more time out. The half or game can end while those 10 seconds are run off on the clock.

If the defensive team is behind in the score and commits a foul when it has no time outs left in the final 30 seconds of either half, the offensive team can decline the penalty for the foul and have the time on the clock expire. Fouls that occur in the last five minutes of the fourth quarter as well as the last two minutes of the first half will result in the clock starting on the snap.

Televised Games

There is another reason play can be stopped. In the case of games that are being televised, play is sometimes interrupted so the network can break to commercials. In recent seasons, professional games being televised have included 25 commercial minutes. Many of the commercials are telecast during normal interruptions when a timeout is called, after a touchdown or field goal, or when a penalty is called. But occasionally, an official will halt play for the sole reason of allowing commercial breaks. Oftentimes, you will see a guy on the sidelines with big orange oven mitt looking things on his hands. This is the guy that signals a network timeout to the officials.

Because official play is stopped so often, there is a big difference between actual playing time and the elapsed time of a game. The elapsed time of the 60-minute professional game is often more than three hours.

Divisions

The original NFL league, you'll remember from the history timeline, was called the American Professional Football Association, originally created in 1920 with 14 teams. After the second season, the league officially changed its name to the National Football League. The NFL as we know it today ends each season with the champions of the two conferences, the AFC (American Football Conference) and the NFC (National Football Conference) battling in the final game, the Super Bowl.

However, in the NFL's beginning, the championship was not decided by the team with the best record, but it was decided by a vote. It wasn't until 1932 that the league decided to actually have a playoff game. In 1933, the NFL divided into the two divisions (conferences) with each team playing the same number of games and the winners of each division playing for the league championship.

The American Football League (AFL) organized in 1960 with eight teams, was the early structure of what became the American Football Conference (AFC). Huge changes occurred in the first nine years of the AFL entering the sport. By the end of the sixties, the expanded sport was a national attraction. Fans filled stadiums in record numbers. Rapidly increasing television coverage introduced pro football to millions of new fans and the pursuit of players by both leagues led to escalating salaries.

When the AFL obtained its own television contract, there was competition for the NFL's top quarterbacks. A merger of the two leagues was established in 1966 under the umbrella of the NFL and the American Football League was then renamed the AFC. After 1967, the two

Rules of Time

1. The stadium game clock is official. In case it stops or is operating incorrectly, the line judge takes over the official timing on the field.
2. Each period is 15 minutes. The intermission between the periods is two minutes. Halftime is 12 minutes in high school and college and 15 minutes in the NFL, unless otherwise specified.
3. On charged team time outs, the field judge starts the watch and blows the whistle after one minute 50 seconds have elapsed, unless television does not utilize the time for a commercial break. In this case, the length of the time out is reduced to 40 seconds.
4. The referee will allow necessary time to attend to an injured player, or repair a legal player's equipment.
5. Each team is allowed three time outs each half.
6. Time between plays will be 40 seconds from the end of a given play until the snap of the ball for the next play, or a 25-second interval after certain administrative stoppages and game delays.
7. Clock will start running when ball is snapped following all changes of team possession.
8. With the exception of the last two minutes of the first half and the last five minutes of the second half, the game clock will be restarted following a kickoff return, a player going out-of-bounds on a play from scrimmage, or after declined penalties when appropriate on the referee's signal.
9. Consecutive team time outs can be taken by opposing teams, but the length of the second time out will be reduced to 40 seconds.
10. When, in the judgment of the referee, the level of crowd noise prevents the offense from hearing its signals, he can institute a series of procedures that can result in a loss of team time outs or a five-yard penalty against the defensive team.

The Chicks' Guide to Football

Denver Bronco cornerback Deltha O'Neal.

leagues held a common draft and began interleague play in the 1970 season.

The two conferences consist of 31 teams and 32 in the 2002 season, with the addition of Houston. It is divided into East, Central and West regions. Ironically, a team city's geographical location is not indicative of which conference they are in.

Conferences develop consistency for teams, as they can expect to be matched against their division rivals each year. To start, the first eight games of the season consist of each team playing the four other teams in its division twice, once at home, and one away game. The next four games are played against teams from the other conference. The final four games are played against teams in their own conference but not in their same division.

The schedule also depends on where the team placed the previous year. For example, a first-place team plays the first place, second place and third-place teams from the other two divisions. The second-place team plays the other second-place teams, plus the first and fourth-place teams in the conference.

Two hundred and forty games are played in the NFL in a season. The three first-place teams from each conference qualify for the conference playoffs, and the winners of each conference plan to meet at the "Big Show" (the Super Bowl, see page 59).

National Football Conference

EASTERN DIVISION	CENTRAL DIVISION	WESTERN DIVISION

Arizona Cardinals	Chicago Bears	Atlanta Falcons

Dallas Cowboys	Detroit Lions	Carolina Panthers

New York Giants	Green Bay Packers	New Orleans Saints

Philadelphia Eagles	Minnesota Vikings	St. Louis Rams

Washington Redskins	Tampa Bay Buccaneers	San Francisco 49ers

American Football Conference

EASTERN DIVISION	CENTRAL DIVISION	WESTERN DIVISION

Buffalo Bills

Baltimore Ravens

Denver Broncos

Indianapolis Colts

Cincinnati Bengals

Kansas City Chiefs

Miami Dolphins

BROWNS

Cleveland Browns

Jacksonville Jaguars

Oakland Raiders

New England Patriots

Pittsburgh Steelers

San Diego Chargers

New York Jets

Tennessee Titans

Seattle Seahawks

2002 NFC Realignment

NFC East

Dallas Cowboys

New York Giants

Philadelphia Eagles

Washington Redskins

NFC North

Chicago Bears

Detroit Lions

Green Bay Packers

Minnesota Vikings

NFC South

Atlanta Falcons

Carolina Panthers

New Orleans Saints

Tampa Bay Buccaneers

NFC West

Arizona Cardinals

St. Louis Rams

San Francisco 49ers

Seattle Seahawks

NFL and the NFL shield design are registered trademarks of the National Football League. The team names, logos and uniform designs are registered trademarks of the teams indicated.

2002 AFC Realignment

AFC East

Buffalo Bills

Miami Dolphins

New England Patriots

New York Jets

AFC North

Baltimore Ravens

Cincinnati Bengals

BROWNS

Cleveland Browns

Pittsburg Steelers

AFC South

Houston Texans

Indianapolis Colts

Jacksonville Jaguars

Tennessee Titans

AFC West

Denver Broncos

Kansas City Chiefs

Oakland Raiders

San Diego Chargers

Jacksonville Jaguars defensive end, Troy Brackens.

Chapter 4
The Season

The Draft

The most important off-season event in the NFL is the annual draft, held during one weekend in mid-April. The build up to this one weekend, though, is a series of strategic meetings, salary reviews, game-day film critiques, scouting and expert consultation for a franchise's administrative and coaching staff. For players, it is a series of physicals, time trials, endurance testing, poking, prodding and comprehensive performance reviews.

This is the process for college-age players to be picked up in the NFL and dispersed to all the teams. Because of such rampant speculation about the rookie crop entering the popular sport, the event has gone from quiet sports page fine print to a full-blown media event with a fan following all its own. Looking past the hype and glossy packaging, the draft is the springtime ritual that is the primary means for organizations to build their teams and replenish areas of need when it comes to on-field personnel. For the athletes, especially those selected as number one and two draft picks, being pursued by a professional football team is a career milestone.

First-round draft picks are key in the annual event. Each team has a first-round pick, where they will obviously pick their trump card — the player they envision as the best fit for the team among the sea of eligible athletes. Needless to say, the first 30 or so players to go are considered relatively important and impressive players. Players, teams and sports agents watch draft day closely, not only to determine which team recruits a player, but also, what type of salary that player can command with his first professional contract.

The records of the previous NFL season determine the order in which the teams draft their rookies. The team that finished with the worst record has the opportunity to make the first selection in the first round and in each subsequent round, while the Super Bowl champion makes the final selection each time through the order. There are seven rounds in the draft, down in number significantly from years gone by. The number makes sense when you consider that what once was a league of 12 to 14 teams in the 1960s is now at 32 teams (when Houston rejoins).

Also, a team may not wish to remain in its assigned position in the draft order, making the trading of one draft slot for other slots and/or other players already belonging to another team a common practice. On the titanic end of this wheeling-and-dealing spectrum, the New Orleans Saints traded all their other picks in the 1999 draft to Washington in order to move up to a first-round slot high enough to select University of Texas running back Ricky Williams. Less than a year later, the entire Saints' "brain trust" that orchestrated the dramatic transaction had been fired.

Creating a scene reminiscent of the old "Let's Make a Deal" game show, a limited number of fans actually attend the draft proceedings. These "draftniks" come decked out in their very best game-day garb and brandish signs that, shall we say, strongly suggest what player they would like to see their favorite team select. The first round, especially the early stages, is famous for fan demonstrations that either lobby for a certain player or, after the pick has been made, express deep feelings of betrayal or joy as to what new player has come into the fold.

With the draft traditionally held in New York City, Jet and Giant fans are especially prevalent, with Philadelphia usually well represented. The next woman to attend as part of the grandstand area peanut gallery may well become the first. If that pioneer should turn out to be you, I suggest wearing a helmet. Needless to say, the emotion and noise level created by the spectators give the draft much of the sensory flavor that networks are looking for when airing a live event. Another plus is that most, if not all, of the prospective first-round selections now attend the draft in person, affording the first photo opportunities and "how does it feel" interviews as the player dons the colors and logo of his new team via hat, jersey or both. Some draftees bring mom or girlfriend along, so the draft is not totally foreign turf for the female population.

Television brought the draft out of the closed-door conference room and into the major media spectacle it is today. The transformation began when ESPN arrived on the scene in September 1979 as a fledgling operation, notably prior to its meteoric rise as the dominant network in the television sports industry. Rodeo and lumberjack competitions were staples of early ESPN programming, as the cable network did not have the capital to compete for major televised sporting events. But, what the network was short on in dollars, it made up for in creativity, as they aligned the network with the NFL by turning the draft into a made-for-TV event. In 1980, a televised draft became a reality, and ESPN, along with sister network ESPN2 in recent years, has broadcast the event since.

One final note. At some point over the years, the final player chosen in the NFL Draft was tagged with the nickname "Mr. Irrelevant," no doubt by a grizzled scribe in the days when the process was colorless and consisted of 17 or more rounds. Many a last pick has indeed disappeared into football oblivion, never to appear on an NFL field. However, some have beaten the odds to have solid, if not Hall-of-Fame careers.

Training Camp

For approximately six weeks starting in mid-July, each NFL team holds training camp to select its roster and prepare the players, both physically and mentally, for the upcoming season. Though 90 to 100 players may be invited to participate at camp, only 53 will remain at the end of what is often a grueling and brutal process.

There was a time when much of training camp was spent working extra weight off bodies that had grown soft during the off season. Keep in mind that 30 or 40 years ago, even an upper-echelon NFL player needed another means of income after the football season concluded, as salaries were less-than-sufficient in those days. In other words, selling cars or tending bar for six months didn't exactly leave guys in game shape, and they sometimes dragged their spare tires onto the field at the start of camp. Factor in the stifling heat of the mid-summer months in a state like Georgia, and you can picture how painful mere survival of camp was in the early years.

Today, a player is expected to show up in better-than-good shape, and even then, the training is rigorous and demanding. Better salaries mean greater expectations from management, and increased competition for these high-paying jobs make no player irreplaceable. Knowing this, most athletes maintain routines of off-season conditioning to avoid being left in the dust once camp swings into gear. To help this process along, and to keep a closer eye on the gigantic investments made in players these days, organizations now hold periodic off-season "mini-camps." These two or three-day sessions spread the conditioning and learning curves throughout nearly the entire calendar year. Thus, an "off season" in pro football is practically extinct.

One distinguishing feature of the summer training camp environment is that it has traditionally been quite fan friendly. NFL teams usually seek a small-town college environment for summer sessions, and spectators can usually attend practices for little or no charge. Such locales serve the obvious purpose of housing and feeding large groups of men in a dormitory setting. Beyond that, finding a training camp home as far away from the lights and night life of any municipality with more than one traffic signal is also a priority. Part of the strict regimen is designed to eliminate any temptations leading to unsuitable behavior or inability to perform. Regardless, training camp is a marvelous opportunity to get an up-close view of what players actually look like under all that equipment. Full pads are often not used as a concession to the heat, and players often walk among the spectators while moving to and from a practice session. In a sport that takes on an ancient gladiator-esque feel on game day, the training camp atmosphere opens the door to observe the more human element of football.

Each team plays four or five preseason games during training camp to get ready for the regular schedule. These used to be called "exhibition" games until team owners decided to include them in season ticket packages and charge full price for admission. Nonetheless, these games allow players a chance to strut their stuff during game conditions, or get used to the feel of the game, which is especially important to the rookies or experienced back-up players on the fringes of the roster. Established players see only enough playing time to shake off the rust for fear of injury. Despite such precautions, many a star player has been lost for an entire year due to an injury suffered in a preseason game.

Training camp location normally stays the same year after year, and the dates are approximately the same each year. Call your team's main office to check on locations and dates.

TEAM	LOCATION
Arizona	Northern Arizona, Flagstaff, Arizona
Atlanta	Furman University Greenville, South Carolina
Baltimore	Western Maryland College, Westminster, Maryland
Buffalo	St. John Fisher College, Pittsford, New York
Carolina	Wofford College, Spartanburg, South Carolina
Chicago	Wisconsin - Platteville, Platteville, Wisconsin
Cincinnati	Georgetown College, Georgetown, Kentucky
Cleveland	Browns Training Facility, Berea, Ohio
Dallas	Midwestern State University, Wichita Falls, Texas
Denver	Northern Colorado, Greeley, Colorado
Detroit	Saginaw Valley State University, Saginaw, Michigan
Green Bay	St. Norbert Colleve, De Pere, Wisconsin
Houston	Houston, Texas, Reliant Park, Houston
Indianapolis	Rose-Hulman Institute, Terre Haute, Indiana
Jacksonville	ALLTEL Stadium, Jacksonville, Florida
Kansas City	Wisconsin - River Falls, River Falls, Wisconsin
Miami	Nova University, Davie, Florida
Minnesota	Mankato State University, Mankato, Minnesota
New England	Bryant College, Smithfield, Rhode Island
New Orleans	Nichols State University, Thibodaux, Louisiana
N.Y. Giants	State University at Albany, Albany, New York
N.Y. Jets	Hofstra University, Hempstead, New York
Oakland	Napa Valley Marriott, Napa, California
Philadelphia	Lehigh University, Bethlehem, Pennsylvania
Pittsburgh	St. Vincent College, Latrobe, Pennsylvania
San Diego	California - San Diego, La Jolla, California
San Francisco	University of Pacific, Stockton, California
Seattle	Eastern Washington University, Cheney, Washington
St. Louis	Western Illinois University, Macomb, Illinois
Tampa Bay	University of Tampa, Tampa, Florida
Tennessee	Tennessee State University, Nashville, Tennessee
Washington	Redskin Park, Ashburn, Virginia

Games

The NFL regular season begins each year in early September and ends around Christmas time in December. It consists of 17 weeks, as each team plays 16 games with one off, or "bye," week. Although byes had existed previously, Cleveland's return to the league in 1999 lifted such weeks to a very practical status. The Browns became the 31st NFL team, meaning that with an odd number of league participants, at least one team has to be idle each week of the season.

One certainty of a given team's schedule is that it will play each team within its division twice during the regular season, once at home and once on the road. For instance, the Minnesota Vikings know that half of their regular-season games will be against Chicago, Detroit, Green Bay and Tampa Bay every year. The rest of any team's schedule is determined by an NFL formula and applied to the results of the previous season. This practice is designed

Super Bowl
facts and figures

SUPER BOWL HOST CITIES:
- New Orleans (8 times)
- Miami (8)
- Los Angeles (7)
- San Diego (2)
- Atlanta (2)
- Arizona (1)
- Detroit (1)
- Houston (1)
- Minneapolis (1)
- Stanford (1)
- Tampa (3)

FUTURE SUPER BOWL SITES:
- Super Bowl XXXVI, Superdome, New Orleans, La., Feb. 3, 2002
- Super Bowl XXXVII, Qualcomm Stadium, San Diego, Calif., Jan. 26, 2003
- Super Bowl XXXVIII, Reliant Stadium, Houston Tx., February 1, 2004
- Super Bowl XXXVIX, Alltel Stadium, Jacksonville, Fla., February 6, 2005
- Super Bowl XL, Ford Field, Detroit, Mi., February 5, 2006

COST OF THE VINCE LOMBARDI TROPHY: $12,000

WHO MAKES THE SUPER BOWL TROPHY: Tiffany & Co. of New York

COST OF SUPER BOWL RINGS: League pays for up to 125 rings at $5,000 per ring (plus adjustments for increases in gold and diamonds). League also pays for 125 pieces of jewelry for the losing team, which may not cost more than one-half the price set for the Super Bowl ring.

to balance the teams, so that first-place teams are asked to play, on paper at least, a more ambitious schedule than a last-place team. A team with a "fifth-place" schedule is one that did not perform well in the previous season and is often matched against another team with similar credentials from the year before.

The importance of each regular-season game in the NFL is magnified by the fact that such a small number of contests determine which teams qualify for the play-offs. Compare 16 NFL games to the 162 games that make up the season in major league baseball, or the 82-game season played in professional basketball. A three-game losing streak in baseball is a blip on the radar screen. In the NFL, dropping three in a row often inspires articles and commentaries calling for the head coach's scalp. There are NFL seasons in which a 10-6 record is not quite good enough to reach the playoffs, although there have been circumstances when an 8-8 mark has been enough to sneak a team into the post-season. Regardless, the small number of regular-season games has a great impact on the intensity level of the team each time it takes the field. One catch, fumble, missed tackle or official's decision in any one game could well determine whether a team gets a chance to compete for the championship.

Playoffs

The road to the Super Bowl begins with 12 teams qualifying for the playoffs, six each from the American Football Conference (AFC) and the National Football Conference (NFC). Each conference is comprised of three divisions of at least five teams each.

The six teams that finish at the top of the NFL's six divisions automatically reach the playoffs. These six account for half of the post-season field. Each conference will also produce three "wild card" teams, or the three teams in each conference with the best records among the teams that are not division winners. Three weeks of playoffs will determine a conference champion for both the AFC and NFC. The two conference champions become the opponents in the Super Bowl.

Of the three division winners in a conference, the two teams with the best records receive a bye during the first week of the playoffs and automatically play at home the following week. Historically, combining the elements of an extra week of rest and preparation time, plus home-field advantage for the conference semi-final game, has been a solid recipe for success. Rarely does a team plow its way through "Wild Card Weekend" and make it all the way to the Super Bowl, although Denver won the championship in January 1998 having done just that.

The home teams for the first round of the playoffs are the division champion with the third-best record and the team with the best record among the wild card contingent. The division champ matches up against the team with the worst record among the three wild card clubs, and the other two wild card teams meet head-to-head.

Week two of the post-season always features at least one surviving wild card team per conference, and sometimes two each. The next round features the week one survivor with the worst record visiting the division winner with the best record, and the division winner with the second best record hosting the other winner from the first round. Thus, consecutive playoff weekends in the NFL trim hopeful teams from 12 to four, with two games (one in each conference) being played on successive Saturdays and Sundays.

The AFC and NFC championship games are played back-to-back on the Sunday of playoff week three. The winners advance to what is perhaps the sports world's most-watched single-day event, the Super Bowl. The Indianapolis 500 was traditionally the largest one-day sporting event.

Super Bowl

The first Super Bowl was played in the Los Angeles Coliseum on January 15, 1967. There were 20,000 empty seats for the 35-10 Green Bay victory over Kansas City. Even so, the game's result seemed to verify that the established NFL was far superior to the upstart American Football League. The 1968 game did little to change anyone's opinion, as the Packers romped again by a 33-14 count, this time against the Oakland Raiders. This time, though, the stands were full. The next year, the game that finally changed the course of professional football history and really put the Super Bowl on the map, roman numerals and all, came along.

The Green Bay/Kansas City game had been billed officially as the "World Championship of Professional Football," with the term "Super Bowl" sort of floating about as an unofficial nickname. But by January of 1969, the annual collision of the powers of the NFL and AFL became officially known as the Super Bowl, with the appro-

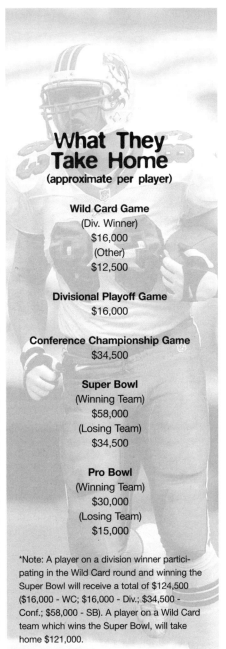

What They Take Home
(approximate per player)

Wild Card Game
(Div. Winner)
$16,000
(Other)
$12,500

Divisional Playoff Game
$16,000

Conference Championship Game
$34,500

Super Bowl
(Winning Team)
$58,000
(Losing Team)
$34,500

Pro Bowl
(Winning Team)
$30,000
(Losing Team)
$15,000

*Note: A player on a division winner participating in the Wild Card round and winning the Super Bowl will receive a total of $124,500 ($16,000 - WC; $16,000 - Div.; $34,500 - Conf.; $58,000 - SB). A player on a Wild Card team which wins the Super Bowl, will take home $121,000.

Grid for Football Pool

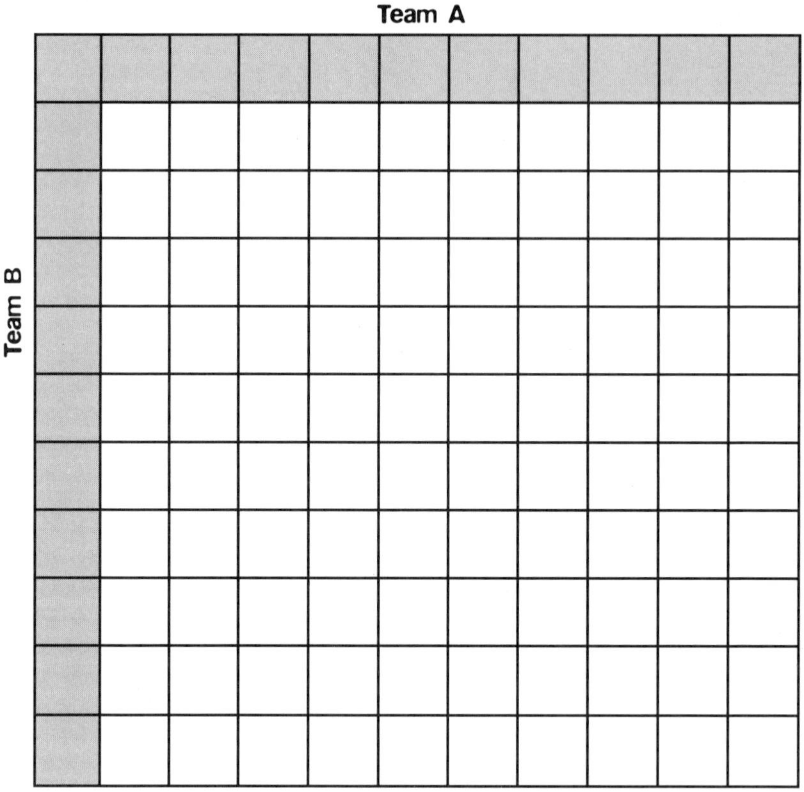

Team A

Team B

A grid is drawn with 100 squares. Each square is $5.00. The pool players write their name in the square they choose. When all the squares have sold, randomly draw numbers zero through nine out of a "hat," and write the numbers vertically. Then draw the numbers one through nine again and place those numbers horizontally. Draw again for AFC and NFC and put the first drawn on the vertical and the second on the horizontal.

Place a value on each quarter ($25), and the half ($50). At the end of the first half, according to the score, the person that has the corresponding square gets the $25. At the end of the game, the balance or "pot" goes to the person whose name is on that square.

priate roman-numeral designation affixed at the end. Thus, it was Super Bowl III, featuring the Baltimore Colts and the New York Jets that remains lodged in the minds of veteran football observers as a major milestone.

Baltimore had terrorized the NFL during the 1968 season. How dominant were the Colts? They defeated the Browns 34-0 in the NFL title game, in Cleveland no less, earning the trip to Miami to meet the Jets for the big game. New York had enjoyed a good season, but it was a surprise to many when the Jets squeaked by the defending champion Raiders on a late touchdown in the AFL championship game. The score was 27-23.

Given the brief history of previous Super Bowl games, and the path of destruction the Colts left in their wake during their regular season, no one was giving the Jets a chance. The most common point spread had Baltimore at an 18 1/2 point favorite to win, or better than two touchdowns and a field goal. Today, you will see such odds on an NFL game maybe once a season, and then it would only occur if the league's very best team is playing the very worst. Writers, broadcasters and fans predicted and braced themselves for a slaughter. The mighty Colts would reign supreme.

Didn't happen. New York won the game. Easily.

Guided by brash and confident quarterback, Joe Namath, the Jets built a 16-0 lead and coasted to the historic 16-7 win that lifted the AFL from amusement park sideshow status to legitimacy. The Jets intercepted five passes, part of a Baltimore meltdown that had seemed impossible. In Super Bowl IV, the last before the NFL and AFL became the NFC and AFC in a unified National Football League, the AFL ruled again, with Kansas City whipping the favored Minnesota Vikings 23-7.

But it was the Jets, based in New York, the world's media capital and led by the young, hip and handsome star that brought the beanstalk crashing down. Even today, many old timers who were associated with the AFL grow misty-eyed and sentimental at the thought of the Jets underdog, but amazing triumph. The Jets have not appeared in the Super Bowl since.

The Colts won Super Bowl V, then never returned before relocating to Indianapolis 13 years later. The Indianapolis Colts have not yet been to the Super Bowl. Through Super Bowl XXXV (that's 35 for those annoyed by long series of letters) in January 2001, Dallas and San Francisco share the honor of posting the most Super Bowl wins with five each.

Pittsburgh is the AFC team that has enjoyed the most success, having won the big game four times from 1975 through 1980. The Saints and Cardinals have been in the NFL the longest without ever having reached the Super Bowl, with Atlanta and Tennessee making maiden voyages (although losing ventures) in 1999 and 2000 respectively. The Baltimore Ravens made their first appearance, and won, in 2001.

Beyond the football, this event has become a two-week (though sometimes there has been only a week between the conference title games and the Super Bowl) extravaganza for the host city, usually located in the Sun Belt. Fanfests, corporate parties, the league dinners and gatherings, the media and, oh yeah, the teams themselves, are all part of the dizzying build up.

Cities most often associated with this scene over the years are Miami, New Orleans and Los Angeles (although now L.A. doesn't have a team). Phoenix hosted a Super Bowl and Atlanta has become a regular in the rotation. Even cold-weather sites Pontiac, Michigan (where the Detroit Lions play) and Minneapolis have been included to host football's premier event. Regardless of the locale, or the team you're cheering for, the game has become a party that rivals New Year's Eve celebrations. It's Super Bowl Sunday. And one item never to be found again in a Super Bowl stadium is an empty seat.

Major College Conferences

More than 100 institutions of higher learning participate in the brand of competition known as "major college" football. It has nothing to do with the size of the university in terms of student population (Notre Dame, for instance, does not have a high enrollment) and everything to do with money. Sure, there's plenty of dough to be made by the powerhouse programs what is termed Division 1-A level, but football is also an expensive sport to finance for recruiting, scholarships, staff salaries, equipment and travel. That being said, the best teams in the major conferences are the ones with the realistic chances to play in the major bowl games (recall holiday football) with an eye on the ultimate prize, a national championship.

The landscape of big-time college football is dominated by six conferences. They are the Big 10, Big 12, Big East, Pacific 10 (Pac), Southeastern Conference (SEC) and the Atlantic Coast Conference (ACC). The popular football program at Notre Dame is known as an independent, really the only major school without a conference affiliation. Ironically, the Fighting Irish basketball team plays in the Big East, but that's an entirely different book.

The Big 10 is widely considered to be the "big dog" of the college football scene. Many Big 10 member schools have participated in intercollegiate athletics for over a century. For years, this conference was labeled the "Big Two," because of the dominance of Ohio State and Michigan over an extended period of time. Recent years have seen Wisconsin, Michigan State and Purdue rise to prominence, and Penn State, a "newcomer" to the conference. Penn State joined the Big Ten in 1993, but nobody dropped out in the process. So, schools with great traditions and high educational standards play in a conference that has 11 teams, but is still called the Big 10. Go figure.

The Big 12 is a hybrid of the old Big Eight and Southwestern Conferences. There is great tradition among member schools such as Nebraska, Oklahoma, Texas and Texas A&M, but not in a structure that finds them under the same umbrella. Kansas State, college football doormat for decade upon decade, has become a Big 12 power too. This conference and the SEC share some unique qualities due to their size. Each conference is split into two six-team divisions, with the respective division winners ultimately meeting in a conference championship game each December. The winner of these showdowns, a new phenomenon within the past few years, is almost surely ticketed for a major bowl game. Florida, Alabama and Tennessee have dominated the SEC for some time, with Georgia, Auburn and Mississippi State barking at their heels.

The Pac 10 champion is usually headed for the traditional Rose Bowl match up against the winner of the Big 10. This conference, known in recent years for wide open, high-scoring games and the lack of a dominant team, houses the likes of Arizona, Arizona State, USC, UCLA and Washington. On the opposite coast, the ACC has one member school that has made the conference championship its own personal domain: Florida State. Only Georgia Tech and Virginia have mounted consistent resistance to FSU over the years. Teams like Clemson and North Carolina have programs with great tradition.

The Big East was a basketball conference at first, and built its reputation in the 80s with hardwood powerhouses like Georgetown, St. John's and Villanova ruling the roost. All these schools have football teams now, too, but they do not compete in Division 1-A or the Big East. This is a distinguishing characteristic of this conference, as mentioned above in regards to Notre Dame. The member schools of the other five conferences are exactly the same regardless of the sport in question.

Obviously, this is not so in the Big East, the baby of them all when in comes to major college football. Still, this conference produced an outstanding Virginia Tech team at the turn of the new century, which lost to Florida State in the championship game in January of 2000. Miami of Florida and Syracuse are other Big East teams that are usually capable of competing with anyone, with Miami having won national titles as an independent before the formation of the conference.

The New Championship Game, created in 1998, guarantees a National Champion among college teams. A combination of coaches and media member polls, as well as complicated, computer-based ranking systems determines which teams will chase the national championship each season. The two top-ranked teams after the regular season (including the Big Twelve and SEC championship games) meet in the championship game, which rotates now among the four major Bowls.

The Bowl BCS games are the Rose, Orange, Sugar and Fiesta Bowls. You will hear this referred to as the Bowl Championship Series, but all that makes it a series is that the three non-title games are played in succession on or around New Year's Day on the same television network, all to better promote the ultimate game a couple days later. The Sugar Bowl in New Orleans had the Virginia Tech/Florida State game on Jan. 4, 2000, a Tuesday night. Wouldn't want to interfere with the NFL's Monday Night Football now would we?

Conferences

ORANGE BOWL: Hosts the winner of the ACC and Big East Conference

ACC - ATLANTIC COAST CONFERENCE
- Clemson Tigers
- Duke Blue Devils
- Florida State Seminoles
- Georgia Tech Yellow Jackets
- North Carolina State Wolfpack
- North Carolina Tar Heels
- Virginia Cavaliers
- Wake Forest Demon Deacons
- Maryland Terrapins

BIG EAST CONFERENCE
- Boston College Eagles
- Miami (Fla.) Hurricanes
- Pittsburgh Panthers
- Rutgers Scarlet Knights
- Syracuse Orangemen
- Temple Owls
- Virginia Tech Hokies
- West Virginia Mountaineers

ROSE BOWL: Hosts the winner of the Big Ten and PAC-10 Conferences

BIG 10 CONFERENCE
- Illinois Fighting Illini
- Indiana Hoosiers
- Iowa Hawkeyes
- Michigan Wolverines
- Michigan State Spartans
- Minnesota Golden Gophers
- Northwestern Wildcats
- Ohio State Buckeyes

- Penn State Nittany Lions
- Purdue Boilermakers
- Wisconsin Badgers

PAC 10 CONFERENCE
- Arizona Wildcats
- Arizona State Sun Devils
- California Golden Bears
- Oregon Ducks
- Oregon State Beavers
- Stanford Cardinal
- UCLA Bruins
- USC Trojans
- Washington Huskies
- Washington State Cougars
- California Golden Bears

SUGAR BOWL: Hosts the winner of the SEC Conference

SOUTHEASTERN CONFERENCE
- Alabama Crimson Tide
- Arkansas Razorbacks
- Auburn Tigers
- Florida Gators
- Georgia Bulldogs
- Kentucky Wildcats
- LSU Tigers
- Mississippi State Bulldogs
- Ole Miss Rebels
- South Carolina Gamecocks
- Tennessee Volunteers
- Vanderbilt Commodores

continued on page 64

FIESTA BOWL: Hosts the
winner of the Big 12 Conference

BIG 12 CONFERENCE
- Colorado Buffaloes
- Iowa State Cyclones
- Kansas Jayhawks
- Kansas State Wildcats
- Missouri Tigers
- Nebraska Cornhuskers
- Baylor Bears
- Oklahoma Sooners
- Oklahoma State Cowboys
- Texas Longhorns
- Texas A&M Aggies
- Texas Tech Red Raiders

WAC
- Boise State Broncos
- Fresno State Bulldogs
- Hawaii rainbow Warriors
- Louisiana Tech Bulldogs
- Nevada Wolfpack
- San Jose State Spartans
- Texas El Paso Miners
- Tulsa Golden Hurricane

MOUNTAIN WEST
- Air Force Falcons
- Brigham Young (BYU) Cougars
- Colorado State Rams
- New Mexico Lobos
- San Diego State Aztecs
- UNLV Rebels
- Utah Utes
- Utep Miners
- Wyoming Cowboys

IA INDEPENDENTS
- Connecticut Huskies
- Navy Midshipman
- Notre Dame Fighting Irish
- South Florida Bulls
- Troy State Trojans

MID AMERICA
- Akron Zips
- Ball State Cardinals
- Bowling Green Falcons
- Buffalo Bulls
- Central Michigan Chippewas
- Eastern Michigan Eagles
- Kent State Golden Flashes
- Marshall Thundering herd
- Miami (Oh) Redhawks
- Northern Ill Huskies
- Ohio Bobcats
- Toledo Rockets
- Western Michigan Broncos

CONFERENCE USA
- Army Cadets
- Cincinnati Bearcats
- East Carolina Pirates
- Houston Cougars
- Louisville Cardinals
- Memphis Tigers
- Southern Mississipp
  Golden Eagles
- Tulane Green Wave
- Alabama-Birmingham Blazers

SUNBELT CONFERENCE
- Kansas St. Indians
- Idaho Vandals
- Louisiana Lafayette
  Ragin Cajuns
- Louisiana Monroe Indians
- Middle Tennessee
  St. Blue Raiders
- New Mexico St. Aggies
- North Texas Eagles

Movies continued from page 11.

The Replacements (2000)
Keanu Reeves, Gene Hackman
When professional athletes go on strike, the league builds a hodge-podge team with replacement players. Comedy ensues. Expect a couple laughs, a warm ending and the annoying urge to hum Gloria Gaynor's "I Will Survive" for a couple days.

Varsity Blues (1999)
James Van Der Beek, Jon Voight
Bud Kilmer has coached his West Canaan, Texas, AAA team to two state championships and 22 district championships in his 35-year tenure. There's a big bronze statue of Coach Kilmer right outside of the stadium which is named for him. The story revolves around Van Der Beek and his girl friend (Amy Smart) who rebel against the football mania gripping everyone around them.

All the Right Moves (1983)
Tom Cruise, Craig T. Nelson
A coming-of-age story that follows Cruise's character struggling to escape the confines of his hometown by way of a football scholarship.

School Ties (1992)
Brendan Fraser, Chris O'Donnell, Matt Damon, Ben Affleck
A thoughtful movie set in the 1950s about a talented college player (Fraser) who must hide his true identity to avoid losing his chance at football glory. Look for early performances from the now-famous Matt-and-Ben duo.

Everybody's All American (1988)
Jessica Lange, Dennis Quaid, Timothy Hutton, John Goodman
A legendary high school football player marries his homecoming queen sweetheart and embarks on a professional career fraught with trials as well as glories.

Best of Times (1986)
Comedy, PG-13
Robin Williams, Kurt Russell
Two high school football players who literally dropped the ball in a championship moment feel the sting years later. They reunite in an inspired attempt to relive their big game by challenging the rival team as adults.

The Longest Yard (1974)
Burt Reynolds
Reynolds plays an imprisoned quarterback who leads his fellow inmates to victory in a wild and crooked football game.

Johnny Be Good (1988)
Anthony Michael Hall, Robert Downey, Jr., Uma Thurman
Graduating from the geek he made famous, Hall portrays hometown football stud, Johnny Walker, the most coveted high school recruit in the country. When universities come calling, Johnny must decide what kind of ball he really wants to play. Light and entertaining, this movie makes fun of the excesses of big-money college programs before the title character redeems himself.

The Last Boy Scout (1991)
Bruce Willis, Damon Wayans
This quick-paced action stars Willis as a private detective who reluctantly partners with an ex-football player to uncover a murder. Once involved, the duo realizes just how deep this rabbit hole goes, as they confront corruption in high places.

Lucas (1986)
Corey Haim, Charlie Sheen
A sweet movie about a nerdy "whiz kid" who intellect places him in high school, but whose maturity puts him in dangerous position on the football field when he tries to impress his older classmate "crush."

Necessary Roughness (1991)
Scott Bakula, Kathy Ireland, Hector Elizondo, Robert Loggia, Jason Batemen
A very funny story about what happens after Texas State University loses their football team due to NCAA violations and scandals.

The Waterboy (1998)
Adam Sandler, Henry Winkler, Kathy Bates
This goofball comedy has Adam Sandler as a socially-retarded 31-year-old Cajun football waterboy who's been tormented all his life by everyone around him — until he joins a losing college football team and learns to transform his anger into awesome tackles.

Pigskin parade (1936)
Judy Garland, Betty Grable, Jack Haley, Patsy Kelly, Stuart ErwinStar
It's musical hijinks on the gridiron when a college coaching team pulls in a dark horse quarterback—a naive local farm boy—to catapult Texas State University to victory against the Yale Bulldogs. Garland's major film debut. Songs include "You Say the Darndest Thing," "It's Love I'm After," and "Down With Everything" (this sung by Alan Ladd in one of his first roles).

Wildcats (1986)
Goldie Hawn
A petite teacher whose father was a coach gets a chance to follow in his footsteps when she is put in charge of an unruly inner-city high school football team.

Air Bud: Golden Receiver. (1998)
Kevin Zegers, Cynthia Stevenson, Gregory Harrison, Nora Dunn
Air Bud is back, this time on the gridiron as he saves the day for his young master's junior high school football team. There's the obligatory villains to attempt to foil Bud's football victory — here in the form of two fumbling Russian circus crooks who steal extraordinary pets for their show — but never fear, the dog conquers all, along the way saving the coach's job as well as mom's romance.

Ace Ventura—Pet Detective (1994)
Jim Carrey, Courteney Cox
The first major showing of Carrey quirkiness, Ace Ventura is the title character who must use his animal-finding detective skills to find the Miami Dolphin's mascot. His adventures ultimately lead him to unmask a scandal involving the real Dan Marino.

Former Miami Dolphins wide receiver Tony Martin, now with the Atlanta Falcons

Chapter 5
The Team

One of the most crucial aspects to understanding the game is to know the positions, and what to look for when the 22 men take to the field. Well, we know what you're looking *at*, but there's a little bit more to it than that.

Professional positions take a lot of talent, a great deal of practice and a tremendous level of specialization. These are big jobs. These are high-pressure positions. And, there's a lot of competition both on and off the field for these coveted spots on game day. Let's take a look at what these guys do and learn more about roles so pivotal, small mistakes can win and lose games.

DEFENSE: THE DEFENSIVE LINE

When you call these guys the "big, bulky" types, it's a compliment. In fact, these guys, who on average weigh 300 pounds, count on it. But, be careful not to confuse their weight with a lack of talent or athleticism. Typically the largest guys on the field, the defensive linemen have to among the most coordinated, quick and agile of all players. Remember, their jobs rely on stopping offensive opportunities before they start.

Player Position	Uniform Number
quarterback, punter, place kicker	1-19
running back, defensive back	20-49
center	50-59 (or 60-79 if needed)
linebacker	50-59 (or 90-99 if needed)
offensive guard, tackle	60-79
defensive lineman	60-79 (or 90-99 if needed)
wide receiver	80-89
tight end	80-89 (or 40-49 if needed)

As the defensive linemen approach the line of scrimmage, they are facing an equally-daunting array of strength and opposition in the offensive line. These two lines will do nothing short of battle, as the defense prepares to invade the territory they protect in order to keep the play-makers safe. To do this, and keep significant offensive gains from happening, they have to take teamwork to another level, and collaborate to stop the run through at least four aggressive, intense attempts. Formations and alignments will change as the linemen use every tactical skill at their command to anticipate the next offensive move. All the while, they will be a human wall of resistance to the offensive attack. The composition of the line is custom-built, since a wall has no strength without considerable reinforcement.

The Line
NOSE TACKLE

This player lines up "nose-to-nose" against the center. Because the center is the foreman of offensive timing, the nose tackle's game has to be precise and decisive. He will not be the defensive player to receive the glory for a sack or tackle that brings down the offensive effort, but he is definitely a staple of the defensive foundation.

The nose tackle is notoriously double-teamed, due mainly to the impending danger if he is released in a too-close-for-comfort position to the quarterback. In his position, he is responsible for securing the gaps on either side of the center. At the snap, the nose tackle erupts into action, attacking the center with his arms and hands. Usually, these two positions will battle it out while the main action of the play occurs around them.

This position requires a keen instinct, as a sneaky center can throw him into penaltyland with a disguised movement or noise. To avoid false start or offsides setbacks, the nose tackle must play hard through each down.

DEFENSIVE TACKLES

Two players generally hold this position, located on the field inside from the defensive ends, and opposite the opposing offensive guards. The job description varies slightly from play to play, but primarily, these players are there to read the play and stop the attack.

This may involve changing alignments, or "stunting," which are maneuvers designed to disrupt and confuse the offensive line and their blocking strategies. It's all about the competition in these positions, a constant shifting, moving and changing plans in order to analyze how the offense is playing and what, if any, weaknesses they can exploit to their benefit. If they find that weakness, look for the defensive tackles to favor that side, whether it's to the right or left, and stop long offensive gains.

DEFENSIVE ENDS

Outside the tackles' shoulders and sometimes over the offensive tackle is where you will find the defensive ends. Their alignment is based on the defensive call or scheme. The two ends are responsible for chasing the quarterback and occasionally come up with the big defensive coups by sacking the passer. For this reason, they are generally the fastest of the defensive team, and even come in under the average weight of the defensive line.

Because most quarterbacks are right-handers, the ends are stacked to maximize chances of eliminating any passer gains, whether aerial or on the run. The left defensive end is a little stronger for the run, a bigger force on the tackle. The right end can usually rush the passer quicker and better, with the ability to slide through and around offensive holes. Destination: ball carrier.

LINEBACKERS

Linebackers must be a combination of high intensity and intelligence to work in a position that requires a wide variety of responsibilities and a sixth-sense instinct about the movement on the field. They will range in size, from tall and fast to match the speed of a running back, or shorter and stout, with the ability to be instrumental in a barrier to the offensive assault.

Some linebackers will specialize in stopping the run, while others are better suited to combat the pass. Defensive strategies rely on the linebackers joining the defensive backfield to literally "mix it up." Depending on the performance of the offense, specifically which part of the game is their strongest, linebackers will move around with the intent to force the quarterback and offensive players to monitor them closely and hopefully, break their offensive stride as they try to stay out of linebacker danger.

If an offensive player gets into linebacker danger, he is likely to be tackled. This is the main objective of this type of back, to get to the ball by getting the ball carrier. Other job descriptions entail blitzing the quarterback, or leaving their position or assignment in order to pressure the passer. They must defend in the zone that is known as short-deep areas on their side of the line of scrimmage.

The middle linebacker is important, as he makes the defensive calls on alignment and movement after anticipating what the offense will do after breaking their huddle. This player has to know every intricacy of the game they are in and quickly adapt to the circumstances as they happen.

In a man-to-man coverage scheme, the linebacker has to be prepared to run along with a quick wide receiver. In other coverage routines, they are responsible for watching and staying with the tight ends and backs. But, as often as they move around in an effort to predict the play, you can spot the linebackers as the leading tacklers against the offense, in constant pursuit of the ball carrier.

THE SECONDARY

This is a group of players that make up the defensive backfield. He is the final line of defense, right behind the defensive line and linebackers, and if the offense breaks through them, scoring is imminent. Their job is to break up the offensive play by tackling the ball carrier or creating an impenetrable wall.

Depending on the defensive scheme a coach opts to employ, this line will consist of three to seven players. The backfield consists of the following positions:

CORNERBACK

He is typically the fastest of the defensive backs, able to move quickly and burst into the field after the offensive run. One of the greatest challenges he faces is on the passing play, and he often goes one-on-one with a receiver. Because he cannot hide in the line, and is often exposed to a ball carrier in an open field, any cornerback must accelerate his performance for successful defense.

In man-to-man coverage, most schemes use two-cornerback coverage on the offense's wide receivers. The cornerback lines up on the far left and right sides of the line of scrimmage, five to 12 yards from their nearest teammate and opposite the offensive wide receiver. In general, it is the best cornerbacks against the best receivers. In this structure, ability is matched against ability, and the friction heightens the competition.

Smaller, slower cornerbacks that don't match up well against the offensive receivers will play more zone coverages so that the fast receivers do not exploit the secondary's weaknesses.

SAFETIES

The safeties lead the secondary in much the same way as the middle linebacker leads the defensive line. He will read the offensive play and formation, and adjust the backfield accordingly, which is why this position is nicknamed "defensive quarterback." His duty does not duplicate the middle linebacker's, as the linebacker focuses on his region, and the safeties, farther in the backfield, see to it that coverage adjustments are made based on what they recognize from the offensive formation.

There are two safeties: a strong safety and a free safety.

Strong safety: the bigger and stronger of the two, but not as quick as linebackers. They are above-average tacklers though, and can make the bone-crushing hits you hear on TV. They must have the ability to drop into pass coverage quickly, which entails backpedaling and retreating to cover a specific area left open to an offensive threat.

The strong safety often aligns to the strong side, which is to the tight end side of the offensive formation and how the position has derived its name. Due to this location, his pass coverage is primarily oriented to the tight end or a running back who leaves the backfield.

GAMEDAY GOURMET

Any football fan will tell you, food and snacks are important gameday accessories. 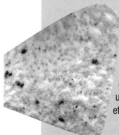 Beyond the typical menu fare of beer and pretzels or nachos and salsa, a buffet of low maintenance items can add a little culinary flair for the game. *The Chicks' Guide to Football* presents unique recipes for the perfect variety to the traditional snack tray.

Spinach & Artichoke Dip   *Serves 8*

3 cups mozzarella cheese
  divided (2 1/4 c. and 3/4 c.)
1/4 cup sour cream
1/4 tsp. black pepper
5 garlic cloves, crushed
1 can artichoke hearts, drained and chopped
2 (8oz.) packages of cream cheese, softened
3/4 package frozen chopped spinach, thawed,
  drained and squeezed dry
1 bag tortilla chips, large
1 french baguette, slices

Preheat oven to 350 degrees. Combine 2 1/4 cups mozzarella cheese, sour cream, black pepper, garlic, artichoke hearts, cream cheese and spinach. Spoon mixture into a 9X13 baking dish. Sprinkle top with remaining mozzarella cheese.

Bake at 350 for 30 minutes, or until cheese is golden brown. Serve with tortilla chips and baguette slices

Seven-Layer Bean Dip with Chipotle Sour Cream   *Serves 8*

2 cans refried beans
1 box spanish rice mix
2 cups cheddar cheese
2 cups guacamole
2 cans black beans
2 cups mozzarella cheese
2 cups salsa
2 cups sour cream
5 chipotle peppers (or any other pepper such as jalapeno or red bell)

Layer first seven ingredients in a 9X13 baking dish. Put in a 350-degree oven until cheese has melted (about 15-20 minutes). Top with chipotle sour cream.

Expect the strong safety to excel against the run offense. He can defend in pass and man-to-man coverage, but it's not his specialty. The strong safety is nearer the line of scrimmage, which is why he is more reliable to stop the run. He is also positioned to defend the tight end when he runs out on a pass pattern.

Free safety: a more athletic, but less physical player, the free safety positions himself 12 to 15 yards deep and off the line of scrimmage. He must be quick, because he will run in prevention of the long touchdown pass while simultaneously covering gaps in the field. He is the final line of defense against a long pass, and has to anticipate that kind of intention from the quarterback. He is trained to watch the QB closely, since a good free safety can get a hint where the ball is going.

This position must be able to defend against a wide receiver in man-to-man coverage. If an offense uses three receivers, there's an extra that goes uncovered (the first two are covered by the cornerbacks) and that receiver becomes the responsibility of the free safety.

NICKEL AND DIME BACKS

It can be complicated, and there are no official designations for nickel and dime backs. They are sometimes the second-string cornerbacks, and sometimes shuffled defensive backs. Essentially, they come in on special plays and replace the linebackers, when the defensive coaches believe the offense plans to throw the football. Sometimes, the offense will start a passing game. Sometimes, though, they've suckered the defense, and pick up a running game against the smaller, weaker nickel and dime backs.

To the defense's benefit, they are prepared for the occasional run and having the extra defensive backs out there gives the team some extra blitzing and coverage options. It's a balancing act, as the offense and the defense show successes in different play variations.

OFFENSE: THE OFFENSIVE LINE

Be careful about jumping to conclusions about these guys. Weighing from 290 to 325 pounds, the offensive linemen are definitely big boys, but not untalented, not lacking in athleticism and definitely not lazy. They are protectors. With giant body masses, huge, muscular legs and tremendous upper-body power, the natural strength of these men on the line give the offense an opportunity on every down to make something happen.

TACKLES

Tackles are traditionally the biggest linemen, and on the offensive front, they are the most athletic as well. Their main function in this position is to seal off the outside, which is to prevent the defense from penetrating around the corner and reaching the ball carrier. That's no small task when you consider the collective weight and momentum trying to disintegrate that barrier. Protective as they are, these linemen must possess agility and presence of mind after every snap, not only to avoid giving up important inches, but to play smart and feel where they need to move the defensive player in order to provide a hole for the ball carrier.

He will move a defensive player to the outside when the play is run up the middle. He is concerned with securing the edge, the outside shoulder of the defensive end or linebacker aligned over him. If that is freed, the runner has open field to get a head start through the middle.

On other plays, the tackles will block toward the inside to allow the ball carrier to run wide and outside the edge. In blocking down on the defensive tackle, with the help of a guard, he will attempt to remove a defender from the running lane.

It's not easy to get through the human barricade of the tackles, which is why many offensive strikes are designed to run through the inside tackles. Off-tackle runs go to the strong side of a formation, where tight ends act as extra blockers, and tackles have to be in place to block his direct opponent and push him inside so a ball carrier can run outside.

To prepare sour cream: puree or finely chop chipotle peppers (peppers can be roasted if desired). Add peppers to sour cream and mix.

Chinese Five Spice Wings

Serves 4 - 8

4 lbs. frozen chicken wings (or pre-packaged buffalo wings or drummettes)
1 1/2 onion
4 tbsp. soy sauce
3 tbsp. medium-dry sherry
2 tbsp. chinese five spice powder (pre-packaged or mix equal parts of cinnamon, cloves, fennel seed, star anise, szechuan peppercorns)
1 1/2 tbsp. sugar
2 tbsp. coarse salt
2 1/4 tsp. black pepper, ground
3/4 cup cornstarch
8 cups vegetable oil
2 1/2 cups sour cream, ranch dressing or bleu cheese dressing

Thaw chicken wings. In a large bowl, combine onion, soy sauce, medium-dry sherry, chinese five-spice powder, sugar, salt and black pepper. In an eight-quart pot, heat eight cups oil to 370 degrees. Dredge chicken wings in flour and fry in oil until golden brown and thoroughly cooked (about four to five minutes).

Toss wings in five-spice sauce and serve with sour cream, ranch dressing or bleu cheese.

Quesadillas with Cilantro-Lime Sour Cream

Serves 4

8 flour tortillas (large)
1 cup mozzarella cheese, grated
1 cup smoked gouda cheese, grated
1 cup scallions, chopped
1 cup tomatoes, diced
4 tbsp. hot sauce
1 cup cilantro, chopped
3 tbsp. fresh lime juice
2 cups sour cream

For each quesadilla: Heat one flour tortilla in nonstick pan. Layer 1/4 cup mozzarella, 1/4 cup gouda, 1/4 cup scallions, 1/4 cup tomatoes and 1 tbsp. of hot sauce. Top with one flour tortilla. Place in 350-degree oven for five minutes or remain cooking in pan on stovetop. Once cheese has melted, carefully flip quesadilla and cook for two minutes on other side.

For sour cream: Mix cilantro, fresh lime juice and sour cream and garnish.

Chili
Serves 4

1 1/2 lb. ground beef or ground turkey
2 packages pre-mixed chili seasonings
1 onion, chopped
1 scallion, chopped
2 jalapeño peppers, diced
3 1/2 cans stewed tomatoes
1 can black beans, drained and rinsed
1 can red kidney beans, drained and rinsed
1 cup sour cream
1 cup grated mozzarella
1/4 cilantro, chopped

Heat six-quart stock pot on medium heat. Add ground beef or turkey to skillet. Cook for three minutes and add chopped onions. As soon as meat is cooked, stir in scallions, chili seasonings and jalapeños. Mix thoroughly. Add tomatoes and stir to combine. Simmer for 30 minutes on medium heat. Add black beans and kidney beans and simmer for 10 minutes.

Ladle into bowls and top with sour cream, mozzarella cheese and cilantro.

Grilled Beef & Chicken Skewers
Serves 4

8 skewers
1 lb. chicken, cubed
1 lb. beef, cubed
1 package cherry tomatoes
1 red onion, quartered
1 package mushrooms
1 cup olive oil
1 tsp. salt
1 tsp. fresh ground black pepper
1/2 tsp. cayenne pepper
1 tsp. red wine vinegar

Soak skewers in water for two minutes. On each skewer, alternate two pieces of chicken, two pieces of beef, cherry tomato, onion, and mushroom. In a bowl, mix oil, salt, black pepper, cayenne pepper and red wine vinegar. Brush all sides of skewer with oil and vinegar mixture and grill until meat is cooked thoroughly.

Culinary Contributor: Jennifer Wittman, Art Institute of Los Angeles, Culinary Program

Their styles — the traditional big, bulky men, or the smaller, quicker line — all reflect the effort to protect their ground, while simultaneously breaking new ground for the running backs. On top of that, he must protect the quarterback and other play-makers from the pursuit of the quick defensive approach.

CENTERS

This is the player that snaps the ball to the quarterback. You will see him directly in front of the QB, crouched in a position with the ball set in another position near his ankles on the ground. The snap, the process of hiking the ball to the quarterback, comes from the center. He is responsible for a timely and sharp snap by listening to the quarterback's signals (that shouting on the line that usually ends with "hut, hut"). Then, he must pop into action after the snap, setting up a wall between his quarterback and the defensive tackle or linebacker trying to break inside.

This is how every offensive play begins, with the quarterback reaching through the legs of the center and pulling back a snap that will eventually become a run, pass, or other variation of an offensive strike. However, it's not always so easy. The center must be preoccupied with the placement of his hands at all times, so that he can pop back into a defensive block. This is a necessary evil, and can result in a situation called short-arming the ball if the center and quarterback are not careful. Short-arming is a poor or clumsy snap that goes back to the quarterback, causing a slip or delay in the preciseness the play requires.

The centers are generals on the field. The center will signal or speak in code as they read the defensive formation. It is his responsibility to get his line in a proper formation, and still deliver a clean ball at the snap. Likewise, he must be quick witted to lead his team and even-keeled to take a hit from the defensive line. If he worries about taking the hit, or is unprepared to do so, he will be less apt to hike a sharp ball to the quarterback, and more apt to watch the ball fumble. It is the most demanding position on the offensive line.

GUARDS

Guards line up on either side of the center, making up the true composition of the line. They need to be the best blockers on the team, because they have to use every muscle in their arms, hands, legs and shoulders to move the defenders out of the way. He has a proactive role, which means he needs to create room for the ball carrier. Moving correct defenders out of the way leaves enough of a hole for a first down or a serious gain.

A guard must also be able to go head-to-head with his man, or his opponent. This is where the guard must be doubly talented: to protect his quarterback and to create play options for the running game.

THE GROUND GAME

Most of the excellent teams in professional football have strong ground games, which mean they can run the ball and advance the short yardage necessary to take advantage of the downs. It's the basic premise in football:

With the Florida sun going down over Pro Player Stadium, Patriots quarterback Drew Bledsoe solitarily watches the last snap of the game by the Dolphins.

get the ball and run with it. But, it's also much, much more, including strategy on how to elude tacklers, create open field opportunities and find ways to put points on the board.

RUNNING BACK

Running backs do so much more than just run with the ball. They have an extremely demanding and brutal position. As primary ball carriers, they are the prey for fierce defenders. This means that will take a lot of hits and have to keep going back for more. More than anything, though, the running back has to be amazingly fast and able to navigate the field with precision to achieve significant gains.

When they receive the handoff, the two most important factors are to avoid fumbling and to protect the ball while they bolt onto the field. Failing at either task can result in a turnover. After he has possession of the ball, the back will grip and tuck and rest it into his body (the protection factor). He needs to be aware of where all the players are positioned on the field. Like eyes in the back of the head, he needs to have a keen sense of who's on his heels and what his options are.

A team expects a lot of performance from a running back. He needs to be mentally and physically present on every play, know the downs and watch the clock. He also needs to have a ready recall of the play variations and the passing routes, an understanding of the defense alignments and strategies and every possible hole number in the playbook that tell a back where to go on a run. That's quite a load to carry.

The running back position is an umbrella for other positions that are more specific to their alignment of the field, but any player in the offensive backfield running with the ball could be determined a running back.

Halfback/Tailback: the team's principle ball carriers. The tailback is the primary running back in the I-formation. The halfback handles the ball more than other running backs.

Fullback: the bigger of two backs in the offensive backfield. He will block and clear the way for the halfback and doesn't carry the ball much. Occasionally, he will swing out of the backfield to catch a pass from the quarterback. In the one-back set offensive formation, another back, the H-back, blocks near the line of scrimmage. Before the snap, he'll pop into action toward the side he intends to block. Better blockers than ball carriers, they will go up against a man anywhere from 50 to 100 pounds heavier.

Buffalo Bills quarterback Rob Johnson throws against the Indianapolis Colts defense.

THE PASSING GAME
QUARTERBACK

It's difficult to say there's one player on a team that's more important than other players, but the quarterback, who drives the offense and is one of the more public players, is arguably the number one guy on the field.

The quarterback is the player directly behind the center. He calls all the plays after communicating with the coaching staff on the sidelines (only on the professional level) through a hearing device in his helmet. He also has a play list on his armband that he can refer to while in the huddle.

Once the play has been established, the quarterback gets possession of the ball and, according to what the play requires, he will hand the ball to a running back, plant a few steps back and try to pass it downfield, or scramble with the ball himself.

The QB operates in the pocket, where the offensive line and running backs will protect him. He rarely moves outside the pocket, and if he's doing so, he's probably already committed to run the ball himself because he cannot find an open receiver. However, there are plays, such as the quarterback sneak, that will make the passer a runner (even though it's just usually a couple yards to the first down).

The main job for the quarterback, though, is to throw the ball and make the plays. A quarterback's arm, a human cannon, can launch the ball 60 or more yards, and that's just on average. They have to have a great capacity to understand both offensive and defensive strategies, quick decision making skills, the instinctive authority to lead the game and a celebrity-style personality.

Throughout the book, you will see that all plays and positions have some kind of relationship with the quarterback. The defense wants to annihilate him, the offense strives to protect him and the plays are designed with him in mind. Remember, the quarterback is there to physically put his team within scoring range, so everything on the field revolves around his position. He is, quite simply, the engineer of the game's success or failure. But his compensation is pretty good, with notoriety and money, and he is one of the most adored figures to step on the field. Not a bad exchange.

Rams running back Marshall Faulk puts on his NFC Championship hat as he walks off the field after the Rams defeated Tampa Bay 11-6 at the Trans World Dome. The Rams will face Tennessee in Super Bowl 34.

RECEIVERS

Without receivers, a quarterback doesn't have a passing game. Period. Wide receivers and tight ends are pass specialists, although running backs can break out and catch the ball. Receivers come in all shapes and sizes, but he will uniformly have able hands, the ability to work under extreme defensive pressure, and speed with a capital "S."

WIDE RECEIVER
TIGHT END

A quarterback can launch the ball down the field all day, but it won't do his team any good unless a receiver is there to catch it. So because their role is pivotal for points, wide receivers and tight ends are principle offensive players. They are the main workhorses when it comes to catching passes, although running backs are used extensively in the passing offense. But, it's the wide receiver and the tight end who must run in strategic patterns against their defensive counterparts, and quickly position themselves to be open and ready to catch what the quarterback has thrown his way. When these two positions have done their jobs successfully, long yardage is gained for the offense, and the glory of a beautiful play is greeted with cheers and on-their-feet approval from the audience.

Receivers come in all sizes and shapes. They are tall, short, lean, fast, and quick. Excellent receivers must have nimble hands (hands that find ways to catch the most difficult, seemingly impossible passes), the ability to concentrate under defensive pressure, courage under fire, and strength enough to withstand the physical punishment of an abrupt defensive assault. Most importantly, though, receivers must be quick-witted about the location of the ball, and have a natural instinct or feel of the field and the direction needed to get open in order to make the big plays.

Receiving is a glamorous job, but one with many specific obligations. Every team expects its receivers to block defensive halfbacks or cornerbacks in addition to their offensive play-making duties. Teams want their receivers to be able to put a defensive cornerback on his back, or at least shield him from making a tackle on a running back.

Tight ends, by design, aren't as fast as wide receivers because they play the role of heavy-duty blockers on many plays. But, they also play double-duty to produce offensive opportunities. If the defense thinks it smells a connection between the quarterback and a certain receiver, they'll swarm all over him, making a potential catch or carry impossible. However, a good tight end with traits of a quick and agile receiver and the strength of a lineman can fool the defense and carry the ball to a first down, or better yet, to the end zone "promised land."

Basic offenses have five possible receivers: two running backs, the tight end, and the two wide receivers. The wide receivers are commonly referred to as X and Z receivers. The X receiver normally aligns to the weak side of the formation (split end) and Z aligns to the strength of the formation (normally called the flanker). The tight end is known as the Y receiver. On definite passing downs, many teams substitute another wide receiver if the tight end isn't a very good receiver.

The split end received his name because he was the end (the offenses of the 1930s used two ends) who aligned 10 yards away from the base offensive formation. Hence, he split from his teammates. The other end, the tight end, aligned next to an offensive tackle. The flanker position was originally a running back, and as offenses developed, he flanked to either side of the formation, but never on the line of scrimmage like the split end and tight end.

Throughout the game, the positions will vary, and you will notice quarterbacks favoring one receiver or end who can most reliably gain yards against the defense. The best way to anticipate this kind of action is to watch a few offensive plays and learn how the quarterback and his ball carriers interact and read each other's body language and non-verbal signals. You'll be better able to determine how defensive pressure causes an offensive reaction. After awhile, you'll be able to predict if a quarterback intends to run the ball, and to which side (or up the middle), or if a passing play is in the works. This is how the game becomes addictive.

THE KICKING GAME
SPECIAL TEAMS

The players who make up special teams are placekickers, punters and field goal kickers. They are highly specialized players with an intense job: the only time their efforts are truly noticed is when they fail. More specifically, the level of expectation on these guys is so high, it's almost a given. It seems a given that a field goal kicker will kick through the uprights and get the extra point for the team. We, as spectators, expect it so much that we could probably bear to look away during the game, banking on the consistency the kicker has shown in his professional career. But, one miss, and wham! The game is lost (for dramatic purposes) and suddenly the kicker is the scourge of the earth. Certainly a high-pressure job.

Special team duties

The kickers have strong, muscular legs, but are some of the smallest players overall on the team. They can kick a ball 70 yards, but you don't match them up to block against any linemen.

Placekicking involves kickoffs, field goal attempts and extra-point attempts or PATs, point-after-touchdown. Unlike the punter, the kicker in a placekick boots the ball from a particular place on the field. The kickoff, the beginning of the game, involves a kick that allows the two teams an attempt to block each other for the first time. One team attempts to help it's returner break through and gain some yardage, while the kicking team is trying to prevent any and all gains. The kick is protected by teammates who hurry downfield in order to cover the kick. The other team (soon to be the offense on the next play) will be trying to advance as closely to scoring range as it can, so the team sets out to limit the return made off the kick. If the kick-

Indianapolis Colts Peyton Manning smiles as he reaches out for the hand of a fan as he leaves the field.

ing team stops the run quickly, kicking has set the competitive tone for the rest of the game.

Punting happens when an offense is hobbling on its last down and can't advance the yards needed for a first down. The punt will occur on the offensive fourth down and necessitates giving up possession of the ball. Rather than risk an unsuccessful attempt on the fourth and final down, the punter comes in to maintain better field position, and keep the opponent away from their end zone. To do this, a punter stands about 15 yards behind the line of scrimmage, catches the snap from the center, takes two or three steps, drops the ball and kicks it before the ball reaches the ground. He is extremely coordinated and usually boots a good, high kick aiming at 45 yards away from the scrimmage line, with a decent hang time (they strive for about 4.5 seconds in the air).

The special teams divisions are extremely specialized at their roles in the games, and usually come out and nail it every time. Inclement weather at outdoor games can have an effect on the outcome of kick, but generally, the kicking game is a secure and smart strategy when used to win games.

COACHING STAFF

With so much at stake and with football becoming more specialized and scientific over the course of time, it's no surprise that coaching staffs have evolved dramatically along with the game. A generation ago, a head coach had a staff of a half dozen or so assistant coaches. Today, it is not unusual for a team to have a coaching staff numbering 15 or 16. Everybody has a specific area of focus because football has become more compartmentalized, with "position" coaches taking on more and more of the teaching load while the head coach acts in more of an administrative capacity. In simplest terms, this makes sense if for no other reason than the fact that the size of football squads has grown significantly over the years. Two platoon football means more than 50 players on NFL rosters — major college programs sometimes suit up close 50 to 100 players for home games. Somebody has to tell these guys what to do, right? And since you're not there ...

HEAD COACH

Make no mistake, while much of the individual teaching of players may now be the domain of assistants, it is the head coach who imposes his will on the entire operation in terms of over-all team philosophy and approach to the game. He is the one who determines whether the team will play a generally conservative or more wide-open style, when and how often a team will practice, how his assistants will help team objectives be reached, what rules and expectations pertain to each player and, lest we forget, who makes the team and who goes off looking for a job somewhere else.

The job of head coach is, without question, a leadership position, which requires balancing the task of bearing the ultimate responsibility for the outcome of games and seasons with the willingness to delegate man vital tasks to others on the staff. No head coach can be as hands-on with players as in the Lombardi era where the sophistication of the game simply does not leave enough hours in the day. The classic modern example of the metamorphosis of the head coach is Dick Vermeil, who led the Rams to victory in Super Bowl XXXIV.

Vermeil's 1980 Philadelphia Eagle team had made it to the big game nineteen years earlier, only to lose to the Raiders. Two years later, in his mid-forties, Vermeil walked away from the game, using in his tearful farewell press conference a term that has since become synonymous with the coaching profession: "burn out." He had been notorious for putting in 18 to 20-hour workdays in endless succession during a season, complete with all the common symptoms of the classic workaholic, such as skipping meals, sleeping in the office, etc. An emotional man known for wearing his heart on his sleeve, Vermeil hit the wall with the Eagles in large part by trying to put his stamp on absolutely every aspect of his team. By comparison, during his reincarnation as a head coach in St. Louis, Vermeil credited his newfound ability to "let go" for his apparently more relaxed demeanor. In other words, he delegated and became more of an administrator with big-picture focus. It worked!

Is Vermeil, now the head coach of the Chiefs, a slacker these days? Hardly. In fact he and other head coaches like him who have made adjustments in their work habits are still logging long hours. After all, the head coach is, and always will be, the guy who ultimately accepts the responsibility for the results on the field. He's the one, whether at a press conference, on the field, or behind a desk, who has microphones and note pads in his face as reporters seek to unearth every angle to every win, loss, decision and transaction. However, maybe today's head coach can work a little smarter (and maybe see his wife and kids at the dinner table once in awhile) by surrounding himself with strong assistants and by entrusting them with many of the major tasks at hand.

OFFENSIVE & DEFENSIVE COORDINATORS

Next to the head coach, these are the two most important positions on any football coaching staff. So much so in fact, that in some organizations you will find the man filling one of these roles also carrying the dual title of "assistant head coach." That's a fancy way of saying that this guy is not just any old assistant coach, he's also the head coach's right-hand man when it comes to philosophy and decision making. Considering the workload coordinators shoulder and the impact their efforts have on a team's ability to succeed, bestowing an extra title (and more dough when the paycheck gets handed out) makes some sense.

The offensive coordinator oversees what a team will do when it is in possession of the football. He designs and, in most cases, calls all the plays. He is a mastermind when it comes to the Xs and Os of football. (Or in our case chips and cookies). In other words, by watching countless miles of game tape and video, he can scheme and create offensive formations, patterns and approaches that can be successful in the on-field chess game against the defense. On most teams this is the man that actually calls each and every offensive play during a game, usually from his perch in the coaches' booth at press box level. Via headset, the offensive coordinator sends his play call for the next down to the sideline, from where it is relayed to the quarterback. With hundreds of plays and variations at this disposal, the coordinator weighs the down and distance, what the opponent's defense is doing, etc., and decides what play will be most effective and what personnel needs to be on the field to enable the offense to execute properly. All this occurs in a mere handful of seconds-remember, the play clock is ticking down toward zero and the next play must begin on time to avoid a penalty. Other than that, there really isn't any pressure at all! (You can watch for the chain smoking that goes on in coordinators' booths during games where unmanned mini-cams are sometimes mounted in front of the coaches so that you can see them agonizing over decisions and reacting to results on the field.)

Similarly, the defensive coordinator is moving his chess pieces around to try to stop the opponent's offense and gain possession of the ball for his team. Third and seven — a passing down. Are we going to blitz to put extra pressure on the quarterback? Who are we going to send? A linebacker? Which one, an inside or an outside? No, let's go with extra defensive backs instead. "Get the dime package in there!" And on it goes. Obviously, both coordinators speak in code a great deal, to save time and for the sake of secrecy. Their fingers are on the pulse of virtually every play. Naturally, some head coaches do have all verbal traffic funnel through them for the purpose of approving or vetoing the calls made from the press box, but over the years the coordinators have assumed more and more responsibility regarding decision on both sides of the ball.

POSITION COACHES

Yeah, we all know some guys who can use some help with this, but it's not what you're thinking! Really, what we're talking about here are specialized coaches who have the sole focus of teaching technique to guys who play a specific position. In other words, all tams now have one (or, in special circumstances, more than one): offensive line coach, receivers coach, tight ends coach, running backs coach, quarterback coach, defensive line coach, linebackers coach, secondary (or defensive backs) coach. In addition, there is a special teams coach to coordinate all punting and kicking plays in terms of coverage ad protection schemes, and, often, a coach that works only with the kickers and punters on technique.

A team will also now have at least one strength coach, in charge of overseeing all the off-field physical preparation that is such a huge part of the sport, i.e. weightlifting, stretching and overall fitness. Is it any wonder that when you guy a team picture at the souvenir stand you can't tell what anyone's face looks like? There are so many guy to squeeze into the shot that everyone's head is a little speck. Such is football today, and we haven't even touched on team psychologists, trainers, equipment guys, and the like. Without question, everyone has defined roles and everyone contributes. If a team can have such a large group of people all on the same page and hitting on all cylinders, it is a powerful phenomenon to behold. Such is the nirvana for which all coaches strive.

Chapter 6
The Officials and
The Chain Gang

OFFICIALS

Let's dispel some rumors here. As a rule, they are not blind. They are not generally involved in a great conspiracy to bring down the home team (or whatever team owns your loyalty). And, despite occasional death threats, boos and jeers from a crowd of several thousand audible fans, NFL officials are only interested in one thing. Football. Played by the rules.

When a yellow flag is thrown on a play, one of these guys is responsible for stopping the game and spotting the infraction. Whenever a player breaks a rule or commits a foul, it's these seven officials in black and white stripes watching from every angle conceivable on the field. Officials are responsible for any decision involving a rule, its interpretation and its enforcement. They also enforce and record all fouls and monitor the clock and all time-outs charged.

An official's uniform consists of black and white vertical striped shirts, white pants, long socks and black athletic shoes, typically with cleats. There is a small NFL insignia and small letters giving the official's position on his shirt. A number will also identify the official. They wear standard black ball caps and the referee is distinguished by wearing a white cap. Each official is equipped with a whistle, which he blows to signal that a play is complete, to stop a play from continuing, or when players begin to fight during or after a play.

All officials carry penalty flags or markers. When an official observes a player committing a penalty during the play of the game, he tosses the flag in the air. The presence of one or more flags on the ground signals that the penalty exists and has been marked. The game clock is stopped, and the official who threw the flag reports the violation to the referee. The penalty is announced to both teams as well as to spectators, and the penalty yardage is marked off, or a penalty ruling announces if the violation has been refused. The flags, soaring through the air on a penalty call, are weighted with whatever is handy on the field: rocks, sand etc., however, due to a recent career-ending injury when a weighted flag hit a player in the eye, unpopped popcorn kernels are in vogue.

In the NFL, there are 16 individuals (all men) that hold each officiating position. These officials have come up through the ranks from high school and college to work for the NFL. NFL personnel

Author

actually scout for NFL officials. Current officials take a weekly exam of the rules to stay educated on the rules and regulations of the NFL. After each game, officials are rated from tapes and only the officials with the highest ratings are considered for duty at the Super Bowl. The officials work on a part-time basis with the NFL, college and high school football, and are paid each week by the games over which they preside. Their regular jobs range from teachers to airline pilots, with some retired guys finding the work an enjoyable vocation.

As you will see from the profile of the responsibilities in judging a professional game, the league has designed the officiating positions to work in tandem and act as back-ups for each other's tasks in order to avoid missing any viable action on the field. This provides as fair a game as possible, even under the high intensity, lightning-fast moves after the snap. Keep an eye on the officials during the games, and you will learn a great deal about how quickly a game can change hands, and what calls and rulings will quickly take a team out of winning favor.

REFEREE

This guy is the only one of the officials that wears a white hat.

On pass plays, the referee stands behind the offensive backfield about 10 to 12 yards behind the line of scrimmage. If the quarterback is a right-handed passer, the "ref" will usually favor the right side. From that perspective, the referee will determine the legality of the snap, observe the deep back for illegal motion and watch for legality of blocks by the linemen. This referee is the guy you see running down the field with the quarterback in order to determine if the hand-off was legal. He will also rule on any possible roughing action against the quarterback, or if the ball becomes loose, rules whether the ball is free on a fumble or dead on an incomplete pass.

During kicking situations, the ref has primary responsibility to rule on a kicker's actions and whether or not any subsequent contact by a defender is legal. He will announce, via a microphone, when each period has ended, indicates penalties through hand signals and announces to the crowd the specific penalty and the number of the player who committed it. In college and high school, a specific player is not singled out for announcement.

UMPIRE

The umpire wears a black cap and arguably has the most dangerous position of all the officials. Because he is located behind the bulky defensive line, up four to five yards downfield, he is in a prime position to be trampled by players running up the middle. His position will vary in front of the weakside tackle to the strongside guard.

The "ump" watches for rule violations at the line of scrimmage, as well as player conduct and actions on the scrimmage line. He looks for possible false starts by eager offensive linemen and observes legality of contact by both offensive linemen blocking and by defensive players as they attempt to ward off blockers. In this position, he has the authority and is prepared to call rule infractions if they occur on offense or defense. It is also a primary responsibility for the ump to confirm that the offensive team has only 11 players on the field at the time of the snap.

Because the umpire calls most of the plays between the offense and defense, he also calls most of the holding penalties. The umpire is in charge of recording the outcome of the pre-game coin toss, records all time-outs, all scores, and makes all the rulings on the legality of the players' equipment. The umpire also wipes the ball dry before the snap, if the weather necessitates that attention.

When a pass play develops, he will move forward to the line of scrimmage in order to insure that the interior linemen do not move illegally downfield. If the offensive linemen indicate a screen pass will be attempted, the umpire will shift his attention toward the screen side, pick up potential receivers in order to ensure that he will legally be permitted to run his pattern and continue to rule on the action of blockers. The umpire also assists in the ruling of incomplete or trapped passes when ball is thrown overhead or short.

HEAD LINESMAN

The head linesman is located on the side of the field opposite the Line Judge. At the ball snap, he straddles the line of scrimmage and watches offside, encroachment, and all other line-of-scrimmage violations. He is responsible for ruling out-of-bounds plays on his side of the field.

On pass plays, the linesman is responsible for ruling on any illegal action taken by defenders on the forward progress by a runner on a play directed toward the middle or into his side. He rules on the pass receivers or runners in or out of bounds and any ruling on legality of action involving the receiver who approaches his side. He will call pass interference when the infraction occurs, and will rule on legality of blockers and defenders on plays involving a live ball. During kicks or passes, he checks for illegal use of hands, and he must know all eligible receivers prior to every play.

He signals the referee or umpire where the forward point of the ball has reached. He is the one that usually runs in after a play and by placing his foot, designates where the forward progress of the ball ended. He also situates the chain for measuring a first down.

Together with the referee, the linesman is responsible for keeping track of the number of downs and is in charge of the mechanics of his chain crew and their duties.

LINE JUDGE

The line judge straddles the line of scrimmage on the side of the field opposite the head linesman and watches for offside, encroachment, and actions such as illegal motion and illegal shifts pertaining to the scrimmage line prior to or at the snap.

He assists the referee with calls regarding false starts and forward laterals behind the line of scrimmage. He also makes sure that the quarterback has not crossed the line of scrimmage prior to throwing a forward pass. He observes the receiver until he moves at least seven yards downfield. Then, he moves toward the backfield side, being especially alert to rule on any back in-motion and on the flight of the ball when the pass is made (he must rule whether forward or backward).

After the pass is thrown, the line judge directs his attention toward activities that occur behind the umpire. He assists the ump with holding calls and watches for illegal use of hands on the end of the line, especially during kicks and pass plays. He also assists in observing actions by blockers and defenders who are on his side of the field.

During punting situations, the line judge remains at the line of scrimmage to be sure that only the end men move downfield until the kick is made. (NFL rule only) He rules on the kick, specifically whether or not it crossed the line. He is also responsible to observe action by the members of the kicking team who are moving downfield to cover the kick. The line judge also supervises substitutions made by the team seated on his side of the field.

This position has the important job of supervising the clock and the timing of the game. He assumes the official timing on the field when the official game clock becomes inoperative. He is the official timekeeper and supervises the scoreboard clock. The line judge advises the referee when time has expired at the end of each period. He also signals the referee when two minutes remain in a half, stopping the clock for the two-minute warning. (NFL only.) The two-minute warning was devised to give the team in possession of the ball an added time-out. (In the NFL, the referee has jurisdiction over stopping the clock, allowing more time for the offensive team to run its plays.) During half-time, he notifies the home team's head coach that five minutes remain before the start of the second half.

Indianapolis Colts Peyton Manning and his offensive line during a preseason game against the Seattle Seahawks.

BACK JUDGE

The back judge positions himself about 20 yards deep behind the defensive side, near the wide receiver on the same side of the field as the line judge. The back judge is responsible for making sure there are no more than 11 defensive players on the field. He watches for violations involving all pass receivers and defensive backs on his side. This official keeps interference and other violations on passes far beyond the line of scrimmage in check. He makes out-of-bounds rulings on his side of the field, concentrating on the action in the area between the umpire and the field judge. He makes calls on trapping, catching, recoveries, or illegal touching of a loose ball beyond the line of scrimmage. He will also call the penalties regarding clipping when it occurs on punts and kickoffs that are caught and returned. With the field judge, he rules on whether field goals and extra point attempts are successful.

SIDE JUDGE

The side judge position was added nearly 12 years ago. This position officiates 20 yards down the field from the line of scrimmage, opposite the back judge and on the same side of the field as the head linesman. He has the same responsibilities as the back judge: watching for violations downfield during long pass attempts, responsible for calling penalties on forward passes and kicks, and counting the number of defensive players on the field. On field goal and extra point attempts, he helps the back judge rule whether a field goal and extra point attempt are successful.

FIELD JUDGE

The field judge positions himself 25 yards down field, behind the defensive side of the ball on the same side as the offensive tight end near the middle of the field. This judge monitors the tight end's pass patterns, calling interference, making decisions involving catching, recovery, out-of bounds, illegal touching of a fumbled ball after it crosses the line of scrimmage and other actions during offensive strikes.

He also watches for violations on punt plays, kickoffs and deep passes. The field judge is responsible for the number of defensive players on the field, and making sure that the players are all onside. He is responsible for forward passes that cross the defensive goal line and any fumbled ball in his area. Along with the back judge, he rules on whether the field goal and extra point attempts are successful. The field judge also indicates when the play clock should be stopped or started; when a play ends, a change of possession, a time-out, an injury, a measurement, or any unusual delay of the game

THE CHAIN GANG

These are not guys in black and white stripes along the highway picking up trash, or with rock picks thrown over their shoulders like some scene from Cool Hand Luke. (Editor's Note: Ah, Paul Newman!) No, no. These are the individuals that make tracking the game a little less complicated.

The chain gang (not a big gang, just three to six members) hang out on the home sideline opposite the press box wearing a vest with a big fluorescent X. Here, they are visible to all interested parties, from the press to spectators, to coaches and players.

You'll see two of these people, called rodmen, each holding a five-foot bright orange rod attached by a 10 yard "chain." This apparatus helps keep track of how many yards the offense needs to advance in order to gain a first down. (Remember the formula: Four downs to advance 10 yards.)

For obscure vantage points along the field, and for the benefit of televised games, the rodmen will mark the field where the play will start and where the play needs to end for a first down. One rodman marks where the possession began, and the other rodman extends the chain to the offensive team's goal, 10 yards downfield.

The third member in the "gang" is called the boxman. This individual carries four different rods. Each of his rods has a marker on top, numbered one through four. This number tells the crowd whether it is first, second, third, or fourth down.

When there is a question regarding whether the offense has made a first down, the chain gang moves toward the hash marks nearest where the ball was "downed." The officials use the rods, extending the chain along the field, to determine whether the ball has made its critical 10 yards and can earn the offense another series of downs.

The home team supplies both the chain crew and the ball boys, who are responsible for keeping available balls on both sidelines and putting new ones in play when needed. Ball boys also keep the footballs clean and free of excessive moisture.

Indianapolis Colts running back Edgerrin James during practice.

The Chicks' Guide to Football

| Touchdown, field goal, or successful try | Safety | First Down |

Chapter 7
Rules and Penalties

RULES AND PENALTIES INTRODUCTION

One of the most crucial characteristics one new to football should understand is that this is a game known for a strict set of rules and regulations, complicated at first, but designed to make the game adhere to its competitive, high-intensity format.

With a firm grasp of the rules, and how they pop in and out of play situations, you will be able to watch or participate in this fast-paced game at any man's level. Even better!

Who makes these rules?

The National Football League rulebook is the main reference manual for regulations and standards for professional teams in the United States. Likewise, Canadian Football procedures play according to the rules of the Canadian Football League.

Most American college teams belong to the National Collegiate Athletic Association (NCAA) or the National Association of Intercollegiate Athletics (NAIA), who set rules for their members. Junior colleges and community colleges follow the rules established by the National Junior College Athletic Association. And, most high schools play according to the rules of the National Federation of State High Associations. The few high schools that haven't accepted the Association rulebook rely on the NCAA rules.

While the rules of play for each level are about the same, there are important differences that distinguish various leagues or classes of the sport. For example, a high school game lasts 48 minutes, while professional and college games are 60 minutes in length. The rules concerning timeouts also vary slightly. In high school and college, four timeouts are permitted each half and college three timeouts per half. In pro play, there can be only three timeouts each half. But, pro rules also permit several timeouts for television commercials.

PENALTIES

Simply put, when a rule of football is broken, the team gets a penalty. Some of the most common penalties, or fouls, are:

Crowd noise, dead ball, or neutral zone established | Ball illegally touched, kicked or batted | Time Out

Offside: called when an offensive or defensive player crosses the line of scrimmage before the ball is snapped. Penalty = five yards.

Holding: called when an offensive player uses his hands or arms to ward off a defensive player. Penalty = ten yards.

Defensive holding: called when a defensive player holds or tackles anyone but the ball carrier. In professional football, defensive holding also means an automatic first down for the offense. Penalty = five yards.

Clipping: occurs when an offensive player blocks a defensive player from behind, particularly by throwing his body across the back of the defensive player's legs. Penalty = 15 yards.

Roughing the passer: committed by a defensive player who runs into or tackles the passer after the pass has been thrown. Penalty = 15 yards and an automatic first down.

Roughing the kicker: foul committed by a defensive player who runs into or knocks down the kicker while he is punting or place-kicking. Penalty = 15 yards and an automatic first down.

Delay of game: the failure to put the ball in play within the time specified. In professional football, the offensive team must put the ball in play within 30 seconds after the referee has signaled play to begin. In high school and college football, the interval is 25 seconds. Penalty = five yards.

PENALTY DEFINITIONS:

Chucking: Warding off an opponent who is in front of a defender by contacting him with a quick extension of arm or arms, followed by the return of arm(s) to a flexed position, thereby breaking the original contact.

Clipping: Throwing the body across the back of an opponent's leg or hitting him from the back below the waist while moving up from behind. This action occurs as a penalty unless the opponent is a runner or the action is in close line play.

Close Line Play: The area between the positions normally occupied by the offensive tackles, extending three yards on each side of the line of scrimmage.

Crackback: Eligible receivers who take or move to a position more than two yards outside the tackle may not block an opponent below the waist if they then move back inside to block.

Dead Ball: Ball not in play.

Double Foul: A foul by each team during the same down.

No time out or time in with whistle

Delay of game or excess time out

False start, illegal formation, or kickoff or safety kick out of bounds or kicking team player voluntarily out of bounds during a punt

Down: The period of action that starts when the ball is put in play and ends when it is dead.

Encroachment: When a player enters the neutral zone and makes contact with an opponent before the ball is snapped.

Fair Catch: An unhindered catch of a kick by a member of the receiving team who must raise one arm a full length above his head while the kick is in flight.

Foul: Any violation of a playing rule.

Free Kick: A kickoff or safety kick. It may be a placekick, dropkick, or punt, except a punt may not be used on a kickoff following a touchdown, successful field goal, or to begin each half or overtime period. A tee cannot be used on a fair-catch or safety kick.

Fumble: The loss of possession of the ball.

Game Clock: Scoreboard game clock.

Impetus: The action of a player that gives momentum to the ball.

Live Ball: A ball legally free kicked or snapped. It continues in play until the down ends.

Loose Ball: A live ball not in possession of any player.

Muff: The touching of a loose ball by a player in an unsuccessful attempt to obtain possession.

Neutral Zone: The space the length of a ball between the two scrimmage lines. The offensive team and defensive team must remain behind their end of the ball. Exception: The offensive player who snaps the ball has the right to be within this zone.

Offside: A player is offside when any part of his body is beyond his scrimmage or free kick line when the ball is snapped.

Own Goal: The goal a team is guarding.

Play Clock: 40/25 second clock.

Pocket Area: Applies from a point two yards outside of either offensive tackle and includes the tight end if he drops off the line of scrimmage to pass protect. Pocket extends longitudinally behind the line back to the offensive team's own end line.

Possession: When a player controls the ball throughout the act of clearly touching both feet, or any other part of his body other than his hand(s), to the ground inbounds.

Post-Possession Foul: A foul by the receiving team that occurs after a ball is legally kicked from scrimmage prior to possession changing. The ball must cross the line of scrimmage and the receiving team must retain possession of the kicked ball.

Punt: A kick made when a player drops the

Personal foul

Holding

Illegal use of hands, arms or body

ball and kicks it while it is in flight.

Safety: The situation in which the ball is dead on or behind a team's own goal if the impetus comes from a player on that team. Two points are scored for the opposing team.

Shift: The movement of two or more offensive players at the same time before the snap.

Striking: The act of swinging, clubbing, or propelling the arm or forearm in contacting an opponent.

Sudden Death: The continuation of a tied game into sudden death overtime, in which the team scoring first (by safety, field goal, or touchdown) wins.

Touchback: When a ball is dead on or behind a team's own goal line, provided the impetus came from an opponent and provided it is not a touchdown or a missed field goal.

Touchdown: When any part of the ball, legally in possession of a player inbounds, breaks the plane of the opponent's goal line, provided it is not a touchback.

Unsportsmanlike Conduct: Any act contrary to the generally understood principles of sportsmanship.

SUMMARY OF PENALTIES
Automatic First Down
Awarded to offensive team on all defensive fouls with these exceptions:
1. Offside; 2. Encroachment; 3. Delay of game; 4 Illegal substitution; 5. Excessive time out(s); 6. Accidental grasp of facemask; 7. Neutral zone infraction; 8. Running into the kicker; 9. More than 11 players on the field at the snap.

Five yards
The team is penalized five yards for any of the following infractions:
- Defensive holding or illegal use of hands (automatic first down)
- Delay of game on offense or defense
- Delay of kickoff
- Encroachment
- Excessive time out(s)
- False start
- Illegal formation
- Illegal shift
- Illegal motion
- Illegal substitution
- First onside kick off out-of-bounds between goal lines and not touched
- Invalid fair catch signal
- More than 11 players on the field at snap for either team

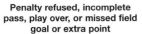

Penalty refused, incomplete pass, play over, or missed field goal or extra point

Pass juggled inbounds and caught out of bounds

Illegal forward pass

- Less than seven men on offensive line at snap
- Offside
- Failure to pause one second after shift or huddle
- Running into kicker (as opposed to "roughing")
- More than one man in motion at snap
- Grasping facemask of the ball carrier or quarterback
- Player out-of-bounds at snap
- Ineligible member(s) of kicking team going beyond line of scrimmage before ball is kicked
- Illegal return
- Failure to report change of eligibility
- Neutral zone infraction
- Loss of team time out(s) or five-yard penalty on the defense for excessive crowd noise
- Ineligible player downfield during passing down
- Second forward pass behind the line.
- Forward pass is first touched by eligible receiver who has gone out of bounds and returned
- Forward pass touches or is caught by an ineligible receiver on or behind line.
- Forward pass thrown from behind line of scrimmage after ball once crossed the line

10 Yards

- Offensive pass interference
- Holding, illegal use of hands, arms, or body by offense
- Tripping by a member of either team.
- Helping the runner
- Deliberately batting or punching a loose ball
- Deliberately kicking a loose ball
- Illegal block above the waist

15 Yards

- Chop block
- Clipping below the waist
- Fair catch interference
- Illegal crackback block by offense
- Piling on (automatic first down)
- Roughing the kicker (automatic first down)
- Roughing the passer (automatic first down)
- Twisting, turning, or pulling an opponent by the facemask
- Unnecessary roughness
- Unsportsmanlike conduct
- Delay of game at start of either half
- Illegal low block
- A tackler using his helmet to butt, spear, or ram an opponent
- Any player who uses the top of his helmet unnecessarily

| Intentional grounding of pass | Interference with forward pass or fair catch | Invalid fair-catch signal |

- A punter, placekicker, or holder who simulates being roughed by a defensive player
- A defender who takes a running start from beyond the line of scrimmage in an attempt to block a field goal or point after touchdown and lands on players at the line of scrimmage

Five yards and loss of down (Combination Penalty)

Forward pass thrown from beyond line of scrimmage.

10 Yards and loss of down (Combination Penalty)

Intentional grounding of forward pass (safety if passer is in own end zone). If foul occurs more than 10 yards behind line, play results in loss of down at spot of foul.

15 Yards and loss of coin toss option

- Team's late arrival on the field prior to scheduled kickoff.
- Captains not appearing for coin toss.

15 Yards (and disqualification if flagrant)

- Striking opponent with fist
- Kicking or kneeing opponent

- Striking opponent on head or neck with forearm, elbow, or hands, whether or not the initial contact is made below the neck area
- Roughing the kicker
- Roughing the passer
- Malicious unnecessary roughness
- Unsportsmanlike conduct
- Palpably unfair act (Distance penalty determined by the referee after consultation with other officials)

Touchdown awarded (palpably unfair act)

When referee determines a palpably unfair act deprived a team of a touchdown. (Example: Player comes off bench and tackles runner obviously en route to touchdown).

15 Yards and automatic disqualification

- Using a helmet (not worn) as a weapon
- Striking or purposely shoving a game official

Suspension from game for one down

Illegal equipment (Player may return after one down when legally equipped)

Ineligible receiver or ineligible member of kicking team downfield

Illegal contact

Offside, encroachment, or neutral zone infraction

Field

- Sidelines and end lines are out of bounds. The goal line is actually in the end zone. A player with the ball in his possession scores when the ball is on, above, or over the goal line.
- The field is rimmed by a white border, six feet wide, along the sidelines. All of this is out-of-bounds.
- The hash marks (inbound lines) are 70 feet, nine inches from each sideline.
- Goal posts must be single-standard type, offset from the end line and painted bright gold. The goal posts must be 18 feet, six inches wide and the top face of the crossbar must be 10 feet above the ground. Vertical posts extend at least 30 feet above the crossbar. A ribbon four inches by 42 inches long is to be attached to the top of each post. The actual goal is the plane extending indefinitely above the crossbar and between the outer edges of the posts.
- The field is 360 feet long and 160 feet wide. The end zones are 30 feet deep. The line used in try-for-point plays is two yards out from the goal line.
- Chain crew members and ball boys must be uniformly identifiable.
- All clubs must use standardized sideline markers. Pylons must be used for goal line and end line markings.
- End zone markings and club identification at 50-yard line must be approved by the Commissioner to avoid any confusion as to delineation of goal lines, sidelines, and end lines.

Ball

Thirty-six approved footballs will be used in games played outdoors (24 indoors).

Coin toss

The coin toss will take place within three minutes of kickoff in the center of field. The toss will be called by the visiting captain. The winner may choose one of two privileges and the loser gets the other:

- Receive or kick
- Goal his team will defend

Immediately prior to the start of the second half, the captains of both teams must inform the officials of their respective choices. The loser of the original coin toss gets first choice in the second half.

Timing

- The stadium game clock is official. In case it stops or is operating incorrectly, the line judge takes over the official timing on the field.

| Illegal motion at snap | Loss of down | Interlocking interference, pushing, or helping runner |

- Each period is 15 minutes. The intermission between the periods is two minutes. Halftime is 12 minutes, unless otherwise specified.
- On charged team time outs, the field judge starts the watch and blows the whistle after one minute 50 seconds, unless television does not utilize the time for a commercial break. In this case the length of the time out is reduced to 40 seconds.
- The referee will allow necessary time to attend to an injured player, or repair a legal player's equipment.
- Each team is allowed three time outs each half.
- Time between plays will be 40 seconds from the end of a given play until the snap of the ball for the next play, or a 25-second interval after certain administrative stoppages and game delays.
- Clock starts running when the ball is snapped following all changes of team possession.
- With the exception of the last two minutes of the first half, and the last five minutes of the second half, the game clock will be restarted for the following reasons: a kick off return, a player going out-of-bounds on a play from scrim-

mage or after declined penalties when appropriate on the referee's signal.
- Consecutive team time outs can be taken by opposing teams, but the length of the second time out will be reduced to 40 seconds.
- When, in the judgment of the referee, the level of crowd noise prevents the offense from hearing its signals, he can institute a series of procedures which can result in a loss of team time outs or a five-yard penalty against the defensive team.

Sudden death

- The sudden death system of determining the winner prevails when the score is tied at the end of the regulation playing time of any NFL game. The team scoring first during overtime play shall win and the game automatically ends upon that score (by safety, field goal, or touchdown) or when a score is awarded by the referee for a palpably unfair act.
- At the end of regulation time, the referee will immediately toss a coin at the center of field in accordance with rules pertaining to the usual pregame toss. The captain of the visiting team will call the toss.

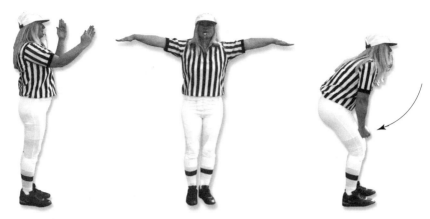

Touching a forward pass or scrimmage kick

Unsportsmanlike conduct

Illegal cut, illegal block below the waist, chop block, clipping

- Following a three-minute intermission after the end of the regulation game, play will be continued in 15-minute periods or until there is a score. There is a two-minute intermission between subsequent periods. The teams change goals at the start of each period. Each team has three time outs per half, and all general timing provisions apply as during a regular game. Disqualified players are not allowed to return.

- In preseason and regular season games, there is a maximum of 15 minutes of sudden death with two time outs instead of three. General provisions that apply for the fourth quarter will prevail. A PAT try is not attempted if a touchdown is scored.

Timing in final two minutes of each half

- On kickoff, the clock does not start until the ball has been legally touched by a player of either team in the field of play (in all other cases, clock starts with kickoff).

- A team cannot buy an excess time out for a penalty. However, a fourth time out is allowed without penalty for an injured player, who must be removed immediately. A fifth time out or more is allowed

for an injury and a five-yard penalty is assessed if the clock was running. Additionally, if the clock was running and the score is tied or the team in possession is losing, the ball cannot be put in play for at least 10 seconds on the fourth or more time out. The half or game can end while those 10 seconds are run out on the clock.

- If the defensive team is behind in the score and commits a foul when it has no time outs left in the final 30 seconds of either half, the offensive team can decline the penalty for the foul and have the time on the clock expire.

- Fouls that occur in the last five minutes of the fourth quarter, as well as the last two minutes of the first half will result in the clock starting on the snap.

Try

- After a touchdown, the scoring team is allowed a try during one scrimmage down. The ball may be spotted anywhere between the inbounds lines, two or more yards from the goal line. The successful conversion counts one point by kick; two points for a successful conversion by touchdown, or one point for a safety.

| Illegal crackback | Player disqualified | Tripping |

- In the NFL the defensive team never can score on a try. As soon as defense gets possession or the kick is blocked or a touchdown is not scored, the try is over.
- Any distance penalty for fouls committed by the defense that prevent the try from being attempted can be enforced on the succeeding try or succeeding kickoff. Any foul committed on a successful try will result in a distance penalty being assessed on the ensuing kickoff.
- Only the fumbling player can recover and advance a fumble during a try.

Players-substitutions

- Each team is permitted to have 11 men on the field at the snap.
- Unlimited substitution is permitted. However, players may enter the field only when the ball is dead. Players who have been substituted are not permitted to linger on the field. Such lingering will be interpreted as unsportsmanlike conduct.
- Twelve men delayed in huddle-illegal substitution.
- Players leaving the game must be out-of-bounds on their own side, clearing the field between the end lines, before a snap or free kick. If a player crosses the end line leaving the field, it is delay of game (five-yard penalty).
- Substitutes who remain in the game must move onto the field as far as the inside of the field numerals before moving to a wide position.
- With the exception of the last two minutes of either half, the offensive team, while in the process of substitution or simulated substitution, is prohibited from rushing quickly to the line and snapping the ball with the obvious attempt to cause a defensive foul. This could cause too many men on the field.

Kickoff

- The kickoff originates from the kicking team's 30-yard line at the start of each half and after a field goal and try-for-point. A kickoff is one type of free kick.
- A one-inch tee may be used (no tee permitted for field goal or try attempt) on a kickoff. The ball is put in play by a placekick or dropkick.
- If the kickoff clears the opponent's goal posts, it is not a field goal.
- A kickoff is illegal unless it travels 10 yards OR is touched by the receiving team. Once the ball is touched by the receiving team, it is a free ball.
- Receivers may recover and advance at

| Uncatchable forward pass | Twelve men in offensive huddle or too many men on the field | Face Mask |

that point. The kicking team may recover, but NOT advance unless the receiver had possession and lost the ball.

- When a kickoff goes out-of-bounds between the goal lines without being touched by the receiving team, the ball belongs to the receivers 30 yards from the spot of the kick, or at the out-of-bounds spot unless the ball went out the first time an onside kick was attempted. In this case the kicking team is to be penalized five yards and the ball must be kicked again.

- When a kickoff goes out-of-bounds between the goal lines and is touched last by receiving team, it is receiver's ball at the out-of-bounds spot.

Safety

- In addition to a kickoff, the other free kick is a kick after a safety (safety kick). A punt may be used (a punt may not be used on a kickoff).

- On a safety kick, the team scored upon puts the ball into play by a punt, drop-kick, or placekick without tee. No score can be made on a free kick following a safety, even if a series of penalties places a team in position. (A field goal can be scored only on a play from

scrimmage or a free kick after a fair catch.)

Fair catch kick

After a fair catch, the receiving team has the option to put the ball in play by a snap or a fair catch kick (field goal attempt), with fair catch kick lines established ten yards apart. All general rules apply as for a field goal attempt from scrimmage. The clock starts when the ball is kicked. (No tee permitted).

Field goal

All field goals attempted (kicker) and missed from beyond the 20-yard line will result in the defensive team taking possession of the ball at the spot of the kick. On any field goal attempted and missed where the spot of the kick is on or inside the 20-yard line, the ball will revert to defensive team at the 20-yard line.

Safety

The important factor in a safety is impetus. Two points are scored for the opposing team when the ball is dead on or behind a team's own goal line if the impetus came from a player on that team.

Examples of Safety:

- Blocked punt goes out of kicking team's

Illegal shift   **Reset play clock-25 seconds**   **Reset play clock-40 seconds**

end zone. Impetus was provided by punting team. The block only changes direction of ball, not impetus.

- Ball carrier retreats from field of play into his own end zone and is downed. Ball carrier provides impetus.
- Offensive team commits a foul and spot of enforcement is behind its own goal line.
- Player on receiving team muffs punt and, trying to get ball, forces or illegally kicks (creating new impetus) it into end zone where it goes out of the end zone or is recovered by a member of the receiving team in the end zone.

Examples of Non-Safety:

- Player intercepts a pass with both feet inbounds in the field of play and his momentum carries him into his own end zone. Ball is put in play at spot of interception.
- Player intercepts a pass in his own end zone and is downed in the end zone, even after recovering in the end zone. Impetus came from passing team, not from defense. (Touchback)
- Player passes from behind his own goal line. Opponent bats down ball in end zone. (Incomplete pass)

Measuring

The forward point of the ball is used when measuring.

Position of players at snap

- Offensive team must have at least seven players on the line.
- Offensive players, not on the line, must be at least one yard back at snap. (Exception: player who takes snap).
- No interior lineman may move after taking or simulating a three-point stance.
- No player of either team may invade the neutral zone before the snap.
- No offensive player may charge or move, after assuming set position, in such manner as to lead the defense to believe snap has started. No player of the defensive team within one yard of the line of scrimmage may make an abrupt movement in an attempt to cause the offense to false start.
- If a player changes his eligibility, the referee must alert the defensive captain after player has reported to him.
- All players of offensive team must be stationary at snap, except one back who may be in motion parallel to the scrimmage line or backward (not forward).
- After a shift or huddle, all players on the

offensive team must come to an absolute stop for at least one second with no movement of hands, feet, head, or swaying of body.

● Quarterbacks can be called for a false start penalty (five yards) if their actions are judged to be an obvious attempt to draw an opponent offside.

Use of hands, arms, and body

● No player on offense may assist a runner except by blocking for him. Interlocking interference is not allowed.

● A runner may ward off opponents with his hands and arms, but no other player on offense may use hands or arms to obstruct an opponent by grasping with hands, pushing, or encircling any part of his body during a block. Hands (open or closed) can be thrust forward to initially contact an opponent on or outside the opponent's frame, but the blocker must work to bring his hands on or inside the frame.

Note: Pass blocking: Hand(s) thrust forward that slip outside the body of the defender will be legal if blocker worked to bring them back inside. Hand(s) or arm(s) that encircle a defender—i.e., hook an opponent—are to be considered illegal and officials are to call a foul for holding.

Blocker cannot use his hands or arms to push from behind, hang onto, or encircle an opponent in a manner that restricts his movement as the play develops.

● Hands cannot be thrust forward above the frame to contact an opponent on the neck, face or head.

Note: The frame is defined as the part of the opponent's body below the neck that is presented to the blocker.

● A defensive player may not tackle or hold an opponent other than a runner. Otherwise, he may use his hands, arms, or body only:

• To defend or protect himself against an obstructing opponent. An eligible receiver is considered to be an obstructing opponent ONLY to a point five yards beyond the line of scrimmage unless the player who receives the snap clearly demonstrates no further intention to pass the ball. Within this five-yard zone, a defensive player may make contact with an eligible receiver that may be maintained as long as it is continuous and unbroken up until a point when the receiver is beyond the defender. The defensive player cannot use his hands or arms to push from behind, hang onto, or encircle an eligible receiver in a manner that restricts movement as the play develops. Beyond this five-yard limitation, a defender may use his hands or arms ONLY to defend or protect himself against impending contact caused by a receiver. In such reaction, the defender may not contact a receiver who attempts to take a path to evade him.

• To push or pull opponent out of the way on the line of scrimmage.

• In actual attempt to get at or tackle a runner.

• To push or pull opponent out of the way in a legal attempt to recover a loose ball.

• During a legal block on an opponent who is not an eligible pass receiver.

• When legally blocking an eligible pass receiver above the waist.

Exception: Eligible receivers lined up within two yards of the tackle, whether on or immediately behind the line, may be blocked below the waist at or behind the line of scrimmage. NO eligible receiver may be blocked below the waist after he goes beyond the line. (Illegal cut)

Note: Once the quarterback hands off or pitches the ball to a back, or if the quarterback leaves the pocket area, the restrictions (illegal chuck, illegal cut) on the defensive team relative to the offensive receivers will end, provided the ball is not in the air.

● A defensive player may not contact an opponent above the shoulders with the palm of his hand except to ward him off on the line. This exception is permitted only if it is not a repeated act against the same opponent during any one contact. In all other cases, the palms may be used on the head, neck, or face, only to ward off or push an opponent in a legal attempt to get at the ball.

- Any offensive player who pretends to possess the ball or to whom a teammate pretends to give the ball may be tackled, provided he is crossing his scrimmage line between the ends of a normal tight offensive line.
- An offensive player who lines up more than two yards outside his own tackle or a player who, at the snap, is in a backfield position and subsequently takes a position more than two yards outside a tackle, may not clip an opponent anywhere nor may he contact an opponent below the waist if the blocker is moving toward the ball and if contact is made within an area five yards on either side of the line.
- A player of either team may block at any time provided it is not pass interference, fair catch interference, or unnecessary roughness.
- A player may not bat or punch:
  - A loose ball (in field of play) toward his opponent's goal line or in any direction in either end zone.
  - A ball in player possession.
    Note: If there is any question as to whether a defender is stripping or batting a ball in player possession, the official(s) will rule the action as a legal act (stripping the ball).
    Exception: A forward or backward pass may be batted, tipped, or deflected in any direction at any time by either the offense or the defense.
    Note: A pass in flight that is controlled or caught may only be thrown backward, if it is thrown forward it is considered an illegal bat.
- No player may deliberately kick any ball except as a punt, dropkick, or placekick.

Forward-pass

- A forward pass may be touched or caught by any eligible receiver. All members of the defensive team are eligible. Eligible receivers on the offensive team are players on either end of line (other than center, guard, or tackle) or players at least one yard behind the line at the snap. A T-formation quarterback is not eligible to receive a forward pass during a play from scrimmage.
  Exception: T-formation quarterback becomes eligible if the pass is previously touched by an eligible receiver.
- An offensive team may make only one forward pass during each play from scrimmage (loss of 5 yards).
- The passer must be behind his line of scrimmage (loss of down and five yards, enforced from the spot of pass).
- Any eligible offensive player may catch a forward pass. If a pass is touched by one eligible offensive player and touched or caught by a second offensive player, pass completion is legal. Further, all offensive players become eligible once a pass is touched by an eligible receiver or any defensive player.
- The rules concerning a forward pass and ineligible receivers:
  - If ball is touched accidentally by an ineligible receiver on or behind his line: loss of five yards.
  - If ineligible receiver is illegally downfield: loss of five yards.
  - If touched or caught (intentionally or accidentally) by ineligible receiver beyond the line: loss of 5 yards.
- The player who first controls and continues to maintain control of a pass will be awarded the ball even though his opponent later establishes joint control of the ball.
- Any forward pass becomes incomplete and ball is dead if:
  - Pass hits the ground or goes out of bounds.
  - Pass hits the goal post or the crossbar of either team.

- Pass is caught by offensive player after touching ineligible receiver.
- An illegal pass is caught by an offensive player.

● A forward pass is complete when a receiver clearly possesses the pass and touches the ground with both feet inbounds while in possession of the ball. If a receiver would have landed inbounds with both feet, but is carried or pushed out of bounds while maintaining possession of the ball, the pass is complete at the out-of-bounds spot.

● If an eligible receiver goes out of bounds accidentally, or is legally forced out by a defender and returns to first touch and catch a pass, the play is regarded as an incomplete pass resulting in a loss of five yards.

● If a personal foul is committed by the defense prior to the completion of a pass, the penalty is 15 yards from the spot where ball becomes dead.

● If a personal foul is committed by the offense prior to the completion of a pass, the penalty is 15 yards from previous line of scrimmage.

Intentional Grounding of Forward Pass

● Intentional grounding of a forward pass is a foul, resulting in a loss of down 10 yards from the previous spot if a passer is in the field of play. Or, a loss of down at the spot of the foul, if it occurs more than 10 yards behind the line or safety, will occur if a passer is in his own end zone when ball is released.

● Intentional grounding will be called when a passer, facing an imminent loss of yardage due to pressure from the defense, throws a forward pass without a realistic chance of completion.

● Intentional grounding will not be called when a passer, while out of the pocket and facing an imminent loss of yardage, throws a pass that lands at or beyond the line of scrimmage, particularly if no offensive is available to catch the ball. This includes the situation if the ball lands out of bounds over the sideline or end line.

Protection of Passer

● By interpretation, a pass begins when the passer—with possession of ball—brings his hand forward. If the ball strikes the ground after this action has begun, the play is ruled an incomplete pass. If a passer loses control of the ball prior to his bringing his hand forward, the play is ruled a fumble.

● No defensive player may run into a passer of a legal forward pass after the ball has left his hand (15 yards). The referee must determine whether an opponent had a reasonable chance to stop his momentum during an attempt to block the pass or tackle the passer while he still had the ball.

● No defensive player who has an unrestricted path to the quarterback may hit him flagrantly in the area of the knee(s) when approaching in any direction.

● Officials are to whistle the play dead as soon as the quarterback is clearly in the grasp and control of any tackler, and his safety is in jeopardy.

Pass Interference

● No interference is permitted with a forward pass thrown from behind the line. The restriction for the passing team starts with the snap. The restriction on the defensive team starts when the ball leaves the passer's hand. Both restrictions end when the ball is touched by anyone.

● The penalty for <u>defensive</u> pass interference in the NFL is an automatic first down at the spot of the foul. In college the maximum defensive pass interference penalty is 15 yards. If interference is in the end zone, it is first down for the offense on the defense's one-yard line. If the previous spot was inside the defense's one-yard line, the penalty is half the distance to the goal line.

● The penalty for <u>offensive</u> pass interference is 10 yards from the previous spot.

● It is pass interference by either team

when any player movement beyond the offensive line significantly hinders the progress of an eligible player or such player's opportunity to catch the ball during a legal forward pass. When players are competing for position to make a play on the ball, any contact by hands, arms, or body are considered incidental unless prohibited. Prohibited conduct occurs when a player physically restricts or impedes the opponent in such a manner that is visually evident and materially affects the opponent's opportunity to gain position or retain his position to catch the ball. If a player has gained position, it is not considered that he impeded or restricted his opponent in a prohibited manner if all of his actions are a bona fide effort to go to and catch the ball. Provided an eligible player is not interfered with in such a manner, the following exceptions to pass interference will prevail:

- Contact by a defender who is not playing the ball and such contact restricts the receiver's opportunity to make the catch.
- Playing through the back of a receiver in an attempt to make a play on the ball.
- Grabbing a receiver's arm in such a manner that restricts his opportunity to catch a pass.
- Extending an arm across the body of a receiver thus restricting his ability to catch a pass, regardless of whether the defender is playing the ball.
- Cutting off the path of a receiver by making contact with him without playing the ball.
- Hooking a receiver in an attempt to get to the ball in such a manner that it causes the receiver's body to turn prior to the ball arriving.

Actions that do not constitute pass interference include but are not limited to:

- Incidental contact by a defenders hands, arms, or body when both players are competing for the ball, or neither player is looking for the ball. If there is any question whether contact is incidental, the ruling shall be no interference.
- Inadvertent tangling of feet when both players are playing the ball or neither player is playing the ball
- Contact that would normally be considered pass interference, but the pass is clearly uncatchable by the involved players.
- Laying a hand on a receiver that does not restrict the receiver in an attempt to make a play on the ball
- Contact by a defender who has gained position on a receiver in an attempt to catch the ball.

Actions that constitute offensive pass interference include but are not limited to:

- Blocking downfield by an offensive player prior to the ball being touched.
- Initial contact with a defender by shoving or pushing off thus creating a separation in an attempt to catch a pass.
- Driving through a defender who has established a position on the field.

Actions that do not constitute offensive pass interference include but are not limited to:

- Incidental contact by a receiver's hands, arms, or body when both players are competing for the ball or neither player is looking for the ball.
- Inadvertent touching of feet when both players are playing the ball or neither player is playing the ball.
- Contact that would normally be considered pass interference, but the ball is clearly catchable by involved players.

Note: If there is any question whether player contact is incidental, the ruling should be no interference.

- Defensive players have as much right to the path of the ball as eligible offensive players.

- Pass interference for both teams ends when the pass is touched.
- There can be no pass interference at or behind the line of scrimmage, but defensive actions such as tackling a receiver can still result in a five-yard penalty for defensive holding, if accepted.
- Whenever a team presents an apparent punting formation, defensive pass interference is not to be called for action on the end man on the line of scrimmage, or an eligible receiver behind the line of scrimmage who is aligned or in motion more than one yard outside the end man on the line. Defensive hold, such a tackling a receiver, still can be called and result in a a five-yard penalty from the previous spot, if accepted. Offensive pass interference rules still apply.

Backward pass

- Any pass not forward is regarded as a backward pass. A pass parallel to the line is a backward pass. A runner may pass backward at any time. Any player on either team may catch the pass or recover the ball after it touches the ground.
- A backward pass that strikes the ground can be recovered and advanced by either team.
- A backward pass caught in the air can be advanced by either team.
- A backward pass in flight may not be batted forward by an offensive player.

Fumble

- The distinction between a fumble and a muff should be kept in mind in considering rules about fumbles. A fumble is the loss of player possession of the ball. A muff is the touching of a loose ball by a player in an unsuccessful attempt to obtain possession.
- A fumble may be advanced by any player on either team regardless of whether recovered before or after ball hits the ground.

- A fumble that goes forward and out-of-bounds will return to the fumbling team at the spot of the fumble unless the ball goes out of bounds in the opponent's end zone. In this case, it is a touchback.
- On a play from scrimmage, if an offensive player fumbles anywhere on the field during fourth down, only the fumbling player is permitted to recover and/or advance the ball. If any player fumbles after the two-minute warning in a half, only the fumbling player is permitted to recover and/or advance the ball. If recovered by any other offensive player, the ball is dead at the spot of the fumble unless it is recovered behind the spot of the fumble. In that case, the ball is dead at the spot of recovery. Any defensive player may recover and/or advance any fumble at any time.

Kicks from scrimmage

- Any kick from scrimmage must be made from behind the line to be legal.
- Any punt or missed field goal that touches a goal post is dead.
- In the NFL during a kick from scrimmage, only the end men, as eligible receivers on the line of scrimmage at the time of the snap, are permitted to go beyond the line before the ball is kicked. *Note:* An eligible receiver who, at the snap, is aligned or in motion behind the line and more than one yard outside the end man on his side of the line, clearly making him the outside receiver, replaces that end man as the player eligible to go downfield after the snap. All other members of the kicking team must remain at the line of scrimmage until the ball has been kicked.
- Any punt that is blocked and does not cross the line of scrimmage can be recovered and advanced by either team. However, if the offensive team recovers it, they must make the yardage necessary for its first down to retain possession if the punt was on fourth down.
- The kicking team may never advance its own kick even though legal recovery is

made beyond the line of scrimmage. Possession only.

- A member of the receiving team may not run into or rough a kicker who kicks from behind his line unless contact is:
  - Incidental to and after he had touched ball in flight.
  - Caused by kicker's own motions.
  - Occurs during a quick kick, or a kick made after a run, or after kicker recovers a loose ball. Ball is loose when kicker muffs snap or snap hits ground.
  - Defender is blocked into kicker. The penalty for running into the kicker is five yards. For roughing the kicker, it is 15 yards, an automatic first down and disqualification if flagrant.
- If a member of the kicking team attempting to down the ball on or inside opponent's five-yard line carries the ball into the end zone, it is a touchback.
- Fouls during a punt are enforced from the previous spot (line of scrimmage). *Exception:* Illegal touching, illegal fair catch, invalid fair catch signal, and fouls by the receiving team during loose ball after ball is kicked.
- While the ball is in the air or rolling on the ground following a punt or field goal attempt and the receiving team commits a foul before gaining possession, the receiving team will retain possession and will be penalized for its foul.
- It will be illegal for a defensive player to jump or stand on any player, or be picked up by a teammate or to use a hand(s) on a teammate to gain additional height in an attempt to block a kick. The penalty is 15 yards and unsportsmanlike conduct.
- A punted ball remains a kicked ball until it is declared dead or in possession of either team.
- Any member of the punting team may down the ball anywhere in the field of play. However, it is illegal touching (official's time out and receiver's ball at spot of illegal touching). This foul does not

offset any foul by receivers during the down.

- The defensive team may advance all kicks from scrimmage (including unsuccessful field goal attempts) whether or not ball crosses defensive team's goal line. Rules pertaining to kicks from scrimmage apply until defensive team gains possession.

Fair catch

- The member of the receiving team must raise one arm a full length above his head and wave it from side to side while kick is in flight. Failure to give proper sign results in the receivers' ball five yards behind spot of signal. *Note:* It is legal for the receiver to shield his eyes from the sun by raising one hand no higher than the helmet.
- No opponent may interfere with the fair catcher, the ball, or his path to the ball. The penalty is 15 yards from spot of foul and a fair catch is awarded.
- A player who signals for a fair catch is not required to catch the ball. However, if a player signals for a fair catch, he may not block or initiate contact with any player on the kicking team until the ball touches a player. The penalty results in a snap 15 yards behind spot of foul.
- If ball hits the ground or is touched by member of the kicking team in flight, a fair catch signal is off and all rules for a kicked ball apply.
- Any undue advance by a fair catch receiver is a delay of game. No specific distance is specified for undue advance, as the ball is dead at spot of catch. If player comes to a reasonable stop, no penalty exists. The violation is five yards.
- If time expires while the ball is in play and a fair catch is awarded, the receiving team may choose to extend the period with one fair catch kick down. However, placekickers may not use tee.

Foul on last play of half or game

- On a foul by defense on last play of half or game, the down is replayed if a penalty is accepted.

- On a foul by the offense on last play of half or game, the down is not replayed and the play in which the foul is committed is nullified.

  Exception: Fair catch interference, foul following change of possession, illegal touching. No score by offense counts.

Spot of enforcement of foul

- There are four basic spots at which a penalty for a foul is enforced:
  - Spot of foul: The spot where the foul is committed.
  - Previous spot: The spot where the ball was put in play.
  - Spot of snap, pass, fumble, return kick, or free kick: The spot where the act connected with the foul occurred.
  - Succeeding spot: The spot where the ball next would be put in play if no distance penalty were to be enforced.
- If a foul occurs after a touchdown and before the whistle for a try-for-point, the succeeding spot is the same spot of the next kickoff.
- All fouls committed by an offensive team behind the line of scrimmage and in the field of play are penalized from the previous spot.
- When a spot of enforcement for fouls involving defensive holding or illegal use of hands by the defense is behind the line of scrimmage, any penalty yardage to be assessed on that play is measured from the line if the foul occurred beyond the line.

Double foul

- If there is a double foul during a down in which there is a change of possession, the team last gaining possession may keep the ball unless its foul was committed prior to the change of possession.
- If double foul occurs after a change of possession, the defensive team retains the ball at the spot of its foul or dead ball spot.
- If one of the fouls of a double foul

involves disqualification, that player must be removed, but no penalty yardage is to be assessed.
- If the kickers foul during a kick before possession changes and the receivers foul after possession changes, the receivers will retain the ball after enforcement of its foul.

Penalty enforced on following kickoff

When a team scores by touchdown, field goal, extra point, or safety and either team commits a personal foul, unsportsmanlike conduct, or obvious unfair act during the down, the penalty will be assessed on the following kickoff

Chapter 8
Plays

All offensive plays in football fall into the category of running plays, passing plays, or those that feature kicking the ball in some manner, known as special-team plays.

The essence of the game is to effectively execute and deploy these plays in a strategic manner that prevents opponents from defending against them. Good plays advance the ball down the field. Moving the ball far enough to cross the goal line or kick a field goal results in points. Scoring more points than the opponent wins games. With this approach, the game becomes easier and easier to understand, doesn't it?

Running Plays

True to their name, running plays are those plays in which the ball is snapped to the quarterback and then handed, in most cases, to one of two running backs for an attempt to run with it in a forward direction.

Sometimes the quarterback will scramble, which involves keeping the ball and running with it himself. But scrambling happens far more often at the college level of the sport than in the NFL. Quarterbacks are not the bulkiest guys on the field, certainly not the fastest, and their main asset is their arm. Because of this, most QBs treat the quarterback scramble gingerly to avoid injury while being taken down by a 300 pound lineman.

Minnesota Vikings quarterback, Daunte Culpepper.

Otherwise, a wide receiver or tight end may also carry the ball on a running play, but this occurs perhaps once or twice a game on a reverse, a type of trick play. Without question, the running game is the meat-and-potatoes of football and centers around the running backs and the ability of the big linemen in front of them to plow open holes for the ball carriers to run through.

In the early 1900s, the forward pass had not yet become an accepted part of the game, so running, or "rushing the football," found its roots at the very

Players

beginnings of the sport. Some of the most basic plays that make up a team's "ground game" (as opposed to "air attack") are, in principle, designed very much like those that have been used for more than 100 years.

Play terminology, too, has evolved as the decades have passed. Blocking schemes for the linemen have varied to account for the changing alignments by defensive personnel. However, the basic idea of handing the ball to a talented running back and trying to figuratively ram it down the other team's throats is very much alive and well.

Here are some of the descriptive terms you will hear when a team is attempting to move down the field by running the football:

Sweep—a handoff or backwards toss to a running back. The back attempts to advance by first running wide toward the sidelines and then cutting up the field. This type of run is slower to develop than standard straight-ahead plays, but it can yield big gains if defenders are stacked to the middle or blocked to the inside by the receivers. A speedy back who can "turn the corner"is most often deployed.

Trap—a quick-hitting handoff up the middle during which the linemen at the point of attack trap the defensive linemen into thinking they are going to be unblocked. Instantaneously, blocks come from players on an angle, as the offensive linemen execute a switch in the traditional blocking pattern. Often, the defender's own momentum against the flow of the play will take him out of any position in which the ball carrier could possibly be tackled.

Drive Block—straightforward blocking technique by which the offensive linemen drive the defenders backwards as best they can so that the [offensive] back can advance after a simple handoff. There is no attempt at deception. The attitude is "here we come, try to stop us."

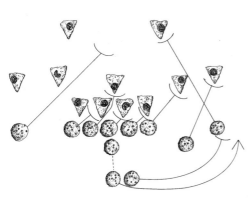

Sweep

Counter or Delay—a running play that proceeds after a fake has been made to one running back heading in another direction. Sometimes, two linemen will start to the right in front of a back on what appears to be a sweep, but the quarterback will merely fake the handoff or backwards toss in that direction. Ultimately, after a second of delay, the ball will be slipped to the second back following the remaining linemen in the opposite or counter direction to the initial flow.

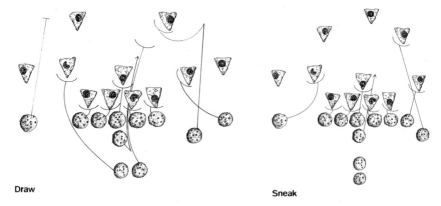

Draw

Sneak

Draw—a running play that finds the ball slipped to the [offensive] back after the quarterback has taken four or five steps back in what appears to be his pre-pass routine. In what may be an obvious passing situation, overzealous defenders may charge right past the ball carrier in their haste to reach and tackle the quarterback.

Sneak—the short-yardage play with the least amount of risk in that the quarterback merely takes the snap and tries to burrow or leap forward for the needed gain. This is usually employed with less than a yard required for either a first down or touchdown.

Dive—the equivalent of the sneak in terms of distance required and simplicity, only the ball is immediately handed to the closest running back for a forward plunge. A few talented and ultra-athletic backs have taken the terminology literally over the years, exhibiting the ability to leap (or dive) over the tangle of linemen at the line of scrimmage, landing beyond the first-down marker or in the end zone.

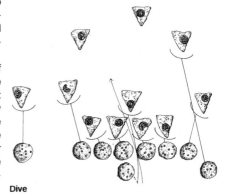

Dive

Pass Plays

If running plays are the neighborhood grocery store where your grandma used to shop, then the passing game of today is the e-commerce world of dot coms and wireless technology. Since the NFL changed the rules more than two decades ago to make passing the football a more attractive option by allowing pass blockers to use their hands more and pass defenders to use them less, passing the football has been compared to everything from fine art to science. Indeed, the intricate coordination of pass patterns and a quarterback's ability to find open receivers and launch the ball in their direction is one of the most exciting aspects of the sport.

Pass plays may allow a team to move the ball quickly and explode upon an opponent with a deluge of points in a short period of time. The "con" is that they may result in incompletions, yielding no-gain plays. Worse, they can cause big losses or interceptions by the opposition. The quarterback is integral since he is the one throwing the football down the field on pass plays. The high-risk, high-reward aspects of many offensive philosophies ultimately rest on his shoulders, which is why quarterbacks are usually the highest-paid players on the team (or, in college, the guy that doesn't have to stand in line at the bookstore). Advanced passing attacks and the excitement that most observers associate with teams that do it well are truly a phenomenon of "modern" football. Just think of the plays that make the highlight reel!

Here are some terms commonly associated with the passing game:

Pattern or Route—the path that receivers run in order to arrive at a prescribed location at the same time that the ball reaches that spot as delivered by the quarterback. The names of patterns often literally describe in what direction the receiver runs after starting up the field, as in "slant,""down and out"and "turn in." Similarly, a "post" pattern finds the receiver starting forward and then slanting toward the goal post. A "flag"pattern sends him up field and then toward the flag (or what is now really a type of pylon) where the sideline and the goal line meet.

Man-to-Man Coverage—any pass defense that assigns defensive backs and linebackers specific offensive players for which to be responsible. Defensive backs commonly cover wide receivers and usually the tight end. Linebackers sometimes cover the tight end and have primary responsibility for running backs coming out into pass patterns.

Zone Defense—any pass defense that calls for defenders to cover both a specific area of the field and any receivers that may venture there. Defender "A"may start out watching a wide receiver, but then pass him on to Defender "B"as that receiver runs out of the initial defender's area of responsibility. Defender "A"may then need to turn his attention to a tight end that has subsequently entered his zone. Offensive teams may attack this type of defensive scheme by "flooding"a zone, or sending three receivers into an area that only one or two men are defending.

Double Coverage—when two defenders are assigned to cover one receiver. This will often occur in man-to-man coverage to defend against the most dangerous receiver on the offensive team. However, complex zone coverage may also result in a type of double team as defenders "roll"or rotate the zone based on their read of the pass patterns. This approach is designed to stop certain types of passes as opposed to shutting down one particularly threatening individual.

Bump and Run or "Press"Coverage—when a wide receiver is challenged by a defensive back at the line of scrimmage at the beginning of a pass play. Defenders may bump or "chuck"receivers only within the first five yards down field from where the play originates. Doing so effectively will obviously disrupt a carefully synchronized pass pattern, forcing adjustments by both receiver and quarterback that are difficult to make on the fly. However, if the receiver eludes the bump at the line, he will likely burst wide open for a potential big gain. Teams that rush the passer well can afford to use this type of coverage more often, because the quarterback is less likely to have a lot of time to read a developing situation and adjust accordingly. Also, defensive backs in this scheme had better be fast, for they will be running with a receiver in man-to-man coverage, and will surely be running after him should the initial bump attempt fail. Hence, the name: Bump and run.

Play action—this pass follows the quarterback pretending to hand the ball off to a running back. Therefore, all aspects of the play for the first second or so make it appear as though a running play is unfolding, with the hope that defenders will be drawn toward the running back in the process. One misstep forward or in the wrong direction by a defender could easily allow a pass receiver to run beyond the defense into an open area to receive the pass. The play action fake may also deter those committed to the pass rush from charging with their usual vigor, as they must respect the prospect of the running back getting the handoff. Thus, this play takes on the aspects of run action in the beginning, only to turn into a passing play. In situations when the down and distance and offensive formation seem to dictate that a run is forthcoming, a play-action pass featuring deft faking and ball handling can

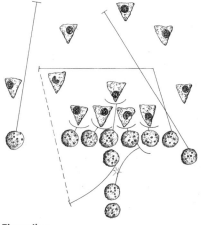

Play action

result in a large gain. Play action, executed adroitly, serves the dual purpose of giving the quarterback a little more time to throw and the receivers a bit more room in which to operate. Remember—when you hear this terminology, just substitute the word "run" for "play."

Deep threat or speed receiver—this is the wide receiver who can outrun people and run the deep pass patterns that result in big chunks of yardage and often touchdowns. The presence of such a receiver allows an offensive team to "stretch"a defense, in that a man running deep can open areas for other receivers running shorter patterns "underneath." Not every team has a legitimate deep threat—those that do have many more offensive options in their arsenal.

Possession receiver—this describes the slower guy who runs the short patterns over the middle and makes the tough catches while two defenders try to abruptly stop him. The term derives from this type of player making catches on third down, thus making a first down and keeping possession of the ball for his team. Sometimes this player is actually a team's third wide receiver, who comes into the game in strategic situations that find defenders paying too much attention to primary and secondary wide receivers.

Bomb—one of the terms that has stood the test of time, this is the most simplistic description of a long pass. It is not unusual for today's athletic quarterbacks to be able to throw the ball 60 or more yards in the air. It's a little more unusual to find a receiver catching a pass more than 30 yards down field on a play.

Screen—a deceptive pass play, during which the defensive linemen are allowed to charge toward the quarterback nearly unmolested by the offensive line. As the quarterback hurries and backpedals, the offensive linemen sift laterally toward the sideline, setting up a wall behind the line but in front of the running back that will receive the pass. As the defensive linemen converge upon him, the quarterback will loop the ball over them to the back, and the back then has a convoy to follow up the field. The timing of the play is difficult to execute, but a well-disguised screen usually results in a large gain.

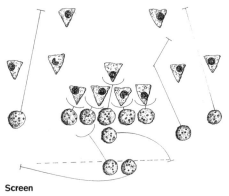
Screen

Quarterback drop—this refers to the distance that the quarterback retreats on any given pass play before setting and releasing the ball. The place where the QB plants his feet to deliver a pass is known as the "pocket." The overall design of a team's air attack determines which type of drop you will see most often from a given quarterback. A "West Coast Attack"features intricate timing routes that require three and five-step drops so that the passes can be delivered quickly. More traditional approaches that look for the option of longer passes more often call for the drop to be a full seven steps back.

Shotgun—the passing formation that finds the quarterback standing five yards behind the center prior to the snap instead of right behind him. This indicates an obvious passing situation, and the alignment gives the quarterback a chance to stand more erect and survey the defense to find a place in which to

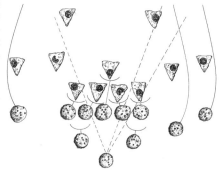
Shotgun

direct the launch. Also, his positioning gives the quarterback a head start on his drop, which is critical since the defensive line will often be charging in an all-out rush. Out of this formation, a QB will sometimes take one step back and then tuck the ball away and run it himself up the middle of the field, often an element of great surprise since a passing situation exists. This is called a "quarterback draw." It's actually a running play, but it fit in nicely here, didn't it?

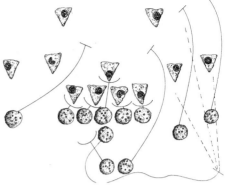

Scramble—when the quarterback Scramble runs, not by design, but to save the play and/or himself. If no receiver is open and the pass rushers are closing in, some quarterbacks have the wherewithal to run away from the pressure and gain yardage down the field. Also, it is possible for a QB to "buy time"by leaving the pocket and moving around behind the line long enough for a receiver to find some open space. The quarterback is still likely to get clobbered after delivering the pass, but it hurts less if the play turns into a significant gain.

Special Team Plays

Once pretty much an afterthought in football, these plays and the men who execute them are now recognized as some of the most important to a team's success. Fifty years ago, rosters were smaller, and the slender, less muscular kickers, whose strength is in their legs, were not cavorting around NFL fields. Someone who played another position for sixty plays a game would drag himself up off the ground and trudge over to try a field goal or punt on fourth down. How times have changed! The kicking game is known as special teams' play because specialists have become the focal point of correct execution.

Each team now has one player just to punt the ball, one just to kick extra points and field goals, and often one player just to snap the ball for such efforts. Some even have a guy whose only job is to kick off, although this is really considered a luxury. Regardless, you get the idea—so many games are decided by a field goal or by field position that entrusting kicking chores to a regular player no longer wins games.

Obviously, part-time kickers or punters cannot devote as much time specializing in these situations because of other offensive or defensive responsibilities. Also, regular players might get hurt tackling or being tackled and are then rendered useless elsewhere on the field. Needless to say, you have a lot to lose if a kicker goes out that cannot perform in a clutch situation.

The most obvious aspect of special team play in terms of affecting the outcome of games is whether or not the place-kicker can put the ball between the uprights of the goal post. This directly accounts for points, and a good field-goal kicker is expected to make around 80% of attempts, with a maximum range of at least 50 yards. Successful field goal—three points and kick off to the other team. Missed field goal—no points and the other team takes over the ball from the spot at which the ball was placed for the kick, not the line of scrimmage. Translation: Missed opportunities for your team and good "field position"for the other team.

Ah, field position. Now we've come to that favorite term among coaches that is the less obvious but very critical underlying theme to what special teams are all about.

Simply put, if you have a punter or kicker who can boom the ball far and high, the other team is likely to have difficulty returning the kick any significant distance. Height comes into play because that translates into more time for the men defending against the return to run down and surround the ball carrier. The farther a team has to march down the field against

Retired Dallas Cowboy Quarterback Troy Aikman.

you to score, the less likely the team will be able to do so without being stopped on downs or by a turnover.

Teams that punt and/or cover punts poorly give the opposition a "short field" on which to operate, meaning that little distance has to be covered to score a touchdown or field goal. With all this in mind, there are now even some specialists who play only as special teams coverage men, such is their value in the area of charging down field like kamikazes trying to make tackles. Each conference now names one special teams' player, above and beyond the kickers, to appear in the post season Pro Bowl Game. A return man is selected for each squad, too. These are well-earned honors.

Fantasy Football

Ah, men's fantasies. As if they're not hard enough to interpret, they begin rambling about salary caps, statistics, team rosters and schedules. My response to this was, "Honey, I have no cap. You can spend as much on me as you want!" Once again, I think we were talking about two different things.

Fantasy football (obviously what HE meant) is another facet of the season made popular by the fact that regular guys around the world, whether wired to their recliners or bar stools, can participate in fantasy play that incites serious competition among fellow football lovers. Did I mention that leagues usually revolve around the almighty dollar? Anyway, now you, too, can take your newfound knowledge of the sport and put it to good use in a fantasy league this season.

The concept is very simple. The team that scores the most points, overall, at the end of the season is the winner. This relies on chance, luck, coincidence and even a bit of strategy in order to make better recruiting decisions than NFL team owners, not to mention all your buddies. However, the premise of the entire fantasy league focuses on watching and following real NFL activities and games in a given season and how those results relate to your standings and picks on a fantasy team. [NOTE: College football fantasy leagues do exist, but for our purposes, we'll stick to the structure of the NFL or professional leagues that are more common and have a wider participant base.]

Fantasy football leagues are everywhere. There are local "bar" leagues, regional leagues, Internet leagues and high-stake national leagues. Several types of leagues exist, including "head-to-head," which means you actually play another team in your league each week, and a "Rotisserie League," which means there is no weekly head-to-head match-up.

A league normally consists of eight to 10 teams to make it easy to schedule games. Each owner (the guys in their "fantasy" roles) submit a team name, or draw a team from a lottery process, and an annual draft day is set up to pick the players for their team. It's important to note that players will be picked at random based on their personal stats and talents. In this league, the drafted players have no allegiance to the team they play for in reality. The players just

Green Bay Packers quarterback Brett Favre leaves the field at Texas Stadium.

contribute on an individual basis for "Joe's team." Remember, this is a fantasy league.

The structure of the fantasy season is based on each participant paying an entry fee in order to secure a team and play in the season-long fantasy league. These fees are pooled together to form a "pot" for the winning team at the end of the season. This organization is one of fantasy league's larger appeals, as it allows a more interactive format, and a more "bang-for-your-buck" experience than betting on individual games throughout the football season. In short, a season of highlights that require thought, strategy, expertise and chance on the individual level is a big attraction to territorial football fans.

During the season, one individual will be chosen or elected league commissioner, with the ability to rule on any disputes that might rear their ugly heads among team owners (again, the guys in their fantasy roles). Statistics are collected each week summarizing the results of the previous week's games, as well as year-to-date stats. Someone from the league might keep the teams statistics or they might pay a stat service for the reporting.

During the league's draft, owners draft NFL players onto teams and compete against each other's teams each week. The players are drafted according to their NFL statistics/performance from the previous year. Players are "paid for" based on a monetary amount when drafted onto a team. If the salary cap (the maximum amount total player salaries must meet per team) is low, only one or two superstars can be afforded. In a national or Internet league, you might start out with $50 million to purchase 11 players; two quarterbacks, three running backs, three wide receivers, one tight end, one kicker and one defensive/special teams unit. That is $4.54 million per player, and a team has just been built based on your financial abilities. Every league has a limited but equal amount of imaginary money to spend on players.

When draft day comes around, the big "owners" (do you know who these are yet?) get together and the games begin. Each owner needs to draft 15 to 18 players. Numbers to determine the draft order are generally pulled out of a hat by the commissioner. The owners make their first round draft choices and the order is usually reversed for the second round and so forth. This goes on until each owner fills a team roster.

During the draft, there are a few things to remember:
- Do **NOT** draft players with the same bye week (week without a game) or from the same team for your roster at the same time. You will not be able to replace them all with reserves when their bye week arrives and you will get ZERO (0) points that week.
- **EVERY PLAYER** on your roster must be a point scorer.
- **NEVER** have someone on your roster that has no real possibility of performing well for you.

Each week, the roster is filled with a starting lineup: One quarterback, two running backs, two wide receivers, one tight end, one kicker, one punt and kickoff return unit (and a partridge in a pear tree). Throughout the season, the performance of players is evaluated and points, yardage and other statistics are tallied based on the happenings by game. Points are earned for a team based on those real-life statistics. For example, fantasy scoring generally follows normal regulations, such as a touchdown is worth six points, a field goal is three points, a safety is two points, and a two-point conversion is two points. Fantasy points also include passing yards at one point per 25 yards, rushing yards at one point per 10 yards and receiving yards are worth one point per 10 yards. If your (or your man's) team outscores an opponents team, you win the game.

And, that's the fantasy. Put in a little time and effort. Count on the professional talent to do the hard stuff. Collect the money. But, most importantly—have fun!

Chapter 10
Arena Football

If the average NFL game is like a backyard barbecue with friends and neighbors, an Arena Football League contest is the fourth hour of a bachelorette party. There is a type of frenzy surrounding AFL games brought about in part by the indoor venues which raise noise levels ñ the pounding music and screaming from fans has no natural means of escape. And why are the fans screaming? Because on a field with only 50 yards separating the two goal lines, every play begins with the possibility of a touchdown being scored. Any play seems to carry the weight of possibly deciding the outcome of a particular game and, with that, the outcome of the entire season. The final score of a game could be 72-71. That outcome could well determine whether or not your team is going to the playoffs. Why not stand up and shout?

Attending an arena game certainly provides a chance to get a better feeling for the intensity of the hitting and the speed of football simply because fans are closer to the action. The playing field runs right up against the boards, just as the rink ends at the boards at a hockey game. The key difference is, fans at a hockey game are separated from the players, and the potential dangers created by flying pucks and swinging stick, by a high pane of unbreakable glass. At an AFL game, you are right there, baby! You are almost literally, in the game, a sensation that can not be duplicated in a 70,000 — seat NFL stadium. Hey ... you might even catch a slightly errant pass from the quarterback as it comes whistling in your direction! If that doesn't keep you on your toes, nothing will!

In an era that finds the cultural gap between pro athletes and the average spectator seeming to grow ever wider, the Arena Football League has taken measures to cultivate and preserve that vital team/fan relationship. Most visible in this endeavor is the Fans' Bill of Rights, which appears below. The Arena Football League released this unique document to the public in 1999.

THE ARENA FOOTBALL LEAGUE'S FANS' BILL OF RIGHTS

In furtherance of our Mission Statement we, the players, coaches, officials, staff and owners of the Arena Football League are thankful to the Fans that we serve, appreciate their support and dedicate ourselves Collectively to protecting their rights as the greatest sports and entertainment Fans in the world.

We believe that every Fan is entitled to a wholesome environment for guests and family members, free of violence, profane gestures and language or rude and invasive behavior that could in any way interfere with a first-class entertainment experience.

We believe that every Fan demands that we maintain absolute respect for the game of Arena Football and maintain the integrity of the finest of fair competition at all times.

We believe that every Fan deserves our very best effort on a consistent basis, on every play on the filed, every action in the stands, every call to our office, and every involvement in our community.

We believe that every fan is entitled to a total entertainment experience at an affordable cost for all members of the family from the time they arrive at the arena to the time they depart.

We believe that every Fan should receive the very best in competitive football, entertainment, merchandise, food and beverage for their purchasing power.

We believe that every Fan is entitled to interact with and have access to players and coaches for autographs and conversation in recognition of their support at every game.

We believe that Fans are entitled to fast, accurate, and complete information about our players, coaches, league, games and performance.

We believe that Fans expect the Arena Football League to be comprised of gentlemen and ladies who are examples and role models for youth, free of physical violence, drugs, alcohol and gambling abuse.

We believe that Fans expect us to honor our country and to be involved in our communities to make contributions for a better, safer, and more positive place to live.

We believe that Fans should know that we are committed to serve and not to be served, to give and not to just take, and to inspire and encourage people to higher levels of personal and professional achievement, growth, maturity, and respect for each other.

Two players have been especially noteworthy for making the transition from the arena game to the National Football League while playing the higher-profile "skill" positions. The success of Miami Dolphin wide receiver Orande Gadsden and St. Louis Ram quarterback Kurt Warner have resulted in the media and public spotlight turning more favorably in the direction of the AFL, flooding the league with positive publicity. Though by no means the only players to have played and played well in both the AFL and NFL, Gadsden and Warner are the first to have gained a great measure of notoriety for doing so.

In 1998 as a player for the Portland Forest Dragons, then a member of the AFL, Gadsden recorded some big numbers. The long and lanky receiver caught 93 passes for 1,335 yards and 37 touchdowns. When the Miami receiving corps was decimated by injuries later that fall, Gadsden became a Dolphin and was soon a favorite target of the NFL's all-time leader in most passing categories, Dan Marino. Gadsden proved to be not merely a stopgap replacement, too. He continued to see regular action as a wide receiver for Miami in 1999 and 2000 as well, becoming known along the way for his ability to make acrobatic catches.

However, the Kurt Warner story tops them all. In 1999, after first-string quarterback Trent Green sustained a season-ending knee injury in an early preseason game, the Rams turned to Warner to lead the team. A virtual unknown, but a veteran of the arena wars as an Iowa Barnstormer, all Warner did was have one of the best seasons in NFL history. St. Louis, a team with a 5-11 record the previous season, won the NFC West, captured playoff contests against the Vikings and Buccaneers, and then won Super Bowl XXXIV by beating Tennessee. In the process, Warner became the only player in the NFL other than Marino to throw for more than 40 touchdowns in a season, was named the league's Most Valuable Player, and took home the MVP trophy from the Super Bowl, too. Do you think a few more NFL scouts are snooping around arena football games these days, hoping to find the next Gadsdens and Warners! You bet!

In fact, the alliance of the NFL and AFL (the former now owns 49% of the arena league) has played a major role in changing the face of what the AFL looks like in terms of franchise location. Teams from Iowa and Albany, NY have moved to New York City and Indianapolis respectively, while the Hartford team now toils in Toronto. New teams have been added in Chicago and Detroit. In other words, more "major market" cities are becoming part of the AFL landscape. There were 29 teams trying to make their way to the ArenaBowl in 2001, divided into two conferences, each with two divisions. This is by no means football in the traditional sense, but having survived for more than a decade the Arena Football League's high-octane brand of play has a significant following and appears to have a healthy future.

The Beginning

During an indoor soccer game on February 11, 1981 at Madison Square Garden, James Foster, then an executive for NFL Properties, watched soccer and saw football. He reasoned that if they can play soccer indoors, why not football? After pulling a large manila envelope from his briefcase, he drew the outline of a miniature football field over a hockey rink, and penciled in some notes on what would evolve into a full-fledged concept for a curiously new and exciting adaptation of an established team sport.

He began with a proven concept, American football. Knowing there was no room for competition with the NFL, he decided instead to hypothesize an indoor and summertime hybrid. He applied the best of the gridiron game with new and interesting twists: 50-yard field, eight vs. eight, single platoon, drop kicks and rebound nets.

Once Arena Football progressed from notes on an envelope to a game with rules and numerous solid and decidedly different innovations, Foster had to take the game one giant step further. He sought to gain acceptance for Arena Football. He took his indoor football ideas to the network NBC, where the-powers-that-be responded positively to the game's potential. However, the USFL, a competitor to the idea, was born shortly thereafter and Foster foresaw an overabundance of summer football. The innovative game was placed on the back burner, where it remained until 1985.

After the rise and fall of the USFL, Foster decided to move forward with the development of indoor football. The first step was to make sure that football could even be executed indoors on a much smaller playing surface. Working with several experienced coaches, it became apparent that the concept could work. The next step was to measure response from the public and sports media through a test game. Five years after the initial sketch, the Arena Football League came to life.

In furthering developing the indoor game, he conducted the "test game" in Rockford, Ill. on April 26, 1986 between the Rockford Metros and Chicago Politicians. The response led to a "showcase game" on February 26, 1987 at the Rosemont Horizon in Chicago. The competition was greeted enthusiastically by 8,200 fans and set the stage for the national debut of the Arena Football League in June of 1987.

Foster pitched the excitement of Arena Football to Bill Grimes, then president of ESPN, and his favorable response sent indoor play on its way. ESPN broadcast, nationally and in prime time, five of 13 games during the league's initial season in the summer of 1987.

The Basics of Arena Football

With the league beginning in May, there are 14-regular season games in this fast-paced, offense-oriented indoor sport. Arena Football is played with only eight players per team on the field at a time. Six of those eight players must play both offense and defense. The field is only 85 feet wide and 66 yards long, with the playing field 50 yards long and the end zones only 8 yards deep.

The indoor padded environment has sideline barriers 48 inches high and made of high-density foam rubber to protect the players. The goal posts are nine feet wide with a crossbar height of 15 feet (NFL goal posts are 18' wide with the crossbar at 10 feet).

Kickoffs occur from the goal line and punting is illegal in Arena football. Kickers sometimes use a one-inch tee. On fourth down, a team may go for a first down, touchdown or field goal. The receiving team may field any kickoff or missed field goal that rebounds off the goal-side rebound nets, which are 30 feet wide by 32 feet high. The bottoms of the nets are eight feet above the ground. Any kickoff that goes out of bounds without being touched will be placed at the 20-yard line or the place where it went out of bounds, whichever is more advantageous to the receiving team.

Each team has just eight players on the field, playing both offense and defense with the only exceptions being the kicker, the quarterback, the kick returner on the defense and two defensive specialists.

Four offensive players line up on the line of scrimmage. Across the line of scrimmage, three defensive players set up in a three-point stance. One linebacker may blitz on either side of the center. Passing rules in Arena Football are the same as outdoor NCAA football, in which receivers must have one foot inbound. A unique exception involves the rebound nets. A forward pass that rebounds off the endzone net is a live ball and is in play until it touches the playing surface. As in NFL football, there are four downs allotted to advance the ball ten yards for a first down, or to score. With a maximum of 50 yards to go for a touchdown, which is a score of six points, the games are very high scoring.

After a touchdown, a place kick is worth one point for a conversion, two points for a drop kick conversion and two points for a successful run or pass after a touchdown. Three points can be obtained for a field goal by placement or four points for a drop kick field goal. A safety is worth two points.

One unusual feature reminiscent of baseball: when a ball is thrown or bounces into the seats surrounding the playing field, the "lucky" fan that catches the ball keeps it. It is estimated that the league gives away 15-20 balls per game. The official football of the Arena League is the Wilson Ironman football. It is the same size and weight of the football used by National Football League players.

Time

There are four 15-minute quarters in Arena football with a 15-minute halftime. Each team is allowed three time-outs per half. The clock stops for out-of-bounds plays or incomplete passes only in the last minute of each half or when the referee deems it necessary for penalties, injuries or timeouts.

Overtime Rules

Overtime periods are 15 minutes during the regular season and the playoffs.

Each team gets one possession to score. If, after each team has had one possession and one team is ahead, that team wins. If the teams are tied after each has had a possession, the next team to score wins.

Arena Football facts

- The popularity of the sport has increased through the years, so much so that the NFL sought a working arrangement with the league in order to develop players, particularly receivers and quarterbacks. NFL owners amended a bylaw to the NFL Constitution to allow NFL owners to acquire Arena League teams within their market
- The average attendance in the 1987 inaugural season was 11,279.
- Iowa became first true expansion team to win a first-round playoff game Sept. 1, 1995 before playoff record crowd of 25,087.

Arena Football's Glossary

Attendance—League attendance in 1998 surpassed one million (1,126,222) for the third consecutive season. The Arizona Rattlers led the circuit for the second straight season, averaging 15,785 per game. ArenaBowl XII, held in Tampa at the Ice Palace, drew the fifth largest crowd in ArenaBowl history.

Ball—The official football of the Arena League is the Wilson Ironman football. It is the same size and weight of the football used by National Football League players.

Ball in the Stands—When a ball is thrown or bounces into the seats surrounding the playing field, the spectator that catches the ball may keep it. Although no official statistic has been recorded, the league estimates 15-20 balls are given away per game.

Defensive Specialists—A pair of players, substituted for the QB and offensive specialist, who are the best "cover-men" on the team. Usually assigned to the opponents' best receiver and offensive specialist.

"Don't Blink!"—The tagline for the league's first-ever national marketing campaign. "Don't Blink!" epitomizes the game. In 1998, the league's combined per game score was a record 97.4 points per game. In fact, six teams averaged better than 50 points. The New Jersey Red Dogs established the professional football record with 91 points against Texas (now Houston) in 1997.

Drop Kick—A field goal that is dropkicked through the uprights is worth four points. An extra point attempt that is dropkicked is worth two points.

Web site—www.arenafootball.com, the league's official web-site contains the latest, news, statistics, rosters, schedules and links to its member teams' web sites.

Ironman—Synonymous with Arena Football, "Ironman" signifies participants playing both offense and defense. Typically, linemen get to pass block as well as rush the passer, wide-outs play either defensive back or linebacker and fullbacks play linebacker. Each year, the league honors an Ironman of the Year.

"Mac and Jack" Linebackers—"Mac" may rush the QB straight on, without stunting, twisting or drop-back coverage. "Jack" must stay within an imaginary box behind the line of scrimmage. Either linebacker may cover the fullback or tight end, but double-teaming is illegal. "Mac" typically plays wide receiver on offense while "Jack" competes at fullback.

Offensive Motion—Unlike more traditional football, one offensive back may go into forward motion prior to the snap of the ball.

Offensive Specialist—This player, substituted for one of the defensive specialists, usually plays wide receiver and kick returner. Simply one of the most dangerous players on the field, the offensive specialist is the first option on offense.

Overtime—Arena Football has a unique overtime rule. If a contest is tied after regulation, teams will play a 15-minute overtime. Each team will have one opportunity to score. If, after each team has had one chance to score, the game is tied, the first team to score is crowned the winner.

Rebound Nets—Goal-side rebound nets extend outward from each upright. The nets are approximately 30-feet wide, 32-feet high and extend to 40-feet above the playing surface. The bottom bars of the frames are positioned eight feet above the surface. Nets are stretched taut so that a missed kick attempt will rebound off the net and back into the field of play. Once the ball bounces off the net, it's live.

Sideline Barriers—Similar to the sideboards that surround a hockey rink, the sideline barrier encircles the playing surface. The barrier is made of a high-density foam pad, measuring three inches thick. The sideline barriers are one to three feet beyond the field perimeter.

Stunting or Twisting—When a defensive lineman is rushing the passer, there's no "stunting" or "twisting." In other words, linemen are required to power past offensive linemen straight on.

Tight End—A position not widely utilized in Arena Football, one offensive lineman can declare himself a tight end prior to the snap by simply raising his arm and "declaring" himself a tight end.

Two-Way Players—One of the most "throwback" features of the Arena League is the fact that the game features eight-on-eight, single-platoon football, where six players on each team must play both offense and defense with limited substitutions, much as was the case with early NFL clubs.

Arena Football History

1998

• League draws more than one million fans for third straight season, with Rattlers leading the circuit in consecutive seasons (15,785 per game).

• League shatters previous mark of 91.6 combined points per game, scoring 97.4 in 1998 (9,541), including record 111.1 in Week 13.

• AFL Board of Directors approves application of New Orleans Saints owner Tom Benson to place a team in New Orleans (June 3).

• Benson is first NFL owner to apply for and purchase an AFL membership.

• NFL bylaws previously prohibited NFL owners from investing in other football leagues or teams, but an amendment to NFL rules was adopted May 22, 1998, allowing exception for AFL teams in NFL club's own market.

• Orlando claims first championship with 62-31 win over Tampa Bay before 17,222 fans at Ice Palace — makes national network debut on ABC's Wide World of Sports, earning a 1.6 rating (Aug. 23).

• AFL completes its purchase of worldwide patent, trademark and copyrights from Gridiron Enterprises, Inc. (Aug. 13). Milwaukee QB Todd Hammel surpassed Jay Gruden as Arena Football's career passing leader (June 6).

• San Jose's Steve Papin becomes the second player to gain over 3,000 all-purpose yards in a season and surpasses Albany's Eddie Brown as the all-time leader in all-purpose yards in a season.

• Texas Terror re-named Houston ThunderBears.

• Grand Rapids Rampage begins play.

• Portland Forest Dragons WR/LB Oronde Gadsden signs with the NFL's Miami Dolphins (Aug. 3).

• Los Angeles awarded team for 2000 season in The STAPLES Center (Nov. 19).

Continued on next page.

1999

• In an historic day for football at all levels (Feb. 8), NFL agrees to exclusive option to purchase an equity interest in Arena Football League. Option can be exercised over next 3 years and would give NFL a minority ownership interest (up to 49.9%) in the AFL and voice in operation of the league (exercising the option is subject to approval of NFL owners).

• Commissioner Baker awarded 5-year contract extension, through 2004 season.

• AFL Board of Directors approves creation of Triple A football league — arenafootball2 — for 1999 season, as part of Baker's five-year strategic plan, Arena Football 2000.

• League unveils Fans' Bill of Rights.

• 15 teams draw over one million fans for fourth consecutive season.

• AFL Board of Directors approves an application to a group including former NFL great Walter Payton to begin play in Chicago in 2001 (July 29).

• Board also approves application for team in Raleigh (July 30) to begin play in 2000 and to a group led by former NFL veteran QB and current ESPN broadcaster Ron Jaworski and former AFL Commissioner Jim Drucker to begin play no later than the 2002 season in a city to be determined.

• Albany Firebirds, celebrating 10-year anniversary, wins ArenaBowl XIII over the defending champion Orlando Predators, 59-48, to claim first title in team history.

• Houston's Clint Dolezel (May 14), Nashville's Andy Kelly (June 18) and Albany's Mike Pawlawski (June 26) tie a league-record with 10 TD passes in a single game.
• Dolezel throws for a league-high 479 yards (May 14).

• Orlando's Barry Wagner becomes first player to achieve 200 career receiving TDs and surpass the 9,000 yard receiving mark.

• New York CityHawks, owned by Madison Square Garden, Corp., relocate to Hartford, CT (known as New England Sea Wolves).

• Expansion Buffalo Destroyers begin play.

• Former Iowa Barnstormer Kurt Warner becomes first NFL QB in 50 years to throw three scoring passes in each of his first three starts (Oct. 3). Eearned Associated Press NFL MVP honors and Super Bowl MVP accolades.

• Board of Directors approves move of Portland to Oklahoma City for 2000 (Nov. 17).

• AFL announces multi-year television contract with TNN, ESPN, ESPN2, and ABC.

• Detroit, under the ownership of Palace Sports & Entertainment and Detroit Lions Chairman, William Clay Ford Jr., announce AFL team to begin play in 2001, making Ford the first NFL owner to field an AFL team (Dec. 1).

• Washington Redskin owners awarded team to begin play in D.C. in 2003 (Dec. 3). AFL unveils expanded playoff format to 12 teams (Dec. 22).

2000
• Federal antitrust lawsuit filed against league by AFL Players Association and its lawyers (Feb. 4).

• Board of Directors vote to cancel AFL season (Feb. 24).

• Board of Directors recognize Arena Football League Players" Organizing Committee as collective bargaining representatives for all AFL players; re-open 2000 season (March 1).

• Owners ratify six-year collective bargaining agreement (July 17).

• NFL agrees to oversee and manage game officials.

• AFL partners up with Total Sports to publish the 2001 Record & Fact Book.

• AFL signs Ford on as its first blue-chip sponsor and "official automobile" partner, press conference is held at the Super Bowl in Tampa Bay (Jan. 25).

• NFL.com and Ignite Internet partnership announced (Feb. 26).

Arena Football American Conference

EASTERN

Buffalo Destroyers

Carolina Cobras

New Jersey Gladiators

New York Dragons

Toronto Phantoms

SOUTHERN

Florida Bobcats

Nashville Kats

Orlando Predators

Tampa Bay Storm

Arena Football American Conference

WESTERN

Arizona Rattlers

Houston Thunderbears

Los Angeles Avengers

Oklahoma Wranglers

San Jose Sabercats

CENTRAL

Chicago Rush

Detroit Fury

Grand Rapids Rampage

Indiana Firebirds

Milwaukee Mustangs

Chapter 11
Stats and Stuff

One of the more common sports cliches, at least when it comes to competition involving teams, is that the only statistics that matter are wins and losses. Of course, such gems are almost always uttered by coaches, whose futures are hanging on the line based on the number of victories produced from year to year. When it comes to athletes, though many will never admit it for fear of being labeled as something other than a "team player," many, many individual stats are likely to play major roles in their futures.

Statistical accomplishments are certainly paramount in landing that new multi-year, multi-million dollar contract. Players are compared to other players during the course of nearly all salary negotiations, and the easiest manner by which to do so is with statistics. And, for those with aspirations of joining the immortals in the Hall of Fame, numbers will almost certainly be a key factor as to whether that status is attained or not. Here then are some important statistical categories and benchmarks that will help you determine who is earning his dough on any given weekend or who instead might be making an untimely exit from professional football.

Offensive Statistics

By the nature of how the game is played, with distinct units for offense and defense along with designed segments of ball possession, most of the eye-catching numbers associated with football have to do with offense. In order to gauge what's happening within the NFL, the stats and milestones exist to measure performances within one individual game. For instance, it is, and has been for decades, considered noteworthy if a player rushes for 100 or more yards in a game. Similarly, a receiver catching passes that total gains of 100 or more yards is also considered to have had a strong game. Catching 10 or more passes is also significant. Back to yardage again, a quarterback reaching or surpassing the 300-yard mark is sure to catch everyone's eye. Falling short of such numbers by no means indicates failure, nor does attaining them always translate into a winning performance. Still, these standards have survived decades of change in football and remain highly significant.

Digging a bit deeper, a running back that averages four yards per rushing attempt is considered to be very valuable. But, is the guy that can do that durable enough to carry the ball 25 times per game to earn 100 yards? Is there value to a more punishing, big back that grinds along at a 3.2 yards per carry pace but can take the pounding and handle the ball 30 times a game?

Yes, depending on what any given offense is looking for from a player in that position. The great ones, of course, bring it all to the table in one package. Cleveland's Jim Brown averaged over five yards per carry for his entire nine-year career, and won the NFL rushing title eight times. He retired after the 1965 season. No one has had a career average up around the 5.0 mark before or since—not Walter Payton, not O.J. Simpson, not Eric Dickerson, not Barry Sanders. In other words, a 4.0 rushing average is very good, and a 5.0 is superhuman—at least through nearly one full century of NFL competition.

Every now and then, a burner comes along at the wide receiver position that can put up some startling numbers. With an excellent quarterback and advanced offensive scheme, it is possible for a receiver to average over 20.0 yards per reception. Realistically, anything in the upper teens is very good, an indication that a receiver has deep-threat ability and that the offense in question has the capabilities to get him the ball down the field. There are many Pro Bowl receivers who do not have such gaudy numbers in terms of yards per catch, but that is because their roles within their teams' frameworks are different. Anything in the 15-yard and above range is certainly significant.

Here's an obscure stat for you that carries a lot of weight within the inner circles of the game. It is yards per pass attempt. Sure, a quarterback could put up a 312-yard game on an afternoon when his team is behind and he's throwing all day, but how efficient was he if it took 52 attempts to reach that figure? On the other hand, a crisp offense led by Joe Montana or Steve Young in the glory days of the San Francisco 49ers might find either quarterback completing 22 of 30 passes for 350 yards. The comparison: the QB with 52 attempts yielded only 6.0 yards per try, while the San Francisco scenario figures to 11.7 per attempt. While you will see yards per completion on many a graphic during a telecast, you will seldom, if ever, see or hear the yards-per-attempt number. This is one you can track for yourself to have the upper hand in rating a team's offensive efficiency. And it makes sense to follow this stat, because yards per carry rushing the ball is a stat that has (here's a pun that simply has to happen) been run into the ground.

It used to be that a punting average of 40.0 yards was considered good—now 45 yards per kick is more what teams are looking for. And, even in this category, the numbers kept have become more complex. A net punting average can be found in most sports sections at least once a week—telling you the distance of the punt minus the distance the other team returned the kick. Also, though an official stat is not kept (yet), "hang time" is a vital category in the measurement of all punters. Simply put, this is the amount of time elapsing from the punter's foot making contact with the ball to the point at which the ball is either caught downfield or hits the ground. Over 4.0 seconds is a legitimate target — 5.0 represents the upper class and cannot likely be maintained for an entire season.

Are you numbered out yet? Just be glad this isn't baseball we're talking about!

Rushing for 1,000 yards in a season still gets a measure of respect, although with the 16-game NFL schedule that now requires gaining only 62.5 yards per game. Only four players, Simpson, Dickerson, Sanders and Terrell Davis, have run for more than 2,000 yards in a season, with only Simpson reaching that milestone during a 14-game schedule. Similarly, having a 1,000-yard season as a receiver will still serve you pretty darn well when sitting down with the suits to talk contract in the off season. So will 100 receptions in a season, although that mark became more attainable in the pass-happy late 1990s. It's still a relatively rare accomplishment—catching 80 or more passes in a year remains mighty good.

A 4,000-yard season for a quarterback means that he has averaged 250 yards over 16 games. This is very good. Another measure of a quarterback is his ratio of touchdown passes to interceptions, a reflection of how well he can play the risk-to-reward game of today's sophisticated aerial offenses. Having 30 touchdown passes in a season is terrific, but if they come in concert with 28 interceptions, the cup will be seen as half empty. Taking care of the football is, after all, a quarterback's responsibility. Obviously, it's far tougher to score when you don't have it.

Defensive Statistics

There are two glamour statistics on the defensive side of the ball. Ironically, neither of them is "tackles," which, as you should surmise, is simply the total number of times a defender brings down a ball carrier.

Of course, playing certain positions put certain players in situations that call for more tackles to be made, and that gives you a read on the value of those athletes to their teams. Anyway, at least one of the glamour stats does pertain to tackling: the category called "sacks."

A sack is recorded when the quarterback is tackled behind the line of scrimmage while attempting to pass. Such plays often result in big losses and can turn around the complexion of a game. Defensive ends and outside linebackers usually record the higher sack totals, and any individual recording a dozen or more in a season is having a strong year. A monster year finds a guy recording close to 20 sacks, which figures to just over one per game. This stat really illustrates how much the game revolves around protecting the passer, and how valuable a defender is who can be a disruptive force. A defensive team averaging four sacks per game over the 16-game season is doing extremely well.

It used to be that the defensive back that led the league in interceptions was automatically considered the best or one of the best at his position. That is no longer necessarily the case. Some DBs have proven themselves to be so adept at pass coverage and also intercepting passes that rival offenses avoid throwing the ball in their direction. This is not to disparage the guys who do have good interception numbers—it is still a highly marketable skill to turn a team's passing attempt into a change of possession favoring your team. But, are you likely to see the same player have seven to 10 interceptions year in and year out? No—his reputation will probably result in offenses throwing the ball away from his half of the field. Taking all this into account, it is rare to see any one player record anywhere in the neighborhood of 10 interceptions in a season.

The Backbone

There are really no significant statistics to rate the backbone of any attack, the offensive linemen. Collectively, they take pride in the rushing totals of the backs for whom they open holes, and in limiting the number of times their quarterback is sacked or hit after releasing a pass. It's ironic that the success of each offensive play hinges upon solid line play while these players receive very little in the way of limelight or individual praise. In college football, you occasionally hear the term "pancake"- referring to a block that is so devastating as to flatten a defender onto his back in flapjack fashion - in association with an offensive lineman who is being touted for all-conference or all-America consideration. But this is a subjective reference, often bestowed following many slow-motion views of the game film in the video room. It's not really a stat, but we can't forget about these play producers up front.

Quarterback Rating System

The NFL also employs something called a quarterback rating system. No one, not even the quarterbacks themselves, understand it. The formula for building nuclear warheads is less complicated. So we won't talk about it, since hardly anybody ever does (although being at 100.0 or above is outstanding and anywhere in the 90.0-99.9 range is really good. According to the numbers, at least). Let's put it this way—if you understand the quarterback rating system calculations, you should not be reading this book. You should be working in the league office.

Sample Stats for year 2000
Yard Leaders through Monday, December 25

Player	Team	G	YDS
Peyton Manning	IND	16	4413
Elvis Grbac	KAN	15	4164
Vinny Testaverde	NYJ	16	3721
Mark Brunell	JAC	16	3640
Rich Gannon	OAK	16	3430
Drew Bledsoe	NWE	16	3291
Steve Mcnair	TEN	16	2865
Brian Griese	DEN	10	2688
Jon Kitna	SEA	15	2658
Jay Fiedler	MIA	15	2402
Rob Johnson	BUF	12	2125
Ryan Leaf	SDG	11	1883
Kordell Stewart	PIT	16	1860
Gus Frerotte	DEN	10	1776
Jeff Garcia	SFO	16	4278
Daunte Culpepper	MIN	16	3937
Brett Favre	GNB	16	3812
Steve Beuerlein	CAR	16	3730
Kerry Collins	NYG	16	3608
Kurt Warner	STL	11	3429
Donovan Mcnabb	PHI	16	3365

Chapter 12
Team Histories

Introduction

Rivalries? It's enemy territory when the Indianapolis Colts play the Buffalo Bills. Same thing when Jacksonville and Carolina meet. Dallas and Green Bay? You betcha.

Fans? The people that show up on game day with war paint streaked on their faces and bare chests exposed in sub-zero temperatures are your NFL "die-hards." These fans dress head to toe in colorful gear, and would rather lose a mouth full of teeth than an argument over their team.

Team colors? Try naming every team in the NFL based on the two or three-color scheme of their identity. Black and gold? The Steelers, of course. Blue and orange? Chicago Bears. The traditional association of mascots, logos and colors can bring instant recall when presented with everything but the team name.

Cities of origin? Los Angeles and Oakland and the Raiders. L.A. again with St. Louis and the Rams. Houston to Tennessee as the Oilers, and then becoming the Titans. No matter where they stay or where they play, every team would be at home for every game if they could. The cities love them, their fans adore them and they see devotion wherever they roam.

What do these things have in common?

More than anything else, these traits survived and were heightened to form a team's history. From the moment they were incorporated into the league, each organization has changed and evolved into what we know as the 32 teams of today. A unified league houses the diverse and unique histories that make for the drama and highlights we anticipate each season.

So, before you buy your next soon-to-be outdated team jersey with what's-his-name emblazoned on the back, check out the team history of each franchise in the NFL. After all, the best way to look into a team's future is to know its past.

ARIZONA CARDINALS

In March 1994, the oldest team of continuous operation in pro football history was christened the Arizona Cardinals. A charter member of the National Football League, the Cardinals trace their history back to 1898 when Chris O'Brien formed the Morgan Athletic Club. A few years later, he bought used jerseys from the University of Chicago. O'Brien termed the faded maroon clothing "Cardinal Red," and the team, then playing at 61st and Racine Streets in Chicago, became the Racine Street Cardinals.

The American Professional Football Association, the direct forerunner of the NFL, began play in 1920. The Cardinals faced an immediate challenge for territorial rights in Chicago from a team named the Tigers, who joined the league after the organizational meeting on September 17 of that year. O'Brien and the Cardinals promptly challenged the Tigers to a game, with the losers destined to leave town. The Cardinals won the game and the franchise rights when the legendary Paddy Driscoll scored the only touchdown in a 6-0 victory.

Except for 1925 when they edged out the Pottsville Maroons for their first NFL championship, the Cardinals experienced only minimal success on the playing field during their first 26 seasons in the league. A Thanksgiving Day game in 1929 did produce an all-time highlight when the Cardinals' superstar running back, Ernie Nevers, scored all 40 points—an NFL record that stands today—in a 40-6 victory over the Chicago Bears.

The Cardinals began a continuous period of family ownership in 1932 when Charles W. Bidwill bought the team. His son, William V. Bidwill, now operates the team. Bidwill kept the Cardinals operating during the depression days of the 1930s and the World War II years of the early 1940s and then finally put together a winning unit just as the war ended. Bidwill's building program produced a team that won a NFL championship in 1947 and the NFL Western division title in 1948. The Cardinals were victorious over Dallas for th 1998 season playoffs. The team's coach, Jimmy Conzelman, is now a member of the Hall of Fame as is Charley Trippi, a key member of the famed "Dream Backfield" that Bidwill fashioned. The unit also included Paul Christman, Pat Harder, Marshall Goldberg and Elmer Angsman when Goldberg moved to defense. In a cruel twist of fate, Bidwell died before seeing that team in action.

Since joining the NFL, the Cardinals have called three cities home. After 40 seasons in Chicago, they moved to St. Louis in 1960. The Cardinals seriously challenged the Cleveland Browns twice for divisional honors in the 1960s, but fell one-half game short both in 1964 and 1968. For a time in the mid-1970s, the St. Louis Cardinals were serious championship challengers. They won NFC Eastern division championships in both 1974 and 1975, but lost in the first round of the playoffs each year. The franchise was moved for a second time in 1988 when William Bidwill selected Phoenix as the new home city. There, the Cardinals play in 73,521-seat Sun Devil Stadium on the Arizona State University campus.

Cardinals Facts

Team Colors: Cardinal Red, Black, White
P.O. Box 888
Phoenix, AZ 85001-0888
(602) 379-0101
www.azcardinals.com
Franchise Granted: September 17, 1920 as the Chicago Cardinals, Charter Member, NFL
First Season: 1920
Moved to St. Louis: 1960
Moved to Phoenix: 1988
Changed Name to Arizona: 1994
Stadium: Sun Devil Stadium
Fifth Street
Tempe AZ 85287
Grass Surface
Capacity 73,273
Training Camp: Northern Arizona University
Flagstaff, AZ 86011
Fan phone: (520) 523-2273
NFL Championships: 1925, 1947
NFL Western Conference Championships: 1947, 1948
NFC Eastern Division Championships: 1974, 1975
Retired Uniform Numbers: #8 Larry Wilson, #77 Stan Mauldin, #88 J.V. Cain, #99 Marshall Goldberg.

ATLANTA FALCONS

The date of June 30, 1965, will always be remembered as a most significant day in Atlanta's sports history. That day, the National Football League awarded its 15th franchise, marking an end to a long struggle by the Georgia capital city to obtain a professional football team. The franchise was allotted to 41-year-old Rankin M. Smith, a successful life insurance executive, for $8.5 million.

One of Smith's first orders of business was announcing a contest to provide a nickname for the new team. The name "Falcons" was suggested by many, but a school teacher from Griffin, Georgia was declared the winner. "The Falcon is proud and dignified," she wrote, "with great courage and fight. It never drops its prey. It is deadly and has a great sporting tradition."

Excited Georgia fans showed their enthusiasm and appreciation by buying season tickets in record numbers. By Christmas Eve, when the Falcons cut off a brief 54-day ticket sale requiring almost no promotion, a NFL record had been established for a new team with the sale of 45,000 season tickets. Minnesota was the previous record-holder with 26,000 sales in 1961.

Midway through the ticket campaign, the Falcons participated in their first NFL draft on November 27, 1965. Their first pick was an Outland Trophy-winning linebacker from the

Falcons Facts

Team Colors: Black, Red, Silver and White
One Falcon Place
Suwanee, GA 30024
(770) 945-1111
Franchise Granted: June 30, 1965
First Season: 1966
Stadium: Georgia Dome
One Georgia Dome Drive
Atlanta, GA 30313
Capacity 71,228
Artificial Turf
Training Camp: Furman University
3000 Poinsett Highway
Greenville, SC 29613
NFC Western Division Championships:
1980, 1998
NFC Championship: 1998
Currently Unused Uniform Numbers: #10
Steve Bartkowski, #31 William Andrews,
#57 Jeff Van Note, #60 Tommy Nobis

University of Texas, Tommy Nobis. Nobis was also drafted by Houston, a member of the American Football League, but he signed a Falcons contract on December 14.

Norb Hecker, an assistant on Vince Lombardi's Green Bay Packers staff, was chosen as the Falcons' first head coach. The new Falcons lost their first nine games before defeating the New York Giants 27-16 on November 20. They finished with three wins, tying an expansion team first-season record at that time.

In 1971, the Falcons recorded their first winning season (7-6-1) under fiery coach Norm Van Brocklin. In 1973, they finished with a 9-5 mark, a new team high. The 1977 team under new coach Leeman Bennett established an NFL team mark that still stands by allowing just 129 total points in a 14-game season. Bennett then led the Falcons to the playoffs three times in a five-year span between 1978 and 1982. In 1980, the Falcons won the NFC Western Division title with a club-record 12 wins, and six Pro Bowl stars, including quarterback Steve Bartkowski and running back William Andrews. In addition to Bartkowski, Nobis and Andrews, as well as stars defensive end Claude Humphrey, center Jeff Van Note, running back Gerald Riggs and Billy "White Shoes" Johnson, the NFL's all-time leading punt returner, made the season exciting for loyal Falcons fans.

Atlanta was one of the first teams to have a year-round practice facility, opening a complex in 1978 in suburban Suwanee. The Falcons closed out their 26-year era at Atlanta-Fulton County Stadium in 1991 with an 11-win season, second most in the team's history. The next year, the team moved into the luxurious Georgia Dome, recognized as one of the country's finest indoor stadiums.

In 1998, the Falcons recorded their most successful season in franchise history. The team won the NFC West with a 14-2 record and marched through the playoffs to claim the NFC championship, earning a trip to Super Bowl XXXIII.

BALTIMORE RAVENS

After an 11-year absence when the Colts moved to Indianapolis, pro football returned to Baltimore, Maryland in 1996 in the form of the new Baltimore Ravens, which were the old Cleveland Browns. "This is a new beginning and a new era for us," Ravens owner Art Modell told fans at the team naming ceremony shortly after moving the franchise. With fans playing an integral role, the selection of the nickname "Ravens" was inspired by the poetry of former Baltimore resident, Edgar Allan Poe. From a list of more than 100 possible nicknames presented by NFL Properties, club executives narrowed the list to 17. Focus groups of 200 people from the Baltimore area trimmed the list to six. A telephone survey of 1,000 fans shortened the list to Ravens, Marauders, and Americans. Fans were then invited to participate in a phone-in poll conducted by the Baltimore Sun. Of 33,288 voters, nearly two-thirds (21,108) picked Ravens.

"Ravens gives us a strong nickname that is not common to teams at any level, and it gives one that means something historically to this community," Modell stressed. While the new team did bring "a new era" of pro football to Baltimore, the team still had to face the on-field "growing pains" of adjustment and settling in. A veteran team that had already played as a unit, the Ravens hired head coach Ted Marchibroda. The popular veteran coach was head coach of the Baltimore Colts from 1975 to 1979. In his first year at the Colts' helm, Marchibroda took a club that had posted a 2-12 mark in 1974 and engineered the then-greatest seasonal turnaround in NFL history by producing a 10-4 record in 1975. The turnaround was the first time in league annals that a team moved from last to first in one season.

The Ravens wasted no time earning their first victory in franchise history. In their inaugural regular season game, the Ravens defeated the Oakland Raiders 19-14 on September 1, 1996. A Memorial Stadium record crowd of 64,124 witnessed the historic moment.

The future looks bright for the Ravens as a young corps of players leads the way. On defense, the team is bolstered by an impressive trio of linebackers in Ray Lewis, Peter Boulware, and Jamie Sharper. On offense, the franchise's first-ever draft pick, Jonathan Ogden, continues to shine from his left tackle position.

Off the field, the Ravens moved into their brand new stadium in 1998. The state-of-the-art PSINet Stadium in downtown Baltimore is adjacent to Camden Yards where the Baltimore Orioles play. In 1999, the coaching reins were handed over to Brian Billick, a long-time NFL assistant coach.

Ravens Facts

Team Colors: Black, Purple, and Metallic Gold

11001 Owings Mills Blvd
Owings Mills, Maryland 21117
(410) 654-6200

Franchise Granted: February 9, 1996

First Season: 1996

Stadium: PSINet Stadium
1101 Russell Street
Baltimore, Maryland 21230
Capacity: 69,354
SportGrass

Training Camp: Western Maryland College
2 College Hill
Westminster, Maryland 21157
(410) 261-FANS

AFC Championships: 2000 Superbowl Champions XXXV

BUFFALO BILLS

The Buffalo Bills began their pro football life as the seventh team to be admitted to the American Football League. The franchise was awarded to Ralph C. Wilson on October 28, 1959. During more than three decades in the AFL, beginning in 1970, the franchise was part of the AFL – NFL merger. The Bills have experienced extended periods of both championship dominance and second-division frustration. The Bills first brush with success came in their fourth season in 1963, when they tied for the AFL Eastern Division crown but lost to the Boston Patriots in the playoffs. But in 1964 and 1965, they not only won their division but defeated the San Diego Chargers each year for the AFL championship.

Head coach Lou Saban, who was named AFL Coach of the Year in 1964-65, departed after the 1965 season. Buffalo lost to the Kansas City Chiefs in the 1966 AFL title game and, in so doing, missed playing in the first Super Bowl. Then, the Bills sank to the depths, winning only 13 games while losing 55 and tying two in the next five seasons. Saban returned in 1972, utilized the Bills' superstar running back, O. J. Simpson to the fullest extent, and made the Bills competitive once again. That period was highlighted by the 2,003-yard rushing record set by Simpson in 1973. But Saban departed again in mid-season 1976, and the Bills again sank into the second division until a new coach, Chuck Knox, brought them to an AFC Eastern Division title in 1980. In 1981, Buffalo advanced to the playoffs again but lost to Cincinnati. The roller coaster ride for Buffalo fans then took another downturn with six straight non-winning seasons in the mid-1980s.

Marv Levy, who took over the coaching reins in 1986, quickly fashioned the Bills into one of today's truly dominant teams. Starting in 1988, the Bills won five AFC Eastern titles in six years and became the only team ever to play in four straight Super Bowls. While three coach-

Bills Facts

Team Colors: Royal Blue, Scarlet Red and White

One Bills Drive
Orchard Park, NY 14127-2296
(716) 648-1800

Franchise Granted: October 28, 1959
First Season: 1960
Stadium: Ralph Wilson Stadium
One Bills Drive
Orchard Park, NY 14127-2296
Capacity: 75,300
Astro Turf
Training Camp: Fredonia State University
Fredonia, NY 14063
AFL Championships: 1964, 1965
AFL Eastern Division Championships:
1964, 1965, 1966
AFC Championships: 1990, 1991, 1992, 1993
Retired Uniform Numbers: None

es, Saban, Knox and Levy have been primarily responsible for the Buffalo's winning years, a handful of superstar players have also been key factors in the Bills' successes. Simpson was the key man in the winning years in the early 1970s, and such stars as quarterback Jack Kemp, who later became a United States Congressman, fullback Cookie Gilchrist, defensive tackle Tom Sestak and Hall of Fame guard Billy Shaw played major roles in the 1960s. Levy's teams in the late 1980s and 1990s were powered by such perennial all-stars as quarterback Jim Kelly, running back Thurman Thomas and defensive end Bruce Smith.

Through it all, Buffalo fan support has been a force factor. Attendance demands forced the expansion of the Bills' first inner-city home, War Memorial Stadium, from 26,000 to 45,748 during the 13 seasons the Bills played there. In 1973, the Bills moved to Rich Stadium in suburban Orchard Park, New York. Buffalo fans set a NFL single-season attendance record of 635,889 in 1991. Wilson remains one of the oldest owners, in terms of longevity, in the entire pro football world. In 1998, civic leaders decided to honor the owner and renamed the home of the Bills, "Ralph Wilson Stadium."

CAROLINA PANTHERS

On October 26, 1993, after six years of hopeful anticipation, the Carolina Panthers became an NFL expansion franchise. Fireworks exploded over downtown Charlotte as jubilant fans gathered to celebrate the news. "This is a dream come true for me and my partners and for the 10 million people in the Carolinas," said Jerry Richardson, the former Baltimore Colts wide receiver turned businessman who led Carolina's bid.

The "dream" began on July 16, 1987, when Richardson met in Charlotte with a group of interested parties to discuss the feasibility of entering the multi-city competition for two NFL expansion franchises. On December 15, Richardson made it official. The Carolinas' hat was in the ring. After a year of planning, Carolinas' bid was bolstered by the addition of Hall of Famer and former Seattle Seahawks general manager/head coach Mike McCormack to Richardson Sports as a consultant for the expansion effort.

One of the first orders of business was to select a stadium site. Although sites in both North and South Carolina were considered, Richardson Sports announced on December 15, 1989, the selection of a site in Uptown Charlotte as the future home of a privately financed stadium that would seat more than 70,000 fans.

Both states' support for the Carolinas' franchise bid poured in at an unprecedented rate. United States Senators Jesse Helms of North Carolina and Ernest Hollings of South Carolina lobbied NFL owners on the Carolinas' behalf. Likewise, South Carolina Governor Carroll Campbell and North Carolina Governor Jim Martin officially announced their support through the formation of a blue-ribbon committee of leading citizens in both states. Fans demonstrated their support at sell-out neutral site exhibition games played in Raleigh, North Carolina in 1989, Chapel Hill, North Carolina in 1990, and Columbia, South Carolina in 1991. At the March 18, 1992 NFL owners meeting, the number of expansion hopefuls was reduced from 11 to seven. Carolinas' bid made the cut. A few months later, on May 20, the NFL reduced the list to five, including Baltimore, St. Louis, Memphis, Jacksonville and the Carolinas. The finalists' enthusiasm was somewhat dampened, however, when on October 20, 1992, the NFL owners, citing complications surrounding the ongoing NFL labor situation, voted to delay the expansion vote until their fall 1993 meeting. Fortunately, on January 6, 1993, the league and its players reached a seven-year Collective Bargaining Agreement. On March 23, 1993, the expansion race officially resumed.

On June 3, Richardson Sports revealed its impressive plan to privately finance a 72,300-seat stadium. Sale of Permanent Seat Licenses, club seats and luxury boxes began on July 1. A remarkable 15,000 pieces of mail from first-day orders were collected. By the end of the first day, all 8,314 club seats were sold out and all 104 luxury suites were reserved and ultimately leased. First-day PSL orders totaled 41,632. Finally, on October 26, 1993, the NFL owners unanimously selected the Carolinas as the 29th NFL franchise and the first expansion team since 1976.

The Panthers played their first-ever game in Canton, Ohio, in the annual AFC-NFC Hall of Fame Game. Their opponent in the pre-season classic was the NFL's other expansion franchise, the Jacksonville Jaguars. Although the Panthers came away with a 20-14 victory, it was apparent that both teams had benefited from the NFL's expansion draft and the free-agent market, and were ready to compete in the NFL. The Panthers not only were competitive in their inaugural season, but established a new NFL record for most wins by an expansion team by posting an impressive 7-9 record. The team improved its second season, winning the NFC Western division with a 12-4 record, and advanced to the NFC Championship Game.

Panthers Facts

Team Colors: Black, Panther Blue and Silver

800 South Mint Street
Charlotte, North Carolina 28202-1502
(704) 358-7000

Franchise Granted: October 26, 1993
First Season: 1995
Stadium: Ericsson Stadium
Charlotte,
North Carolina 28202-1502
Capacity: 73,250
Grass
Training Camp: Wofford College
Spartanburg,
South Carolina 29303
NFC Western Division Championship: 1996

CHICAGO BEARS

The Chicago Bears are one of only two charter members of the National Football League still in existence. Their 1,000-game history started in Decatur, Illinois, in 1920 when the Staley Starch Company decided to sponsor a football team. Then, on September 17, 1920, the Staleys, with George Halas as their representative, joined the American Professional Football Association, which was renamed the National Football League in 1922. The franchise fee was $100.

In 1921, the Staley Starch Company gave Halas the team and $5,000, along with permission to move the team to Chicago if he would agree to keep the Staleys name for a year. The Staleys won the 1921 league championship. A year later, the team was renamed the Chicago Bears.

From the very start, the Bears were one of pro footballs most successful and innovative franchises. They were the first to buy a player from another team, $100 for Ed Healey from Rock Island in 1922. The Bears signed the fabled collegiate all-American, Red Grange, in 1925 and then showcased him before the first huge pro football crowds. In 1932, they defeated the Portsmouth Spartans 9-0 to win the championship in the first NFL game to be played indoors. The next year, they inaugurated the NFL championship series by defeating the New York Giants 23-21.

The Bears kicked off the 1940s with four straight NFL championship appearances. The Bears won three, including the famous 73-0 annihilation of the Washington Redskins in 1940. Despite winning nearly 60 percent of their games in the 1950s, the Bears did not win an NFL title and made only one playoff appearance. They finally broke a 17-year championship

Bears Facts

Team Colors: Navy Blue, Orange, and White

Halas Hall at Conway Park
1000 Football Drive
Lake Forest, Illinois 60045
(847) 295-6600

Franchise Granted: September 17, 1920 as the Decatur Staleys, Charter Member, NFL

First Season: 1920 Moved to Chicago, 1921; changed nickname to Bears, 1922

Stadium: Soldier Field
425 McFetridge Place
Chicago, Illinois 60605
Capacity: 66,944
Grass

Training Camp: University of Wisconsin Platteville
Platteville, Wisconsn 53818

Super Bowl Championship: XX

NFL Championships: 1921, 1932, 1933, 1940, 1941, 1943, 1946, 1963, 1985

NFC Championship: 1985

NFL Western Division Championships: 1933, 1934, 1937, 1940, 1941, 1942, 1943, 1946, 1956, 1963

NFC Central Division Championships: 1984, 1985, 1986, 1987, 1988, 1990

All-Time Record: 620-432-42

Retired Uniform Numbers: #3 Bronko Nagurski, #5 George McAfee, #7 George Halas, #28 Willie Galimore, #34 Walter Payton, #40 Gale Sayers, #41 Brian Piccolo, #42 Sid Luckman, #51 Dick Butkus, #56 Bill Hewitt, #61 Bill George, #66 Bulldog Turner, #77 Red Grange.

drought with a 14-10 win over the New York Giants in 1963. Almost all of the successes on and off the field for the Bears in the 64-year period between 1920 and 1983 can be attributed to George (Papa Bear) Halas, who served the Bears as an owner, player, coach, general manager, traveling secretary, and virtually every other capacity imaginable. Halas split his 40-year coaching into four 10-year segments. When he retired after the 1967 season, he ranked as the all-time leader in coaching victories with 324, a record that stood for 27 years.

Halas died on October 31, 1983 but the Bears tradition is carried on today by grandson Michael McCaskey, who served as club president and chief executive officer and is now Chairman of the Board. In its first 74 years, the team compiled a 586-384-42 overall record. Chicago qualified for the playoffs 21 times, won 19 division titles, eight NFL championships and Super Bowl XX. The Bears also have the proud distinction of listing the most long-time team members as Pro Football Hall of Fame enshrinees. Such names as Red Grange, Bronko Nagurski, Sid Luckman, Dick Butkus, Gale Sayers, Walter Payton, Bulldog Turner, Danny Fortmann and Halas himself are true legends not only of the Bears, but of pro football. For their first 51 seasons in Chicago, the Bears played in Wrigley Field, the famous home of the Chicago Cubs baseball team. Since 1971, they have played in Soldier Field in downtown Chicago.

CINCINNATI BENGALS

Planning for the Cincinnati Bengals franchise began three full years before the team began playing in the American Football League in 1968. Paul Brown, who had enjoyed exceptional success as the head coach of the Cleveland Browns for 17 seasons before departing in 1962, had the urge to get back into pro football. In 1965, he met with then-Governor Jim Rhodes and the two agreed that Ohio could accommodate a second pro football team.

A year later in 1966, Cincinnati's city council approved the construction of 60,389-seat Riverfront Stadium, which was scheduled for completion by 1970. The next year, a group headed by Brown was awarded an American Football League franchise that would begin play in 1968. Brown named his team the Bengals in recognition of previous Cincinnati pro football franchises with the same name in the 1930s and 1940s. Brown returned to the coaching ranks on the Bengals sidelines for the first eight years. He retired after the 1975 season but continued to serve as general manager until his death in 1991. Mike Brown then succeeded his father as general manager.

The 1968 Bengals won their first two home games in 28,000-seat Nippert Stadium against Denver and Buffalo and finished with a 3-11 record, the most an expansion team of the 1960s recorded. Cincinnati improved enough in 1969 that Brown was named the AFL Coach of the Year. In 1970, they captured the AFC Central division title and became the first expansion team to win a championship of any kind in just three years.

In 1971, the Bengals selected Ken Anderson, a quarterback from little-known Augustana College, in the third round of the draft. For the next 16 seasons, Anderson was the key man of the Cincinnati offense and a four-time AFC individual passing champion. Cincinnati won its second AFC Central championship in 1973 and a wildcard berth in the 1975 playoffs in Browns final year as coach. The Bengals missed the playoffs for the next five seasons, but won big in 1981, the year the Bengals unveiled their new uniforms with tiger-striped helmets, jerseys and pants. Cincinnati, with Forrest Gregg as coach, won the AFC Central with a 12-4 record and defeated San Diego 27-7 in the AFC championship game. However, they lost the Super Bowl XVI showdown with the San Francisco 49ers 26-21.

The Bengals had a second shot at the Super Bowl following the 1988 season when, under Coach Sam Wyche and quarterback Boomer Esiason, they improved from the dismal 4-11 record in 1987 to a 12-4 regular-season record. They then defeated Buffalo 21-10 for the AFC championship. But in Super Bowl XXIII, they lost 20-16 to the 49ers on a last-minute touchdown pass by Joe Montana.

In addition to Anderson and Esiason, the Bengals have been able to boast many outstanding players since their first game in 1968. None, however, was more outstanding than tackle Anthony Muñoz, a first-round draft pick in 1981. A perennial all-pro choice, the USC graduate was selected to play in 11 straight Pro Bowls from 1982 to 1992 and was inducted into the Pro Football Hall of Fame in 1998.

Bengals Facts

Team Colors: Black, Orange, and White
One Bengals Drive
Cincinnati, Ohio 45204
(513) 621-3550
Franchise Granted: May 24, 1967
First Season: 1968
Stadium: Paul Brown Stadium
200 Cinergy Field
Cincinnati, Ohio 45202
Capacity: 60,389
AstroTurf-8
Training Camp: Georgetown College
Georgetown, Kentucky 40324
AFC Championships: 1981, 1988
AFC Central Division Championships:
1970, 1973, 1981, 1988, 1990
Retired Uniform Numbers: #54 Bob Johnson

CLEVELAND BROWNS

BROWNS

The Cleveland Browns were born in 1944 when Cleveland businessman Arthur B. McBride acquired a franchise in the new All-America Football Conference that would begin play in 1946. McBride's first act after acquiring the team was to hire Paul Brown, who had been a very successful high school, college and service coach, as coach and general manager.

The teams of the AAFC basically were of comparable quality to those of the NFL but, in the first 10 years of post-World War II pro football, the Cleveland Browns proved to be the best in either league. With such all-time greats as quarterback Otto Graham, fullback Marion Motley and tackle-kicker Lou Groza leading the way, Cleveland won all four AAFC championships and amassed a 52-4-3 winning record. When the AAFC folded after the 1949 season, many insisted a major reason focused on the Browns' dominance that eliminated any viable competition.

The AAFC-NFL settlement called for the Browns, San Francisco 49ers and Baltimore Colts to join the NFL. Many NFL die-hards, still not convinced the Browns were for real, expected Cleveland to fail badly when they played against the established NFL teams. But the Browns quickly proved their domination was no fluke by opening the 1950 season with a stunning 35-10 victory over the defending NFL champion Philadelphia Eagles. Cleveland then

Browns Facts

Team Colors: Brown, Orange, and White
76 Lou Groza Blvd
Berea, Ohio 44017
(440) 891-5000
Franchise Granted: June 4, 1944 as
Charter Member of AAFC
First Season: 1946
Merged into NFL: 1950
No Team: 1996, 1997, 1998
Stadium: Cleveland Browns Stadium
1085 West 3rd Street
Cleveland, Ohio 44114
Capacity: 72,000
Grass
Training Camp: Browns Training and
Administrative Complex
76 Lou Groza Boulevard
Berea, Ohio 44017
1-877-6-BROWNS
NFL Championships: 1950, 1954, 1955,
1964
AAFC Championships: 1946, 1947, 1948,
1949
AAFC Western Divisional Championships:
1946, 1947, 1948, 1949
NFL Eastern Conference Championships:
1950, 1951, 1952, 1953, 1954, 1955, 1957,
1964, 1965, 1968, 1969
NFL Century Division Championships:
1967, 1968, 1969
AFC Central Division Championships:
1971, 1980, 1985, 1986, 1987, 1989
Retired Uniform Numbers: #14 Otto
Graham, #32 Jim Brown, #45 Ernie Davis,
#46 Don Fleming, #76 Lou Groza

won the NFL Eastern Conference championship for six straight years from 1950 to 1955 and NFL titles in 1950, 1954 and 1955.

The Browns won another divisional title in 1957, a year that saw the great running back from Syracuse, Jim Brown, join the team. In his nine-season career, Jim Brown rushed for 12, 312 yards, a lifetime record that stood for more than 20 years.

The Paul Brown era ended after the 1962 season, and he was replaced by former assistant, Blanton Collier. Collier gave the Browns their last NFL championship in 1964, when they defeated the Baltimore Colts 27-0.

The Browns reached the post-season playoffs 22 times in their first 40 years in the NFL. In addition to their four NFL championships between 1950 and 1964, they won 11 NFL Eastern Conference championships, three NFL Century Division titles and AFC Central Division championships in 1971, 1980, 1985, 1986, 1987 and 1989.

In 1961, Arthur B. Modell purchased the Browns for a then-unheard-of price of $4 million. From the start, he was recognized as one of the NFL's more progressive leaders. But, Modell stunned the pro football world in 1995 when he announced that he would transfer his Cleveland franchise to Baltimore to begin play in 1996.

Determined to keep the team in Cleveland, Browns fans and Cleveland city officials orchestrated an unprecedented grass-roots campaign to block the move. The NFL quickly responded and, with city officials, developed a unique solution that not only provided for a new state-of-the-art stadium, but guaranteed the return of pro football to Cleveland by no later than 1999. Additionally, Art Modell agreed to relinquish the "Browns" name, colors, and team history to the new owner of the suspended franchise.

In 1998, the NFL awarded the Browns' franchise to Al Lerner to begin play in 1999, under the guidance of team President/CEO Carmen Policy and coach Chris Palmer.

DALLAS COWBOYS

In 1960, the Dallas Cowboys became the NFL's first successful new team since the collapse of the All-America Football Conference 10 years earlier. Clint Murchison Jr. was the new team's majority owner and his first action was to hire Tex Schramm as general manager, Tom Landry as head coach and Gil Brandt as player personnel director.

This trio was destined for almost unprecedented success in the pro football world but the "glory years" didn't come easily. Playing in the storied Cotton Bowl, the 1960 Cowboys had to settle for one tie in 12 games and Dallas didn't break even until its sixth season in 1965. But in 1966, the Cowboys began a NFL-record streak of 20 consecutive winning seasons. That streak included 18 years in the playoffs, 13 divisional championships, five trips to the Super Bowl and victories in Super Bowls VI and XII.

Dallas won its first two divisional championships in 1966 and 1967, but lost to the Green Bay Packers in the NFL championship game each year. Similar playoff losses the next seasons were followed by a 16-13 last-second loss to Baltimore in Super Bowl V following the 1970 season. The Cowboys were typified as "a good team that couldn't win the big games."

But they dispelled that thought for good the very next year with a 24-3 win over the Miami Dolphins in Super Bowl VI. The Cowboys were Super Bowl-bound three more times from 1975 to 1978. They lost to Pittsburgh in extremely competitive games in Super Bowls X and XIII but defeated the Denver Broncos 27-10 in Super Bowl XII. During their big years of the 1970s, the Cowboys were led by such future Pro Football Hall of Fame members as quarterback Roger Staubach, defensive tackles Bob Lilly and Randy White, defensive back Mel Renfro and running back Tony Dorsett.

In 1967, Murchison announced that the Cowboys would build their own stadium in suburban Irving, Texas. A new Dallas pro football era began on October 24, 1971, when 65,024-seat Texas Stadium was opened.

Cowboys Facts

Team Colors: Royal Blue, Metallic Silver Blue, and White

Cowboys Center
One Cowboys Parkway
Irving, Texas 75063
(972) 556-9900

Franchise Granted: January 28, 1960

First Season: 1960

Stadium: Texas Stadium
Irving, Texas 75062

Capacity: 65,675

Sportfield Turf

Training Camp: Midwestern State University
Wichita Falls, Texas 76308

Super Bowl Championships: VI, XII, XXVII, XXVIII, XXX

NFC Championships: 1970, 1971, 1975, 1977, 1978, 1992, 1993, 1995

NFL Eastern Conference Championships: 1966, 1967

NFL Capitol Division Championships: 1967, 1968, 1969

NFC Eastern Division Championships: 1970, 1971, 1973, 1976, 1977, 1978, 1979, 1981, 1985, 1992, 1993, 1994, 1995, 1996, 1998

Retired Uniform Numbers: None

The Cowboys of the 1970s and early 1980s were known as "America's Team." The organization was just a step ahead of almost every other club when it came to image-enhancing promotions such as The Dallas Cowboys Newsweekly with a circulation of 100,000, sales of Cowboys souvenirs and wearing apparel and the famous Dallas Cowboys cheerleaders.

The Cowboys suffered their first losing season in two decades in 1986 and fell all the way to 3-13 in 1988. H. R. "Bum" Bright, who had purchased the Cowboys from Murchison in 1984, sold the team to Jerry Jones in 1989. Jones named former University of Miami coach Jimmy Johnson to replace Landry, who finished his career with 270 victories, third most by any coach in history.

Johnson's first team won only once in 16 games, but some daring trades and shrewd selections in the annual NFL draft quickly returned the Cowboys to championship status in Super Bowl XXVII in the fourth season of the Jerry Jones regime. They followed with a second straight world title in Super Bowl XXVIII. In March 1994, college coach Barry Switzer replaced Johnson as the Cowboys third head coach. The winning continued under Switzer, as the "Team of the Nineties" won its third Super Bowl in four years with a 27-17 victory over the Pittsburgh Steelers in Super Bowl XXX. In 1998, Chan Gailey replaced Switzer as the Cowboys' head coach. Two years later, Dave Campo became only the fifth head coach in team history.

DENVER BRONCOS

The Denver Broncos have been one of pro football's biggest winners since the merger of the American and National Football Leagues in 1970. The Broncos on-field success is more than matched by a spectacular attendance record of sellout crowds (except for strike-replacement games) every year since 1970. Denver's annual sale of approximately 74,000 season tickets is backed by a waiting list in the tens of thousands.

Bob Howsam, a successful minor league baseball owner who built Bears Stadium in the 1940s, was awarded an AFL charter franchise on August 14, 1959. Severely limited financially, Howsam clothed his first team in used uniforms from the defunct Copper Bowl in Tucson, Arizona. Making the uniforms particularly joke-worthy were the vertically-striped socks that completed the Broncos' dress. Two years later when Jack Faulkner took over as head coach and general manager, the socks were destroyed in a public burning ceremony.

While Denver's on-field experience during the 10 years of the AFL was for the most part bleak, the Broncos did have some bright moments. On September 9, 1960, they won the first-ever AFL game with a 13-10 victory over the Boston Patriots. On August 5, 1967, they scored the first win ever for an AFL team against a NFL opponent with a 13-7 triumph over the Detroit Lions. But at the end of the AFL's decade, Denver's 39-97-4 record was the worst for any of the original eight AFL teams.

Denver's current attendance bonanza can be traced to a remarkable turn of events in 1965 that first threatened, but then assured the future of pro football in the city. Several minority partners formed a majority-voting block to sell the Broncos to Atlanta interests but, at the last minute, the Phipps brothers, Gerald and Allan, who had been left out of the voting block, bought the team and 34,657-seat Bears Stadium. Excited fans showed their appreciation by purchasing almost 23,000 season tickets, compared to 7,996 the year before.

Before the 1968 season, Bears Stadium was purchased by the city and renamed Denver Mile High Stadium. It was expanded to 51,706 capacity that year, then to 63,532 in 1976 and to 75,100 in 1977. As the stadium grew, so too did season ticket sales.

In their 14th season in 1973, the Broncos, under coach John Ralston, finished 7-5-2 for their first winning season ever. This started a trend that saw the Broncos fall below the .500 mark only three times in the next 20 seasons. In the 14-year period between 1977 and 1991, the Broncos won seven AFC Western Division titles and AFC championships in 1977, 1986, 1987 and 1989. It was the kind of success the Broncos' founders could not, with good reason, possibly have imagined.

The Broncos reached the pinnacle of the pro football world, as the team captured its first world championship with a victory over the Green Bay Packers in Super Bowl XXXII. With a victory over the Atlanta Falcons in Super Bowl XXXIII, Denver accomplished what only five other teams have achieved— back-to-back Super Bowl championships.

Broncos Facts

Team Colors: Orange, Broncos Navy Blue, and White

13655 Broncos Parkway
Englewood, Colorado 80112
(303) 649-9000

Franchise Granted: August 14, 1959 as Charter Member of AFL

First Season: 1960

Stadium: Invesco Field at Mile High
1900 West Eliot
Denver, Colorado 80204
Grass

Training Camp: University of Northern Colorado
Greeley, Colorado 80639

Super Bowl Championships: XXXII, XXXIII

AFC Championships: 1977, 1986, 1987, 1989, 1997, 1998

AFC Western Division Championships:
1977, 1978, 1984, 1986, 1987, 1989, 1991, 1998

Retired Uniform Numbers: #18 Frank Tripucka, #44 Floyd Little, #7 John Elway

DETROIT LIONS

After three unsuccessful attempts at establishing a professional football team in Detroit in the 1920s, football took a firm foothold in the city beginning in 1934, when Detroit radio executive George A. Richards purchased the Portsmouth, Ohio, Spartans for the then-astounding sum of $8,000 and moved the franchise to the Motor City.

The Spartans had joined the NFL in 1930 and, in 1932, played in one of history's most pivotal games, a hastily-scheduled championship game against the Chicago Bears that was played indoors at Chicago Stadium. From that game came three major rule changes and the division of the league into two divisions and the establishment of an annual NFL title showdown.

Unlike previous Detroit pro football teams, the new Lions team was loaded with some of the finest players of the day, and the team leader was Dutch Clark, a true triple-threat superstar and the last NFL dropkicker, who became a charter member of the Pro Football Hall of Fame. Playing in the University of Detroit Stadium before crowds of 12,000, the Lions won the NFL championship their second year, 1935. Those early successes firmly established pro football in Detroit and for more than 60 years the sport has been an integral part of the Michigan sports scene.

The Lions also made their lasting mark by scheduling a Thanksgiving Day game in their first season in 1934 and, except for a six-year gap between 1939 and 1944, the team continues the tradition today. Both before and after 1934, other NFL teams have tried Turkey Day games without significant success, excluding the Dallas Cowboys.

In the 1950s, the Lions enjoyed their finest years ever with four divisional titles and three league championships in 1952, 1953 and 1957. Stars of those glittering teams, whose annual showdowns against the archrival Cleveland Browns fascinated the pro football world, included such future Pro Football Hall of Famers as quarterback Bobby Layne, running back Doak Walker, tackle-guard Lou Creekmur and safety Jack Christiansen.

Since their last title in 1957, the Lions have been looking in vain for the top spot. While outstanding players such as Joe Schmidt, Yale Lary, Lem Barney and Dick "Night Train" Lane earned election to the Pro Football Hall of Fame, the best the Lions were able to accomplish as a team for the next 26 seasons were wild-card berths in 1970 and 1982. The Lions finally ended their long championship drought by winning the NFC Central Division championship in 1983. The Lions, under coach Wayne Fontes, and paced by superstar running back Barry Sanders, the team's all-time rushing leader, won divisional titles in 1991 and 1993. Detroit's first playoff victories since 1957

Lions Facts

Team Colors: Honolulu Blue and Silver
Pontiac Silverdome
120 Feattherstone Road
Pontiac, Michigan 48342
(248) 335-4131
Franchise Granted: July 12, 1930 as the Portsmouth Spartans
First Season: 1930
Moved to Detroit: June 30, 1934
Stadium: Pontiac Silverdome
1200 Featherstone Road
Pontiac, Michigan 48342
Capacity: 80,311
AstroTurf
Ford Field - 2002
Detroit, Michigan
Capacity: 65,000
Field Turf
Training Camp: Saginaw Valley State University, University Center, Michigan 48710
Fan Hotline: (248) 972-3700
NFL Championships: 1935, 1952, 1953, 1957
NFL Western Division Championships: 1935, 1952, 1953, 1954, 1957
NFC Central Division Championships: 1983, 1991, 1993
Retired Uniform Numbers: #7 Dutch Clark, #22 Bobby Layne, #37 Doak Walker, #56 Joe Schmidt, #85 Chuck Hughes, #88 Charlie Sanders

took the Lions all the way to the 1991 NFC championship game for the first time in franchise history.

The Detroit team moved from the University of Detroit Stadium to Briggs Field, home of the baseball Tigers, in 1938, where they stayed for 37 years. In 1975, the Lions moved into a new home, the 80,494-seat Pontiac Silverdome. William Clay Ford, who in 1964 purchased sole ownership of the Lions for $4.5 million, is the owner and president.

INDIANAPOLIS COLTS

In 1953, the city of Baltimore was awarded a new National Football League franchise. The team was nicknamed the Colts, the second pro football club to bear that name in a seven-year period. Earlier in 1947, a Baltimore Colts team was founded in the All-America Football Conference. Three years later, as part of the peace agreement between the AAFC and NFL, the Colts became a member of the NFL. But this venture failed and the franchise was disbanded after the 1950 season.

Baltimore was presented with a second chance for an NFL team three seasons later when the Dallas Texans franchise was canceled by the league. NFL Commissioner Bert Bell challenged the city to sell 15,000 season tickets within six weeks. The successful sale took just over four weeks and, on January 23, 1953, Carroll Rosenbloom became the principle owner of the new Baltimore Colts.

In 1954, Weeb Ewbank was named the Colts' head coach and he began a steady building program that put his team over .500 for the first time in 1957. The Colts didn't have another losing season for the next 14 years. Powered by a sensational young quarterback, Johnny Unitas, and a strong supporting cast that included such future Pro Football Hall of Famers as Artie Donovan, Gino Marchetti, Raymond Berry, Lenny Moore and Jim Parker, the Colts won NFL championships in 1958, 1959 and 1968.

The 1958 NFL title clash against the New York Giants, played before the largest television audience ever at that time, increased fan enthusiasm for pro football. With Unitas craftily engineering long drives that led to the tying field goal and winning touchdown, the Colts won 23-17 in overtime.

Both the Colts and Ewbank were involved in a second game 10 years later that would share ranking as a pivotal game in creating far-reaching fan enthusiasm. The game was Super Bowl III, and the Ewbank-led New York Jets stunned the heavily-favored Colts 16-7.

Under Don Shula, who replaced Ewbank in 1963, the Colts won NFL Western conference championships in 1964 and 1968. Shula moved to Miami in 1970, but the Colts, who had moved to the new American Football Conference at the time of the merger, won the first AFC Eastern division title and Super Bowl V. Baltimore, with Ted Marchibroda as coach, won three straight divisional titles in 1975, 1976 and 1977. The franchise then fell on hard times with a 19-53-1 record in the five years between 1978 and 1982.

Colts Facts

Team Colors: Royal Blue and White
P.O. Box 535000
Indianapolis, Indiana 46253
(317) 297-2658
Franchise Granted: January 23, 1953 as the Baltimore Colts
First Season: 1953
Moved to Indianapolis: 1984
Stadium: RCA Dome
100 South Capitol Avenue
Indianapolis, Indiana 46225
Capacity: 56,637
AstroTurf
Training Camp: Rose-Hulman Institute
5500 Wabash Avenue
Terre Haute, Indiana 47803
Super Bowl Championship: V
NFL Championships: 1958, 1959, 1968
AFC Championship: 1970
NFL Western Conference Championships: 1958, 1959, 1964, 1968
AFC Eastern Division Championships: 1970, 1975, 1976, 1977, 1987, 1999
Retired Uniform Numbers: #19 Johnny Unitas, #22 Buddy Young, #24 Lenny Moore, #70 Art Donovan, #77 Jim Parker, #82 Raymond Berry, #89 Gino Marchetti

Robert Irsay, who acquired the Los Angeles Rams franchise in 1972, engineered an historic trade of teams with Carroll Rosenbloom that year. Twelve years later on March 28, 1984, Irsay moved the Colts to Indianapolis, where they now play in downtown Indianapolis at the RCA Dome.

The Indianapolis Colts won the AFC East title in 1987 and 1999, and also earned playoff berths in 1995 and 1996. In 1996 the Colts met Pittsburg in the AFC Championship Game.

GREEN BAY PACKERS

The Green Bay Packers story began in August 1919, when the Indian Packing Company agreed to sponsor a local pro football team under the direction of Earl (Curly) Lambeau. In 1921, the Packers were granted a membership in the new National Football League. Today, they rank as the third oldest team in pro football. With a long and storied history, the Green Bay team encountered much struggle, until comparatively recently, as a result of financial survival off the field and playing stability on the field. The Packers' record has been punctuated with periods of both the highest success and the deepest depths of defeat.

Many great football players have performed for the Green Bay team but two coaches, Lambeau and Vince Lombardi, rank as the most dominant figures in the Packers' epic. Between the two, Lambeau and Lombardi brought the Packers 11 NFL championships, including two record strings of three straight titles, the first in 1929, 1930 and 1931 and the second in 1965, 1966 and 1967. Those last three championships completed the Packers' dynasty years in the 1960s, which began with Green Bay also winning NFL championships in 1961 and 1962. During the late 1930s and early 1940s, the Lambeau-led Packers were annual championship contenders. They won four divisional crowns and NFL titles in 1936, 1939 and 1944.

Individually, Lambeau, Lombardi and 17 long-time Packers players are enshrined in the Pro Football Hall of Fame. Hall of Fame players from the early years include Don Hutson, history's first great pass receiver, Arnie Herber, Clarke Hinkle, Cal Hubbard, John (Blood) McNally, Mike Michalske and Tony Canadeo. The great Packers of the 1960s produced Jim Taylor, Forrest Gregg, Bart Starr, Ray Nitschke, Herb Adderley, Willie Davis, Jim Ringo, Paul Hornung, Willie Wood and Henry Jordan for the Hall.

Green Bay, Wisconsin, home of the Packers, is a city of less than 100,000, but viewed as sort of a sports "dinosaur" as the only remaining small city in the big-city world of major league professional sports franchises. Green Bay is unique in another way—the team is the only community-owned, non-profit organization in the NFL. From 1937-1994 the Packers played their home games in two cities. Five of their eight home games were played in Green Bay's Lambeau Field and the remaining three at Milwaukee County Stadium in Milwaukee. Today, the Packers play exclusively at Lambeau Field.

The Packers first played on a couple of small fields in Green Bay and then in 6,000-seat City Stadium beginning in 1925. Eventually, the City Stadium capacity reached 25,000. On September 29, 1957, the Packers dedicated a modern $1 million stadi-

Packers Facts

Team Colors: Dark Green, Gold, and White
1265 Lombardi Avenue
Green Bay, Wisconsin 54304
(920) 496-5700
Franchise Granted: August 27, 1921
First Season: 1921
Stadium: Lambeau Field
1265 Lombardi Avenue
Green Bay, Wisconsin 54304
Capacity: 59,543
Grass
Training Camp: St. Norbert College
De Pere, Wisconsin 54115
Super Bowl Championships: I, II, XXXI
NFC Championships: 1996, 1997
NFL Championships: 1929, 1930, 1931, 1936, 1939, 1944, 1961, 1962, 1965, 1966, 1967
Retired Uniform Numbers: #3 Tony Canadeo, #14 Don Hutson, #15 Bart Starr, #66 Ray Nitschke

um with a 32,150-seat capacity. Subsequent expansions have brought the Green Bay facility, officially named Lambeau Field in 1965, to its current 59,543 capacity. Off the field, the Packers remain a competitive and historically-rich franchise. On the field, the glory years are back. In 1996, the Packers returned to the top of the pro football world when they won Super Bowl XXXI.

HOUSTON TEXANS

In 1997 Houston lost their NFL team when they made their move to Tennessee.

It was then that Bob McNair made it his passion to bring NFL back to Houston. The Houston Livestock Show and Rodeo (HLS&R) gave its full support of NcNair's efforts and pushed for the building of a new domed stadium to be shared with the NFL team. By September of that year the NFL owners voted 29-0 to award the 32nd NFL franchise to Houston and Bob McNair.

Houston NFL, as they were called, had a lot of work ahead of them to get ready for the 2002 season, a new team, a new name, logos and plans for the world's first retractable roof football stadium. Focus groups and fans were asked for their opinions on the team name and logo, it was finally narrowed to five choices: Apollos, Bobcats, Stallions, Texans and Wildcatters. The NFL's 32nd franchise was officially christened the Houston Texans at a rally on Texas Avenue.

In January 2000 Charley Casserly was hired as Executive Vice President/General Manager. Casserly came to Houston after 23 years with the Washington Redskins, the last 10 as general manager. The Redskins captured Super Bowls XVII, XXII and XXVI during his tenure in Washington. Dom Capers was hired as the club's first head coach. Capers came from Jacksonville, where he served the previous two seasons as the Jaguars' defensive coordinator. From 1995-98, Capers was the head coach of the expansion Carolina Panthers, leading the team to the NFC West title and a berth in the NFC Championship Game in 1996. Chris Palmer was hired as the Texans' first offensive coordinator. Palmer spent the previous two seasons as head coach of the expansion Cleveland Browns.

When the team begins play in 2002 the team and their new 69,500-seat state-of-the-art facility, the world's first retractable-roof football stadium, will be ready. Reliant Energy acquired the naming rights for the stadium and the sports, entertainment and convention complex formerly known as the Astrodomain Complex. Reliant Energy's 32-year agreement to acquire the naming rights for five different buildings and the complex is the most comprehensive naming rights agreement in history. Reliant Park will be a partnership of mutual support between the Harris County Sports and Convention Corporation, the Houston Texans, RodeoHouston and Reliant Energy. The facilities at Reliant Park will include Reliant Stadium, Reliant Astrodome, Reliant Arena, Reliant Hall and Reliant Center. Reliant Stadium will host Super Bowl XXXVIII on February 1, 2004.

Through the realignment of the divisions to accommodate the new expansion team, the league will realign into eight four-team divisions. The Texans are placed in the AFC South with Indianapolis, Jacksonville and Tennessee.

Texan Facts

Team Colors: Deep Steel Blue, Battle Red and Liberty White
The Houston Texans
711 Louisiana, 33rd Floor
Houston, TX 77002-2716
(713) 336-7700
Franchise Granted: October 6, 1999
First Season: 2002
Stadium: Reliant Stadium
Capacity: 69,500
Retractable Roof
Grass
Training Camp: Texans Practice Complex

JACKSONVILLE JAGUARS

On November 30, 1993, at 4:12 p.m., an incredible four-year campaign was over and a team became official. The Jacksonville Jaguars were the 30th franchise of the National Football League. Jacksonville's incredible drive actually began on August 17, 1989, when Touchdown Jacksonville Ltd., a partnership, was formed to lead the community effort to win an NFL franchise. Jacksonville businessman Tom Petway led the group.

On September 16, 1991, armed with a $60 million commitment from the Jacksonville City Council to renovate the Gator Bowl, Touchdown Jacksonville!, Ltd. filed an expansion application with the NFL. The application listed a nine-member partnership that included Petway and J. Wayne Weaver, who now serves as the club's Chairman and CEO. One of 11 cities to apply, many considered Jacksonville to be the longest shot on the board. Still, that didn't keep the Jacksonville group from confidently announcing that the team would be named "Jaguars" if awarded one of the two available expansion franchises.

Jacksonville survived the first round of applicant cuts, when on March 17, 1992, at the NFL's annual winter meeting, the list of 11 was reduced to seven. Two months later, the expansion race was narrowed to five possible choices: Jacksonville, Baltimore, St. Louis, Charlotte and Memphis. The remaining applicants' spirits were somewhat dampened, however, when on October 20, 1992, the NFL owners delayed the expansion vote until their fall 1993 meeting. Fortunately, on January 6, 1993, the league and its players reached a seven-year Collective Bargaining Agreement. On March 23, 1993, the expansion race officially resumed.

The Jacksonville contingent quickly scheduled a tour of the Gator Bowl for NFL officials, after which Touchdown Jacksonville!, Ltd. managing general partner J. Wayne Weaver was informed that additional renovations beyond those already planned would be necessary to renovate the stadium to NFL standards. Unable to come to a satisfactory solution to the stadium renovation financing problems with the City Council, Touchdown Jacksonville!, Ltd. announced it was withdrawing from the NFL expansion race.

However, community spirit and Weaver's sense of vision prevailed. Less than a month after renovation financing talks broke off, a new plan was proposed that would cap renovation costs at $121 million. Both sides agreed that $53 million would come from city funds and $68 million from team and team-related sources. Additionally, a committee of civic and business leaders agreed to help by selling 9,000 club seats. Weaver, with the new public / private partnership, met with NFL Commissioner Paul Tagliabue, who welcomed Jacksonville back into the expansion race.

The Jaguars played their first-ever game in Canton, Ohio in the annual AFC-NFC Hall of Fame Game. Their opponent in the preseason classic was the NFL's other expansion franchise, the Carolina Panthers. From the start, it was apparent that the NFL's expansion draft and the free-agent market had allowed both Jacksonville and Carolina to develop more quickly than expansion teams of the past. The Jaguars' impressive 4-12 inaugural season record was one win better than the NFL's previous best for an expansion team. The Jaguars have quickly become one of the dominant teams in the NFL and perennial playoff participants. The team reached the AFC Championship game in 1996 and 1999.

Jaguars Facts

Team Colors: Teal, Black and Gold
One ALLTEL Stadium Place
Jacksonville, Florida 32202
(904) 633-6000
Franchise Granted: November 30, 1993
First Season: 1995
Stadium: Alltel Stadium
One ALLTEL Stadium Place
Jacksonville, Florida 32202
Capacity: 73,000
Grass
Training Camp: ALLTEL Stadium
(904) 633-6525
AFC Central Division Championship: 1998, 1999

KANSAS CITY CHIEFS

In 1959, a 26-year-old Texan, frustrated by his unsuccessful attempts to gain a pro football franchise in the National Football League, embarked on an alternate course that was to drastically change the face of pro football forever. The young man was Lamar Hunt, who founded the American Football League that season and served as the league's first president when its eight new teams began play in 1960.

Hunt's own team, the Dallas Texans, was located in his hometown where he would face direct competition from the NFL's newest expansion team, the Dallas Cowboys. In spite of this opposition from the established NFL, the Texans quickly made their mark as one of the new league's strongest teams. In their third season in 1962, they won the AFL championship with a 20-17 win over the Houston Oilers in a 77-minute, 54-second, two-overtime game, the longest ever played up to that time.

Although the Texans fared well in Dallas, Hunt decided that, for the good of the league, it would be best to move his franchise to Kansas City in 1963. There, the team was renamed the Chiefs and continued to enjoy the success the team had experienced in Dallas. The Chiefs won a second AFL title in 1966 and was the first team to represent the AFL in Super Bowl competition.

Kansas City won another title in 1969, and became the only team in AFL history to win three championships. Although the Minnesota Vikings were heavily favored in Super Bowl IV, Kansas City upset the NFL champions 23-7 to complete the AFL vs. NFL portion of the Super Bowl series tied at two wins each. It was the last game ever played by an AFL team.

The Texans-Chiefs' 10-season AFL record 92 – 50 – 5 was the best of any AFL team. Head coach Hank Stram became the only man to serve as a head coach throughout the AFL's history. Thanks to Hunt's wise player-procurement policies, his teams were loaded with potential superstars, including five, quarterback Len Dawson, defensive end Buck Buchanan, linebackers Bobby Bell and Willie Lanier and kicker Jan Stenerud, who have been elected to the Pro Football Hall of Fame. Hunt himself was the first Chief elected for his role in forming a new league that helped pro football to grow from 12 teams to 26 teams in the 1960s.

When they first moved to Kansas City, the Chiefs played in 49,002-seat Municipal Stadium. But in 1972, they moved into their current home, 78,097-seat Arrowhead Stadium, considered to be one of the world's finest.

The Chiefs won the AFC Western Division title in 1971, but their Christmas Day double-overtime playoff loss to Miami that year marked their last playoff appearance until the 1986 Chiefs captured a wild-card playoff berth. The Chiefs were perennial playoff contenders under coach Marty Schottenheimer from 1989-1998. In 1999, Gunther Cunningham

Chiefs Facts

Team colors: Red, Gold, and White
One Arrowhead Drive
Kansas City, Missouri 64129
(816) 920-9300
Franchise Granted: August 14, 1959 as the Dallas Texans and Charter Member of AFL
First Season: 1960
Moved to Kansas City and changed nickname: 1963
Stadium: Arrowhead Stadium
One Arrowhead Drive
Kansas City, Missouri 64129
Capacity: 79,451
Grass
Training Camp: University of Wisconsin-River Falls
River Falls, Wisconsin 54022
Fan info: 1-800-452-2522
Founder: Lamar Hunt
Super Bowl Championship: IV
AFL Championships: 1962, 1966, 1969
AFL Western Division Championships: 1962, 1966, 1968 (tie)
AFC Western Division Championships: 1971, 1993, 1995, 1997
Retired Uniform Numbers: #3 Jan Stenerud, #16 Len Dawson, #28 Abner Haynes, #33 Stone Johnson, #36 Mack Lee Hill, #63 Willie Lanier, #78 Bobby Bell, #86 Buck Buchanan.

took over the reins as Chiefs head coach, who in turn was replaced by Dick Vermeil in 2001.

MIAMI DOLPHINS

No pro football club in history ever advanced more quickly from the first-year challenges expansion teams face to the ultimate achievement in its sport than the Miami Dolphins did in the six-year period between 1967 and 1972. In 1967, they began their pro football life as the ninth member of the American Football League. Six years later, Miami became the only National Football League team ever to record a perfect season. The 1972 Miami Dolphins won the AFC Eastern division and AFC championships, and then defeated the Washington Redskins 14-7 in Super Bowl VII to complete an unblemished 17-0-0 record.

The Dolphins, who were founded by Joseph Robbie, also got off to a perfect start in the first game of their first AFL season when running back Joe Auer returned the opening kickoff for a 95-yard touchdown against the Oakland Raiders. But the Miami team returned to reality even before the end of its first game. Oakland rallied to win, and the Dolphins finished their first season with a 4-10 record.

George Wilson was the Dolphins' first coach. He finished his four-year AFL tenure after the 1969 season with a 15-39-2 record. But those were not wasted years for the Dolphins because they were steadily adding new talent such as quarterback Bob Griese in 1967, running back Larry Csonka in 1968 and guard Larry Little in 1969 that would eventually turn them into winners.

The transition from losing to winning came in just one season in 1970 when new coach Don Shula led the Dolphins to an AFC wild-card playoff berth with a 10-4 record. Miami then followed with three straight AFC championships in 1971, 1972 and 1973 and victories in Super Bowls VII and VIII. Their combined 1972-1973 record was 32-2, also an all-time mark. From 1970 to 1974, their cumulative record was 65-15-1.

There is no telling what heights the Dolphins might have reached had not three of their finest stars, Csonka, Jim Kiick and Paul Warfield, defected to the rival World Football League after the 1974 season. Miami never again reached the world championship level the Dolphins attained in 1972 and 1973. But Shula, who in 1993 surpassed George Halas' record of 324 coaching victories to become the all-time leader, kept the Dolphins among the league's elite year after year.

The Dolphins, since 1970, have won 11 AFC Eastern division championships and five AFC titles, the last two coming in 1982 and 1984. In the 1984 season, quarterback Dan Marino threw an all-time record 48 touchdown passes. Since 1970, Miami has had losing seasons only in 1976 and 1988.

The Dolphins' first playing home was the Orange Bowl in Miami. Fan support was excellent, and in 1973 the Dolphins established a NFL record with 74,961 season ticket sales. But Robbie had long dreamed of his own privately-funded stadium and, on August 16, 1987, he proudly unveiled a new 73,000-seat stadium. Two years later, the

Dolphins Facts

Team Colors: Aqua, Coral, Blue, and White
7500 S.W. 30th Street
Davie, Florida 33314
(954) 452-7000
Franchise Granted: August 16, 1965
First Season: 1966
Stadium: Pro Player Stadium
2269 N.W. 199th Street
Miami, Florida 33056
Capacity: 75,192
Grass
Training Camp: Nova University
7500 S.W. 30th Street
Davie, Florida 33314
Super Bowl Championships: VII, VIII
AFC Championships: 1971, 1972, 1973, 1982, 1984
AFC Eastern Division Championships: 1971, 1972, 1973, 1974, 1979, 1981, 1983, 1984, 1985, 1992, 1994
Retired Uniform Numbers: #12 Bob Griese, #13 Dan Marino

stadium served as the site for Super Bowl XXIII and again hosted a Super Bowl in January, 1995. The Joe Robbie era ended with his death on January 7, 1990. Early in 1994, the NFL approved the acquisition of the Dolphins by H. Wayne Huizenga, a well-known Florida sportsman. Following the 1995 season, the legendary Shula retired as coach of the Dolphins. Jimmy Johnson succeeded the all-time winningest coach, but after four years with the Dolphins, he retired. The coaching reins were handed to Dave Wannstedt, the former head coach of the Chicago Bears.

MINNESOTA VIKINGS

Over the past quarter-century, the Minnesota Vikings have consistently been at the top of their division. During that same period, only Dallas has made more playoff appearances. In addition, only four teams have played in more Super Bowls than Minnesota, which participated in Super Bowls IV, VIII, IX and XI.

The pro football saga in the Twin Cities began in August 1959, when five Minnesota businessmen were awarded a franchise in the new American Football League. Five months later in January 1960, the same ownership group made up of Bill Boyer, Ole Haugsrud, Bernie Ridder, H. P. Skoglund and Max Winter first forfeited its AFL membership and then was awarded the National Football League's 14th franchise that was to begin play in 1961.

The Vikings had a spectacular debut in their first game ever on September 17, 1961. Rookie Fran Tarkenton made a once-in-a-generation debut when he came off the bench to throw four touchdown passes and run for a fifth score to lead his Vikings to a 37-13 thrashing of the fabled Chicago Bears. Two-and-a-half decades later in 1986, Tarkenton became the first Vikings player to be elected to the Pro Football Hall of Fame.

General manager Bert Rose and head coach Norm Van Brocklin led Minnesota's first management team. From the start, the Vikings embraced an energetic marketing program that produced a first-year season ticket sale of nearly 26,000 and an average home attendance of 34,586, about 85 percent of the capacity of 40,800 Metropolitan Stadium. Eventually, the stadium capacity was increased to 47,900. Rose resigned from his position in 1964 and Van Brocklin quit abruptly in the spring of 1967. The Vikings went to Canada to get their replacements. Jim Finks, then general manager of the Calgary Stampeders, was named as the new general manager. Bud Grant, head coach of the Winnipeg Blue Bombers, became the new Vikings field leader.

The success of the Vikings over the next two decades always will be highlighted by the image of the stone-faced Grant on the sidelines of the frozen field at old Metropolitan Stadium. In only their second year under Grant, the Vikings began a stretch of 11 division titles in 13 years. They won the NFL championship in 1969 and NFC titles in 1973,

Vikings Facts

National Football Conference
Central Division
Team colors: Purple, Gold and White
9520 Viking Drive
Eden Prairie, Minnesota 55344
(612) 828-6500
Franchise Granted: January 27, 1960
First Season: 1961
Stadium: Hubert H. Humphrey Metrodome
500 11th Ave South
Minneapolis, Minnesota 55415
Capacity: 64,121
AstroTurf
Training Camp:
Minnesota State-Mankato
Mankato, Minnesota 56001
NFL Championship: 1969
NFC Championships: 1973, 1974, 1976
NFL Central Division Championships:
1968, 1969
NFL Western Conference Championship:
1969
NFC Central Division Championships:
1970, 1971, 1973, 1974, 1975, 1976,
1977, 1978, 1980, 1989, 1992, 1994, 1998
Retired Uniform Numbers: #10 Fran
Tarkenton, #88 Alan Page , #70 Jim
Marshall

1974 and 1976. He first retired in 1983, but came back for a year in 1985 before making his retirement permanent. Grant's 168-108-5 record makes him the eighth winningest coach of all time.

In 1982, the Vikings moved into the Hubert H. Humphrey Metrodome, the site of Super Bowl XXVI, with a capacity of 63,000. There they have continued to enjoy an approximately .600 home winning record. From Bud Grant, Fran Tarkenton, Chuck Foreman and Alan Page to the stars of the 1990s—coach Dennis Green, Randall McDaniel, Steve Jordan and Cris Carter—the names have changed over the years but the Vikings' tradition has remained constant.

NEW ENGLAND PATRIOTS

Billy Sullivan Jr., a Boston businessman with a strong sports promotional background, secured an American Football League franchise on November 22, 1959. In keeping with the New England heritage, the nickname "Patriots" was selected by a panel of Boston sports writers in a contest to name the team. The Boston team was involved in two significant "firsts" in 1960. The Patriots defeated the Buffalo Bills in the first AFL pre-season game on July 30. On September 9, the Patriots lost to the Denver Broncos 13-10 in the first-ever AFL regular-season game.

During the Patriots' first decade, finding a suitable playing home in the Boston area was almost as urgent as putting a competitive team on the field. The Patriots played at Boston University Field in the 1960 and 1961, and at Harvard in 1962 and 1970. From 1963 to 1969, the Patriots played at Fenway Park, the Red Sox baseball stadium. Then in 1971, two significant things happened. The team changed its name to the New England Patriots and moved to a new 60,764-seat stadium in the town of Foxboro, about 25 miles south of Boston. After two name changes, the Stadium is now called Foxboro Stadium.

In spite of their stadium problems, the Patriots were frequent contenders during their AFL days. Mike Holovak, who replaced Lou Saban midway into the 1961 season, ranks as the winningest coach in team history with a 53-47-9 record. His best season came in 1963, when the Patriots defeated Buffalo 26-8 in a playoff for the AFL Eastern crown. In the AFL championship game the next week, however, they lost to San Diego 51-10. Holovak had few stars to build a team around, but Gino Cappelletti, the team's placekicker and ace wide receiver, became the AFL's all-time high scorer with 1,100 points, 252 on touchdown receptions and the remainder on kicking. Running back Jim Nance won AFL rushing titles when he rushed for an AFL-record 1,458 yards in 1966 and 1,216 yards in 1967.

Following a string of losing seasons after the AFL-NFL merger, the Patriots became serious contenders in the late 1970s. The 1976 Patriots finished 11-3 and just barely lost to eventual-Super Bowl champion

Patriots Facts

Team Colors: Blue, Red, Silver, and White
Foxboro Stadium
60 Washington Street
Foxboro, Massachusetts 02035
(508) 543-8200
Franchise Granted: November 22, 1959 as the Boston Patriots
First Season: 1960
Changed name to New England Patriots: 1971
Stadium: Foxboro Stadium
60 Washington Street
Foxboro, Massachusetts 02035
Capacity: 60,292
Grass
Training Camp: Bryant College
Route 7
Smithfield, Rhode Island 02917
AFC Championships: 1985, 1996
AFL Eastern Division Championship: 1963
AFC Eastern Division Championships: 1978, 1986, 1996, 1997
Retired Uniform Numbers: #14 Steve Grogan, #20 Gino Cappelletti, #40 Mike Haynes, #57 Steve Nelson, #73 John Hannah, #79 Jim Hunt, #89 Bob Dee

Oakland Raiders in a first-round playoff game. They won the AFC Eastern championship in 1978 and finished a close second in 1979. Raymond Berry took over the coaching reins in 1984 and led the Patriots to a 51-41-0 record the next five-and-a-half years. Berry's 1985 team had an 11-5 record, earned a wild-card playoff berth and won three straight AFC play-off games on the road and advanced to Super Bowl XX, where the Patriots lost to the Chicago Bears. That game marked the final appearance of guard John Hannah, who in 1991 became the first Patriot to be elected to the Pro Football Hall of Fame.

In recent years, Patriots ownership has changed often, from Sullivan to Victor K. Kiam II in 1988, to James B. Orthwein in 1992 and finally to Robert Kraft in 1994. With the highly-regarded veteran coach Bill Parcells in charge and the successful stockpiling of quality talent through the NFL draft, the Patriots won the AFC Championship in 1996 and earned a trip to their second Super Bowl. With new coach Bill Belichick and stars such as Drew Bledsoe and Terry Glenn, the Patriots anticipate the future with confidence and enthusiasm.

NEW ORLEANS SAINTS

The National Football League awarded its 16th franchise to New Orleans on November 1, 1966. Appropriately, it was All Saints Day. In mid-December, 28-year-old John W. Mecom Jr., a successful Texas and Louisiana businessman, became the majority stockholder. Less than a month later on January 9, 1967, no one was surprised when the team was named the "Saints."

On March 8, the Saints launched their first season-ticket drive that produced 20,000 sales on opening day and 33,400 before the 1967 NFL season began. Eager to create as much pre-season fan enthusiasm as possible in a city not previously exposed to pro football, the Saints obtained three future Pro Football Hall of Famers for their 1967 roster. Paul Hornung and Jim Taylor, a Louisiana State hero, came from Green Bay and defensive end Doug Atkins came in a trade with the Chicago Bears.

The Saints literally took "The City That Care Forgot" by storm. They won five of their six preseason games and opened the regular season on September 17, 1967, against the Los Angeles Rams before a packed house of 80,879 in Tulane Stadium. New Orleans fans will always remember John Gilliam's 94-yard touchdown return with the opening kickoff even though the Rams eventually won 27-13. A final game victory over the Washington Redskins allowed the Saints to match the 3-11 first-year record attained by Minnesota in 1961 and Atlanta in 1966. Most significant of all, however, was the average home attendance—75,463 per game!

Saints Facts

Team Colors: Old Gold, Black, and White
5800 Airline Drive
Metairie, Louisiana 70003
(504) 733-0255
Franchise Granted: November 1, 1966
First Season: 1967
Stadium: Louisiana Superdome
1500 Poydras Street
New Orleans, Louisiana 70112
Capacity 70,200
AstroTurf
Training Camp: John L. Guidry Stadium
Nicholls State University
Thibodaux, Louisiana 70310
NFC Western Division Championship:
1991, 2000
Retired Uniform Numbers: #81 Doug Atkins, #8 Archie Manning, #57 Rickey Jackson

The Saints made each home game a special event, a so-called "Mardi Gras in Autumn," with cheerleaders, jazz bands, precision-marching routines by high school and college bands, and weekly appearances of "The King" himself—part-owner, chief cheerleader and trumpet wizard Al Hirt. New Orleans was destined to falter year-after-year on the field. Still, they managed to thrill their fans with some exciting victories and memorable moments first at Tulane Stadium and later at the 69,056-seat Superdome, which opened in 1975.

One of the most famous plays in the team's history was Tom Dempsey's record 63-yard field goal in 1970 that enabled New Orleans to beat Detroit 19-17 during the game's final moment. Outstanding players such as quarterback Archie Manning, running back George Rogers, linebacker Rickey Jackson, wide receiver Eric Martin and placekicker Morten Andersen were among those who played important roles as the Saints advanced toward respectability.

The Saints finished 8-8 in both 1979 and 1983, but didn't have a winning year until their 21st season in 1987. That year, under coach Jim Mora, the Saints won 12 of 15 games for a second-place finish in the NFC West. The Saints reached the playoffs four times in six seasons from 1987 to 1992 and won their only NFC West Championship in 1991.

The winning era in New Orleans was ushered in on June 3, 1985, when a New Orleans businessman, Tom Benson, acquired the franchise from Mecom. Benson immediately hired Jim Finks, a future Hall of Fame administrator, as president and general manager, and Mora as head coach. The pair soon turned the Saints into one of the NFL's most potent franchises. Mike Ditka, the Hall of Fame tight end and former Chicago Bears coach, guided the team from 1997-1999. In 2000, former NFL linebacker and long-time assistant Jim Haslett was hired as the new head coach.

NEW YORK GIANTS

The history and tradition of the New York Giants is linked to pro football itself, for one might have perished without the other in the early days of the National Football League. The late Tim Mara, now a member of the Pro Football Hall of Fame, purchased a franchise for $500 in 1925, and before the Giants' first season had ended, he had invested another $25,000 to keep the franchise alive. A team in New York was assured. To the young NFL, which was seeking national media and fan attendance, a team in the nation's largest city was an absolute "must."

The value of New York exposure was clearly demonstrated in December of the first season when more than 70,000 turned out at the Polo Grounds to see the Giants play the Chicago Bears, who had just signed Red Grange, the most famous pro football player of the 1920s.

The very next season in 1926, Grange and his agent formed a rival American Football League and placed their flagship team, the Yankees, in New York to battle the Giants head-to-head. It proved to be a costly battle but the Giants and the NFL won. The AFL lasted only one year.

In their third season, in 1927, the Giants won their first NFL championship behind a defense led by tackle Steve Owen that permitted an all-time low of 20 points in 13 games. Owen became the Giants' coach in 1931. He held the job for 23 seasons and wound up with a 153-108-17 record. He still ranks ninth in all-time coaching victories. The Giants enjoyed some of their finest seasons during the Owen years. Beginning with the start of divisional play in 1933, the Giants won eight Eastern division titles in 14 seasons and NFL championships in 1934 and 1938. Ken Strong, a triple-threat halfback and a premier placekicker, and Mel Hein, a center-linebacker who didn't miss a game in

Giants Facts

Team Colors: Blue, Red, and White
Giants Stadium
East Rutherford, New Jersey 07073
(201) 935-8111
Franchise Granted: August 1, 1925
First Season: 1925
Stadium: Giants Stadium
East Rutherford,
New Jersey 07073
Capacity: 79,469
grass
Training Camp: University at Albany
1400 Washington Avenue
Albany, NY 12222
Super Bowl Championships: XXI, XXV
NFL Championships: 1927, 1934, 1938, 1956
NFC Championships: 1986, 1990, 2000
NFL Eastern Conference Championships: 1933, 1934, 1935, 1938, 1939, 1941, 1944, 1946, 1956, 1958, 1959, 1961, 1962, 1963
NFC Eastern Division Championships: 1986, 1989, 1990,1997, 2000
Retired Uniform Numbers: #1 Ray Flaherty, #4 Tuffy Leemans, #7 Mel Hein, #11 Phil Simms, #14 Y.A. Tittle, #32 Al Blozis, #40 Joe Morrison, #42 Charlie Conerly, #50 Ken Strong, #56 Lawrence Taylor

15 seasons, were Giants standouts through most of the 1930s and 1940s.

With the coaching of first Jim Lee Howell in the late 1950s and Allie Sherman in the early 1960s, the Giants won the NFL title in 1956 and six NFL Eastern championships in eight years from 1956 to 1963. Such stars as Y. A. Tittle, Frank Gifford, Roosevelt Brown, Emlen Tunnell and Andy Robustelli led New Yorkπs annual chase to the title game. From 1964 to 1985, the Giants remained out of championship contention. With Bill Parcells at the helm, they won NFC Eastern division crowns in 1986, 1989 and 1990. They concluded the 1986 and 1990 campaigns with victories over Denver in Super Bowl XXI and Buffalo in Super Bowl XXV.

From the start, the Giants have been a family enterprise. Founder Tim Mara's sons, Jack and Wellington, succeeded him and Tim Mara II served for many years as the club's vice president. Wellington Mara and Preston Robert Tisch, who purchased 50 percent of the club in 1991, are now co-chief executive officers.

NEW YORK JETS

The history of the New York franchise in the American Football League is the story of two distinct organizations, the Titans and the Jets. Interlocking the two in continuity is the player personnel which went with the franchise in the ownership change from Harry Wismer to a five-man group headed by David "Sonny" Werblin in February, 1963.

The three-year reign of Wismer, who was granted a charter AFL franchise in 1959, was fraught with controversy. The on-field happenings of the Titans were often overlooked, even in victory, as Wismer moved from feud to feud with the thoughtlessness of one playing Russian roulette with all chambers loaded. In spite of it all, the Titans had reasonable success on the field but they were a box office disaster. Werblin's group purchased the bankrupt franchise for $1 million, changed the team name to Jets and hired Weeb Ewbank as head coach. In 1964, the Jets moved from the antiquated Polo Grounds to newly-constructed Shea Stadium, where the Jets set an AFL attendance mark of 45,665 in the season opener against the Denver Broncos.

Ewbank, who had enjoyed championship success with the Baltimore Colts in the 1950s, patiently began a building program that received a major transfusion on January 2, 1965, when Werblin signed Alabama quarterback Joe Namath to a rumored $400,000 contract. The signing of the highly regarded Namath proved to be a major factor in the eventual end of the AFL-NFL pro football war of the 1960s.

The 1968 season was the culmination of the New York AFL hopes as the Jets, under the guidance of Ewbank and the play of Namath, Don Maynard and a host of other major contributors, raced to the AFL East title with an 11-3 record. They defeated the Oakland Raiders 27-23 in the AFL championship, and then stunned the entire sports world with a 16-7 victory over the overwhelmingly favored Baltimore Colts in Super Bowl III. It is considered to be one of the two most pivotal games ever in the building of fan enthusiasm for pro football. The Jets won the AFL East again in 1969, but lost to Kansas City in a first-round playoff game and did not

Jets Facts

Team Colors: Green and White
1000 Fulton Avenue
Hempstead, New York 11550
(516) 560-8100
Franchise Granted: August 14, 1959 as the New York Titans and Charter Member of AFL
First Season: 1960
Changed nickname to Jets: 1963
Stadium: Giants Stadium
East Rutherford, New Jersey
Capacity: 78,739
grass
Training Camp: Hofstra University
1000 Fulton Avenue
Hempstead, New York 11550
Fan phone: (516) 560-8288
Super Bowl Championship: III
AFL Championship: 1968
AFL Eastern Division Championships: 1968, 1969
AFC Eastern Division Championships: 1998
Retired Uniform Numbers: #12 Joe Namath, #13 Don Maynard

seriously challenge for a divisional championship for 12 seasons until 1981.

The next decade saw the Jets return to the playoffs five times, in 1981, 1982, 1985, 1986 and 1991. Their high-water marks during those years came in 1981 and again in 1986, when they won first-round playoff encounters before being eliminated. In the strike-shortened 1982 season, the Jets advanced to the AFC championship game, losing to Miami 14-0. Through it all, the Jets have maintained an excellent attendance record. They have not fallen below an average-per-game attendance of 54,051 since 1964, the second season in Shea Stadium. The Jets moved into the Meadowlands stadium across the Hudson River in New Jersey in 1984, and they have sold out every seat since that time.

Coach Ewbank in 1978 and two players in the 1980s, all of whom stand out in Jets history, have been elected to the Pro Football Hall of Fame. Namath was elected in 1985 and Maynard in 1987.

OAKLAND RAIDERS

The American Football League was formally organized on August 14, 1959. However, the Oakland Raiders did not become the eighth member of the new league until January 1960, when they were selected as a replacement for the Minneapolis franchise, which defected to the NFL. A major initial stumbling block was the lack of an adequate stadium in Oakland. Until the 54,616 capacity Oakland Coliseum was opened in 1966, the Raiders had to play in Kezar Stadium and Candlestick Park across the bay in San Francisco and in a temporary stadium, Frank Youell Field in Oakland. Oakland's record for the first three years was a miserable 9-33-0. Average home attendance was just under 11,000.

In 1963, the Raiders hired a San Diego assistant coach, Al Davis, as the new head coach and the reversal in fortunes was both rapid and dramatic. From a 1-13 mark in 1962, Oakland improved to 10-4 in 1963 and Davis was named the AFL Coach of the Year. Since that time, the Raiders' destiny has been the exclusive responsibility of Davis, who left the team only briefly for a short term as AFL commissioner in 1966. After the AFL-NFL merger was complete, Davis returned to the Raiders as managing general partner and immediately transformed the Oakland franchise into one of pro football's premier organizations. Starting in 1965, the Raiders posted winning records 19 of the next 20 years. During that period, they won 12 divisional championships, the 1967 AFL championship, AFC championships in 1976, 1980 and 1983 and victories in Super Bowls XI, XV and XVIII.

The Raiders are the only original AFL team to win a Super Bowl since Kansas City won Super Bowl IV. They also are the only AFC team to win a Super Bowl since the Steelers won Super Bowl XIV NFL or AFL, to play in a Super Bowl in the 1960s, 1970s and 1980s.

In the 30-year period dating back to when Davis took over in 1963 up through 1992, the Raiders' winning record of .661 with 285 victories, 146 losses and 11 ties ranks as the

Raiders Facts

Team Colors: Silver and Black
1220 Harbor Bay Parkway
Alameda, California 94502
(510) 864-5000
Franchise Granted: January 30, 1960 as the Oakland Raiders
First Season: 1960
Played in Los Angeles: 1982-1994
Stadium: Network Associates Coliseum
7000 Coliseum Way
Oakland, CA 94621
Capacity: 63,142
Grass
Training Camp: Napa Valley Marriott
Napa, California 94558
President, General Partner: Al Davis
Head Coach: Jon Gruden
Super Bowl Championships: XI, XV, XVIII
AFL Championship: 1967
AFC Championships: 1976, 1980, 1983
AFL Western Division Championships:
1967, 1968, 1969
AFC Western Division Championships:
1970, 1972, 1973, 1974, 1975, 1976, 1983, 1985, 1990, 2000
Retired Uniform Numbers: None

best among all major sports teams.

While Davis stresses "Commitment to Excellence" for his entire organization, some of the Raiders' unprecedented success can be attributed to outstanding individual players and coaches who have worn the Silver and Black. In addition to Davis, eight players—Jim Otto, George Blanda, Willie Brown, Gene Upshaw, Art Shell, Fred Biletnikoff, Ted Hendricks and Mike Haynes have been elected to the Pro Football Hall of Fame. Five Raider coaches have been named either AFL or NFL Coach of the Year. In addition to Davis, they are John Rauch, John Madden, Tom Flores and Art Shell.

The Raiders made headlines of a different nature when they moved from the Oakland Coliseum to the more spacious Los Angeles Coliseum in 1982. After 12 seasons in Southern California, the team moved back to its original city.

PHILADELPHIA EAGLES

The Eagles have been a Philadelphia institution since their beginning in 1933, when a syndicate headed by the late Bert Bell and Lud Wray purchased the former Frankford Yellowjackets franchise for $2,500. In 1941, a unique swap took place between Philadelphia and Pittsburgh that saw the clubs trade home cities with Alexis Thompson becoming the Eagles owner.

In 1943, the Philadelphia and Pittsburgh franchises combined for one season because of the manpower shortage created by World War II. The team was called both Phil-Pitt and the Steagles. Greasy Neale of the Eagles and Walt Kiesling of the Steelers were co-coaches, and the team finished 5-4-1.

Counting the 1943 season, Neale coached the Eagles for 10 seasons, and he led them to their first significant successes in the NFL. Paced by such future Pro Football Hall of Fame members as running back Steve Van Buren, center-linebacker Alex Wojciech-owicz, end Pete Pihos and beginning in 1949, center-linebacker Chuck Bednarik, the Eagles dominated the league for six seasons. They finished second in the NFL Eastern Division in 1944, 1945 and 1946, won the division title in 1947 and then scored successive shutout victories in the 1948 and 1949 championship games.

A rash of injuries ended Philadelphia's era of domination and, by 1958, the Eagles had fallen to last place in their division. That year, however, saw the start of a rebuilding program by a new coach, Buck Shaw, and the addition of quarterback Norm Van Brocklin in a trade with the Los Angeles Rams. In just three years, Shaw gave Philadelphia another championship. Behind Van Brocklin's expert on-field leadership, the Eagles won the Eastern Division with a 10-2 record and then defeated the Green Bay Packers 17-13 for the NFL championship. Bednarik saved the day for the Eagles with an open field tackle of Green Bay's Jimmy Taylor on the game's final play. The Eagles fell just a half-game short of another NFL Eastern Conference championship in 1961, but didn't reach the playoffs again for 18 years until 1978, their third sea-

Eagles Facts

Team Colors: Midnight Green, Silver, Black and White

Veterans Stadium
3501 South Broad Street
Philadelphia, Pennsylvania 19148
(215) 463-2500

Franchise Granted: July 8, 1933

First Season: 1933

Stadium: Veterans Stadium
3501 South Broad Street
Philadelphia, Pennsylvania 19148
Capacity: 65,352
AstroTurf

Training Camp: Lehigh University
Bethlehem, Pennsylvania 18015
Fan phone: (215)463-2500 or
(610) 758-6868

NFL Championships: 1948, 1949, 1960

NFC Championship: 1980

NFL Eastern Conference Championships: 1947, 1948, 1949, 1960

NFC Eastern Division Championships: 1980, 1988

Retired Uniform Numbers: #15 Steve Van Buren, #40 Tom Brookshier, #44 Pete Retzlaff , #60 Chuck Bednarik, #70 Al Wistert, #99 Jerome Brown

son with Dick Vermeil as the coach. Vermeil's teams played in four straight post-season games between 1978 and 1981. In 1980, Philadelphia won a club-record 12 games, edged out Dallas for the Eastern Division title and defeated the Cowboys 20-7 for the NFC championship. However, the Eagles lost to the Oakland Raiders 27-10 in Super Bowl XV.

Vermeil's successful tenure was followed by some lean years, until Norman Braman took control of the club in 1985. His program hit full stride in 1988 when the Eagles won the NFL Eastern Division. Starting with that 1988 season, Philadelphia, which was particularly dominating on defense, won 10 or more games for five straight years up to 1993. In four of those years, the Eagles entered the playoffs as a wild-card team, a feat they repeated in 1995.

Since 1971, when the Eagles left the University of Pennsylvania's Franklin Field, they have played in 65,356-seat Veterans Stadium before capacity or near-capacity crowds each week.

PITTSBURGH STEELERS

The Pittsburgh Steelers were founded by Arthur J. Rooney on July 8, 1933. Now the sixth-oldest franchise in the NFL, the Pittsburgh team was known as the Pirates until 1940. The Steelers struggled through their first 40 years without winning a championship of any kind until they won the AFC Central Division title in 1972. Two years later, the entire sports world cheered when Art Rooney, one of the world's most popular sports figures, received the Vince Lombardi Trophy after the Steelers' victory in Super Bowl IX.

In the 1970s, after so many years of frustration, the Steelers began one of the most incredible streaks in sports history when they earned eight consecutive playoff berths, seven AFC Central titles and four AFC championships from 1972 to 1979. The Steelers became the first team to win four Super Bowls and the only team to win back-to-back Super Bowls twice. The team of the '70s became the first AFC team to win its division 10 times since the NFL's 1970 merger.

The list of Pittsburgh Steelers heroes of the 1970s is long, but it begins with head coach Chuck Noll, who took control of the team in 1969. Such stars as defensive tackle Joe Greene, linebackers Jack Ham and Jack Lambert, quarterback Terry Bradshaw, cornerback Mel Blount and running back Franco Harris were the backbone of a team that many insist was the finest ever in pro football. All, including Noll, were accorded membership in the Pro Football Hall of Fame in their first years of eligibility.

Pittsburgh's success in the last two decades is the antithesis of the Steelers' experiences in their early years. The team won only 22 games its first seven seasons. Rooney, seeking a way to make ends meet, often took his team from Forbes Field to such neutral cities as Johnstown and Latrobe in Pennsylvania, Youngstown, Louisville and New Orleans so as to avoid competition with baseball and college football in Pittsburgh. Through it all, Rooney never wavered in his determination to make pro football successful in his city.

In 1938, Rooney made Colorado All-America Byron "Whizzer" White the NFL's first "big money" player with a $15,800 contract. The 1942 Steelers, boosted by the NFL-leading rushing of rookie Bill Dudley, enjoyed their first winning season. With ros-

Steelers Facts

Team Colors: Black and Gold
4200 South Water Street
Pittsburgh, Pennsylvania 15203
(412) 432-7800
Franchise Granted: July 8, 1933 as the Pirates
First Season: 1933
Changed Nickname to Steelers: 1940
Stadium: Heinz Field
100 Art Rooney Avenue
Pittsburgh, Pennsylvania 15212
Capacity: 65,000
Grass
Training Camp: St. Vincent College
Latrobe, Pennsylvania 15650
Super Bowl Championships: IX, X, XIII, XIV
AFC Championships: 1974, 1975, 1978, 1979, 1995
AFC Central Division Championships: 1972, 1974, 1975, 1976, 1977, 1978, 1979, 1983, 1984, 1992, 1994, 1995, 1996, 1997
Retired Uniform Numbers: None

ters depleted by the manpower shortage of World War II, Rooney merged the Steelers with the Eagles (Phil-Pitt) in 1943 and the Cardinals (Card-Pitt) in 1944. Coach Jock Sutherland led the Steelers to a first-place tie with the Philadelphia Eagles in 1947, but they lost their first post-season game ever, 21-0, to the Eagles.

From 1957 to 1963, the Steelers, coached by Buddy Parker, with quarterback Bobby Layne, defensive tackle Ernie Stautner and running back John Henry Johnson playing key roles, were legitimate divisional championship contenders. But the "dynasty years" that coincided with the move to the AFC at the time of the AFL-NFL merger and forever brightened Pittsburgh Steelers history were still a decade away.

ST LOUIS RAMS

One of the National Football League's oldest franchises, the Rams began life in Cleveland in 1937. They did no better than a .500 mark during their first six seasons. They disbanded for a year in 1943 because of the manpower shortages of the World War II era. When they finally did record a winning season, they hit the jackpot with a 15-14 victory over the Washington Redskins in the NFL championship game. A sensational rookie quarterback from UCLA, Bob Waterfield, was the league's Player of the Year.

That championship game proved to be the last the Rams would ever play in Cleveland. Dan Reeves, a shrewd businessman and a master innovator who had bought the team in 1941, decided to move the Rams to Los Angeles for the 1946 season. He then signed Kenny Washington and Woody Strode, making them the first two African-American athletes with an NFL contract since 1932. Reeves also instituted the famed "Free Football for Kids" program, providing the groundwork for today's successful TV policies, and became the first to employ a full-time scouting staff.

In their first four seasons on the West Coast, the Rams had to wage a costly head-to-head battle with the intra-city Dons of the All-America Football Conference. Reeves and the Rams suffered mammoth financial losses. But the AAFC folded after the 1949 season just as the Rams were embarking on a string of outstanding seasons on the field. They won four NFL Western Division championships in seven years and captured their second NFL title in 1951. With Waterfield and Norm Van Brocklin connecting regularly on long bombs to Elroy "Crazylegs" Hirsch and Tom Fears, the Rams played an exciting, glamorous brand of football.

The effect at the gate was outstanding. Topped by a crowd of 102,368 for a San Francisco 49ers game in 1957, turnouts in the Coliseum topped 80,000 on 22 occasions during the Rams' first 20 years in Los Angeles.

The heady successes of the early 1950s produced one final divisional championship under a rookie coach, Sid Gillman, in 1955. Then, the Rams slipped into the second division, not to return to championship contention again until 1967.

By that time, George Allen had taken over the coaching reins. Allen fashioned the high-

Rams Facts

Team Colors: Royal Blue, Gold and White
One Rams Way
St. Louis, Missouri 63045
(314) 982-7267
Franchise Granted: February 12, 1937 as the Cleveland Rams
First Season: 1937
Moved to Los Angeles: 1946
Moved to St. Louis: 1995
Stadium: Trans World Dome
701 Convention Plaza
St. Louis, Missouri 63101
Capacity: 66,000
AstroTurf
Training Camp: Western Illinois University
Thompson Hall
Macomb, Illinois 61455
NFL Championships: 1945, 1951
NFC Championships: 1979
Superbowl XXXIV Champions 2000
NFL Western Conference Championships: 1945, 1949, 1950, 1951, 1955
NFL Coastal Division Championships: 1967, 1969
NFC Western Division Championships: 1973, 1974, 1975, 1976, 1977, 1978, 1979, 1985
Retired Uniform Numbers: #7 Bob Waterfield, #74 Merlin Olsen

ly publicized Fearsome Foursome line that included future Hall of Famers Merlin Olsen and Deacon Jones. Allen's five-year record was 49-19-4, best ever for a Rams coach. The Rams continued their winning ways through the 1970s. They won five straight NFC Western Division championships from 1973 to 1977 with Chuck Knox at the helm and then two more divisional titles after Ray Malavasi replaced Knox in 1978. The 1979 Rams won the NFC championship before losing to Pittsburgh, 31-19, in Super Bowl XIV.

In 1972, the Baltimore Colts' Carroll Rosenbloom traded franchises with Bob Irsay and took control of the Rams. Rosenbloom died in 1979 and his widow, Georgia, replaced him as owner/president. In 1995, the Rams moved to St. Louis, where they play in the Trans World Dome. In 1997, the Rams hired former Philadelphia Eagles coach Dick Vermeil. Two years later, in 1999, the Rams were transformed into Super Bowl champions. Guided by quarterback Kurt Warner and running back Marshall Faulk, the team beat Tennessee 23-16 in a thrilling Super Bowl XXXIV. Following the victory, Vermeil retired and was replaced by Mike Martz, the team's offensive coordinator.

SAN DIEGO CHARGERS

CHARGERS

The Chargers were born on August 14, 1959, when Barron Hilton, a 32-year-old hotel executive, was awarded a franchise for Los Angeles in the new American Football League. Even though they won the AFL Western Division championship in 1960, the Los Angeles Chargers received meager fan support. So, Hilton, buoyed by the encouragement of San Diego sports editor Jack Murphy, moved his team 120 miles south to San Diego in 1961. Historic Balboa Stadium was expanded to 34,000 capacity to accommodate the Chargers.

In San Diego, the Chargers, spurred by coach Sid Gillman, developed into one of the true glamour teams of any decade. Gillman's first teams were high-scoring, crowd-pleasing juggernauts that won divisional championships five of the AFL's first six years and the AFL title with a 51-10 win over Boston in 1963. Such stars as wide receiver Lance Alworth, running backs Keith Lincoln and Paul Lowe and quarterback John Hadl not only made the Chargers a winning team but they also provided image, impetus and respect for the entire AFL that was fighting a life-and-death struggle with the established and well-financed NFL. Gillman, Alworth and tackle Ron Mix, another 1960's superstar, are now members of the Pro Football Hall of Fame.

In 1967, the Chargers moved into a new 60,835-seat stadium, now called Qualcomm Stadium. While the new home assured the future of pro football in San Diego, the team itself did not win another championship until 13 years later in 1979. In 1969, after nine games, Gillman suddenly retired from coaching because of failing health. He did coach 10 more games for the Chargers in 1971, but the glory days of the early 1960's could not be duplicated. Gillman's 87-57-6 record in 11 seasons in San Diego is easily the best in Chargers history.

Only one other long-term San Diego coach, Don Coryell, had a winning record. Coryell compiled a 72-60-0 record during his 1978-1986 tenure. The Chargers won AFC Western Division championships in 1979,

Chargers Facts

Team colors: Navy Blue, White and Gold

P.O. Box 609609
San Diego, California 92160-9609
(619) 874-4500

Franchise Granted: August 14, 1959 as the Los Angeles Chargers and Charter Member of AFL

First Season: 1960

Moved to San Diego: 1961

Stadium: Qualcomm Stadium
9449 Friars Road
San Diego, California 92108
Capacity: 71,000
Grass

Training Camp: University of California-San Diego
Third College
La Jolla, California 92037
Fan info: (858) 455-1984

AFL Championship: 1963

AFC Championship: 1994

AFL Western Division Championship:
1960, 1961, 1963, 1964, 1965

AFC Western Division Championship:
1979, 1980, 1981, 1992, 1994

Retired Uniform Numbers: #14 Dan Fouts

1980 and 1981 and reached the AFC championship game the last two seasons. During that period, Coryell's Chargers played the same kind of exciting football that made the team so popular in the 1960s. Like Gillman, Coryell emphasized the forward pass and a future Hall of Fame quarterback, Dan Fouts, was the man who made his offense go. His targets included such Hall of Famers as wide receiver Charlie Joiner and tight end Kellen Winslow. San Diego advanced to the second round of the AFC playoffs in the strike-shortened 1982 season, but then dropped out of contention for the next 10 years.

In 1992, Bobby Ross from Georgia Tech became the coach and immediately led the Chargers back to the playoffs, capturing the AFC Western Division title. Two years later, the Chargers defeated the Pittsburgh Steelers 17-13 in the AFC championship game before losing to the San Francisco 49ers 49-26 in Super Bowl XXIX.

Hilton sold the Chargers to Eugene V. Klein in 1966. Klein in turn sold the team to Alex G. Spanos, a successful Stockton, California, businessman, in 1984. Spanos serves today as Chairman of the Board of the Chargers.

SAN FRANCISCO 49ERS

The San Francisco 49ers were charter members of the All-America Football Conference, which began play in 1946. Had it not been for the Browns, who won four championships and lost only four games in the league's four years of operation, the 49ers would have been the AAFC's dominant team. Their cumulative record was an excellent 39-15-2. They handed the Browns two of their four defeats, but finished second each year. Even in attendance, the 49ers were second best in the AAFC, next to Cleveland.

49ers Facts

Team Colors: Forty Niners Gold and Cardinal

4949 Centennial Boulevard
Santa Clara, California 95054
(408) 562-4949

Franchise Granted: June 4, 1944 as Charter Member of AAFC

First Season: 1946

Merged into NFL: 1950

Stadium: 3Com Park
San Francisco, CA 94124
Capacity: 70,140
San Francisco, California 94124

Training Camp: University of the Pacific Stockton, California 95211

Super Bowl Championships: XVI, XIX, XXIII, XXIV, XXIX

NFC Championships: 1981, 1984, 1988, 1989, 1994

NFC Western Division Championships: 1970, 1971, 1972, 1981, 1983, 1984, 1986, 1987, 1988, 1989, 1990, 1992, 1993, 1994, 1995, 1997

Retired Uniform Numbers: #12 John Brodie, #16 Joe Montana, #34 Joe Perry, #37 Jimmy Johnson, #39 Hugh McElhenny, #70 Charlie Krueger, #73 Leo Nomellini, #87 Dwight Clark

When the 49ers moved to the NFL in 1950 following the collapse of the AAFC, their original management team co-owners Anthony J. Morabito and Victor P. Morabito and general manager Louis Spadia remained intact. In the 1950s, the 49ers boasted some of the game's great individual stars, including quarterbacks Frankie Albert and Y. A. Tittle, running backs Hugh McElhenny, Joe Perry and John Henry Johnson, tackle Bob St. Clair and defensive tackle Leo Nomellini. But, the closest they came to a championship in their first two decades of NFL play was in 1957, when they tied Detroit for the NFL Western Division crown but lost in a playoff.

San Francisco flirted with success in 1970, 1971 and 1972, when the 49ers won three straight NFC Western Division titles. Every year, they were eliminated by the Dallas Cowboys, in the NFC championship games 1970 and 1971, and in the first playoff round in 1972. In 1971, the 49ers moved their home games from antiquated Kezar Stadium to 68,491-seat Candlestick Park.

A bright new era dawned for the 49ers on March 31, 1977, when Edward J. DeBartolo Jr. bought the team. He dedicated himself to transforming a team that never won a league championship into a pro football power. In 1979, DeBartolo selected Bill Walsh, renowned as an offensive specialist, as head coach. It took Walsh just three seasons to bring San Francisco its first-ever league championship with a 26-21 win over Cincinnati in Super Bowl XVI.

San Francisco also won the NFC West in 1983, and did even better in 1984 with 18 wins in 19 games and a 38-16 Super Bowl XIX victory over the Miami Dolphins. Walsh concluded his pro coaching career after a last-second 20-16 victory over Cincinnati in Super Bowl XXIII. In 10 years, Walsh compiled a 102-62-1 record and won six NFC West titles and three Super Bowls.

The 49ers of the 1980s were loaded with a group of young superstars such as quarterback Joe Montana, wide out Dwight Clark and Jerry Rice statistically, the greatest receiver of all-time, running back Roger Craig and defensive back Ronnie Lott. George Seifert, who replaced Walsh, continued to take full advantage of the existing talent. Careful personnel planning paid off as capable new players were on hand when veteran stars retired. A perfect example is the quarterback position where capable and talented Steve Young was on hand to replace Montana, who had battled a series of injuries before leaving the 49ers.

Seifert's record as the 49ers head man was excellent, with two Super Bowl wins, a 55-10 win over the Denver Broncos in Super Bowl XXIV and a 49-26 victory over the San Diego Chargers in Super Bowl XXIX. Stewardship of the franchise is now in the hands of Steve Mariucci.

SEATTLE SEAHAWKS

When the Seattle Seahawks took the field for the first time in the 1976 season, it marked the culmination of a long quest for a National Football League franchise that had its roots in the Pacific Northwest metropolis. As early as 1957, discussion first began about the possibilities of constructing a domed stadium that would assure a professional sports franchise for the city. On June 4, 1974, the NFL awarded its 28th franchise to Seattle to play in the 64,984-seat Kingdome.

A civic suggestion campaign netted 20,365 entries, and 1,741 different names, but "Seahawks" was selected and announced on June 17, 1975. Just a little more than two months later, after a 27-day sale, a campaign ended with the 59,000 season tickets.

On January 3, 1976, Jack Patera, who had been a Minnesota assistant coach, was named the team's first head coach. The Seahawks finished 2-12 in 1976, when they played in the NFC, and 5-9 in 1977, when they moved permanently into the AFC. The Seahawks had winning 9-7 records in both 1978 and 1979, and Patera was named NFL Coach of the Year in '79.

The strike-shortened 1982 season proved to be a transitional year for all of pro football, but no club fit the transitional description better that year than the Seahawks. Patera was removed after six-plus years as head coach. Mike McCormack finished the season as interim head coach and was replaced in 1983 by Chuck Knox, who guided the Seahawks to an 83-67-0 record in nine seasons through the 1991 campaign.

Knox led the Seahawks to the AFC championship game in his first season. Seattle won an AFC West wild-card berth for the first time in its eight-year history and then knocked off Denver and Miami before losing

Seahawks Facts

Team Colors: Blue, Green and Silver
11220 N.E. 53rd Street
Kirkland, Washington 98033
(425) 827-9777
Franchise Granted: June 4, 1974
First Season: 1976
Stadium: The Kingdome was demolished in 2000. The Seahawks are playing at the University of Washington stadium, on new innovative turf. The new Facility opens in 2002.
Training Camp: Eastern Washington University
Cheney, Washington 99004
Fan info: 1-888-NFL-HAWK
AFC Western Division Championship: 1988
Retired Uniform Numbers: #12 (fans/the twelfth man), #80 Steve Largent

to the Los Angeles Raiders 30-14 in the title game.

Once again, in 1984, Knox guided the Seahawks to the playoffs with a 12-4 season. Seattle's success came without ace running back Curt Warner, who led the AFC in rushing as a rookie in 1983 with 1,449 yards. Warner was injured in the first game and missed the rest of the season. Knox led Seattle back to the playoffs in 1987 and to the team's only AFC Western Division championship in 1988. That year, they lost to the eventual AFC champion, the Cincinnati Bengals, in the first playoff round.

The greatest individual star in Seahawks history, wide receiver Steve Largent, retired after the 1989 season as the NFL's all-time leading receiver. At the time of his retirement, Largent held six all-time NFL receiving records. In 1995 he was the first Seahawk to be elected to the Hall of Fame.

During the 1988 season, Ken Behring purchased the majority ownership of the club from the Nordstrom family. On February 11, 1989, he named former Los Angeles Raiders head coach Tom Flores as the team's new president and general manager. Three years later, in January 1992, Flores was named the Seahawks new head coach. In 1995, Flores was replaced by Dennis Erickson, the highly successful coach from the University of Miami. The future of the Seahawks in the Pacific Northwest was secured after Paul Allen purchased the team in 1997 and two years later hired Mike Holmgren as their head coach and general manager.

TAMPA BAY BUCCANEERS

Awarded the National Football League's 27th franchise in 1974 with the first kickoff scheduled for 1976, owner Hugh Culverhouse, a successful Florida tax lawyer and broker, hired John McKay as the first coach of the Tampa Bay Buccaneers. McKay had achieved great success at the University of Southern California with four national championships in his 16 years, and it was McKay who orchestrated the building process that led to the Buccaneers' stunning early success.

After losing a league-record 26 consecutive games, the Bucs broke into the win column at New Orleans on December 11, 1977. Two years later, the Tampa Bay team stunned the football world when it reached the 1979 NFC championship game in only its fourth season. The Bucs clinched the NFC Central title with a dramatic 3-0 win over Kansas City in a driving rainstorm and then defeated Philadelphia 24-17 in playoff action to advance to within one game of the Super Bowl. But in the NFC championship, the Los Angeles Rams prevailed with a hard-fought 9-0 victory.

One of the hallmarks of Tampa Bay's early success was an excellent defense led by Hall of Fame defensive end Lee Roy Selmon, who was the Bucs' first draft choice and the number one pick of the 1976 NFL draft. In his nine-season career, Selmon was named to the NFC Pro Bowl team six times and was named the NFL Defensive Player of the Year in 1979. Offensively, the 1979 Buccaneers were led by quarterback Doug Williams and running back Ricky Bell, who gained 1,263 yards. The Buccaneers reached the playoffs for the second time just two years later in 1981. After winning the NFC Central division championship with a 9-7 record. Similar to 1979, it took a dramatic 20-17 final-week win over the Detroit Lions to secure the title. Selmon on defense and Williams at quarterback once again were key players for the Buccaneers.

Buccaneers Facts

Team Colors: Buccaneer Red, Pewter, Black and Orange
One Buccaneer Place
Tampa, Florida 33607
(813) 870-2700
Franchise Granted: April 24, 1974
First Season: 1976
Stadium: Raymond James Stadium
4201 North Dale Mabry Highway
Tampa, FL 33607
Capacity: 66,321
Grass
Training Camp: University of Tampa
Tampa, Florida 33606
NFC Central Division Championships:
1979, 1981, 1999
Retired Uniform Numbers: #63 Lee Roy Selmon

Although no divisional championships were awarded in the strike-shortened 1982 season, the Bucs qualified for postseason play for the third time in four seasons by winning five of their final six games. A first-round playoff loss to Dallas ended Tampa Bay's season.

McKay retired as coach following the 1984 season after nine years of leading the Buccaneers. In the years since McKay's departure, Leeman Bennett, Ray Perkins, Richard Williamson and Sam Wyche have served as the Tampa Bay head coach but their cumulative record in the first nine post-McKay years was 37-106-0, a .259 winning percentage. With head coach Tony Dungy at the helm and young stars leading the way, the new-look Buccaneers are building a bright future. The Bucs reached the NFC championship game in 1999 before falling to eventual champion St. Louis.

TENNESSEE TITANS

Franchise Owner-President K. S. "Bud" Adams Jr. was one of the founding fathers of the American Football League in 1959. Heisman Trophy winner Billy Cannon from Louisiana State was the first big-name signing of both the Oilers and the AFL. The Oilers were the AFL's first champions, winning back-to-back titles in 1960 and 1961. The team missed a third straight championship in 1962 when it lost 20-17 to the Dallas Texans. At the time, the historic six-quarter contest was the longest professional football game ever played at 77 minutes, 54 seconds.

The Oilers have qualified for the post-season a total of 15 times in the club's history, with AFL playoff appearances coming in 1960, 1961, 1962, 1967 and 1969. Since the AFL-NFL merger in 1970, Houston reached the playoffs 10 times. Included are three straight appearances in 1979, 1980, 1981 and a seven-game string starting in 1987.

The AFL championships Houston won in its first two years of play remain the only league titles the Oilers have claimed. They won four AFL Eastern Division championships in that league's 10-year existence and AFC Central Division titles in 1991 and 1993.

Several coaches contributed to winning seasons in Houston. Lou Rymkus led the Oilers to their first championship in 1960. Wally Lemm coached the 1961 AFL title team. Frank "Pop" Ivy won a divisional championship the next year. Lemm returned to guide the Oilers' 1967 AFL East championship. "Bum" Phillips led the Oilers to three straight playoff appearances in 1979, 1980 and 1981 and Jerry Glanville took the Oilers to post-season play three times in four seasons from 1986 to 1989. Houston turned to Jack Pardee to lead the team in the 1990s. He guided his first four teams to the playoffs. The Oilers won their first divisional championship in 24 years in 1991 and repeated in 1993. Jeff Fisher was named interim head coach in November 1994 and officially given the position in 1995.

Three former Oilers stars are now members of the Pro Football Hall of Fame. The fabled George Blanda, who played 26 years and was the Oilers' quarterback from 1960 to

Titans Facts

Team Color: Navy, Titans Blue, Red, Silver
460 Great Circle Road
Nashville, Tennessee 37228
(615) 565-4000
Franchise Granted: August 14, 1959 as Charter Member of AFL
First Season: 1960
First Season in Tennessee: 1997
First Season as Titans: 1999
Stadium: Adelphia Coliseum
One Titans Way
Nashville, TN 37213
Capacity: 67,000
Natural Grass
Training Camp: Baptist Sports Park
460 Great Circle Road
Nashville, TN 37228
(615) 565-4000
AFL Championships: 1960, 1961
AFC Championships: 1999
AFL Eastern Division Championships:
1960, 1961, 1962, 1967
AFC Central Division Championships:
1991, 1993, 2000
Retired Uniform Numbers: #34 Earl Campbell, #43 Jim Norton, #63 Mike Munchak, #65 Elvin Bethea

1966, was the first to be inducted in 1981. Ken Houston, one of history's great safeties, was elected in 1986 and Earl Campbell, a pile-driving fullback from Texas, was picked in 1991. Four former Oilers stars have had their jerseys retired, including safety Jim Norton, defensive end Elvin Bethea, Campbell and guard Mike Munchak.

In the 1960s, Blanda was a big-yardage maker with his throws to such receivers as Charlie Hennigan, who caught a then-record 101 passes in the 1964 season. The Oilers of the 1980's and early 1990's were powered by quarterback Warren Moon and a host of outstanding receivers.

Houston started its AFL life in Jeppesen Stadium, a high school facility that seated 33,000, before moving to 70,000-seat Rice Stadium in 1965. In 1968, the Oilers moved into the nation's first domed stadium, the air-conditioned Astrodome, becoming the first team in professional football to play indoors on synthetic turf. In 1997, the Oilers became the first NFL team to call Tennessee home when the franchise relocated to the Volunteer State. Two years later, in 1999, the franchise retired the nickname Oilers and became known as the Titans. The change seemed to bring good luck, as the Titans went on to win the AFC Championship that year and earned a trip to Super Bowl XXXIV.

WASHINGTON REDSKINS

Three Super Bowl championships and 13 playoff appearances since 1971 make the Washington Redskins one of the NFL's most dominant teams of the past quarter-century. But the organization's glorious past dates back almost 60 years and includes five world championships overall and some of the most innovative people and ideas the game has ever known. From George Preston Marshall to Jack Kent Cooke, from Vince Lombardi to Joe Gibbs, from Sammy Baugh to John Riggins, plus the NFL's first fight song, marching band and radio network, the Redskins can be proud of an impressive professional football legacy.

George Preston Marshall was awarded the inactive Boston franchise in July, 1932. He originally named the team "Braves" because it used Braves Field, home of the National League baseball team. When the team moved to Fenway Park in July 1933, the name was changed to Redskins. A bizarre situation occurred in 1936, when the Redskins won the NFL Eastern division championship, but Marshall, unhappy with the fan support in Boston, moved the championship game against Green Bay to the Polo Grounds in New York. Their home field advantage taken away by their owner, the Redskins lost. Not surprisingly, the Redskins moved to Washington, D.C. for the 1937 season. Games were played under flood lights in Griffith Stadium with the opener on September 16, 1937. That season also saw the debut of "Slinging Sammy" Baugh, a quarterback from Texas Christian who literally changed the offensive posture of pro foot-

Redskins Facts

Team Colors: Burgundy and gold
Redskin Park
P.O. Box 17247
Washington, D.C. 20041
(703) 478-8900
www.redskins.com
Franchise Granted: July 9, 1932 as the Boston Braves
First Season: 1932
Changed Nickname to Redskins: 1933
Moved to Washington: 1937
Stadium: FedExField
Landover, Maryland 20785
Capacity: 85,000
Grass
Training Camp: Redskin Park
20147 Redskin Park Drive
Ashburn, Va 20147
Super Bowl Championships: XVII, XXII, XXVI
NFL Championships: 1937, 1942
NFC Championships: 1972, 1982, 1983, 1987, 1991
NFL Eastern Division Championships: 1936, 1937, 1940, 1942, 1943, 1945
NFC Eastern Division Championships: 1972, 1982, 1983, 1984, 1987, 1991, 1999
Retired Uniform Numbers: #33 Sammy Baugh

ball with his forward passing in his 16-season career.

The Redskins won five NFL Eastern division titles and NFL championships in 1937 and 1942 during Baugh's tenure. Ray Flaherty was Baugh's first pro coach from 1936-1942 and his 56-26-3 record (.701 percentage) is the best in team history. In 1944, the Redskins formed a radio network to broadcast their games throughout the Southern United States. By 1950, all Redskins games were televised over a network of Southern stations, making Washington the first NFL team to have an entire season of televised games. D.C. Stadium (later changed to Robert F. Kennedy Memorial Stadium) was opened in 1961 and the 55,683-seat stadium was the Redskins home through 1996. In 1997, the Redskins moved into new Jack Kent Cooke Stadium., now called the Fed Ex Field. The state-of-the-art stadium is named in honor of Cooke, who passed away in April 1997. A consecutive sellout streak began in 1966 and is still alive today. No other NFL team can claim that long of a string of sellouts.

In 1969, the legendary Vince Lombardi guided the Redskins to their first winning record in 15 years, but he died of cancer before the 1970 season. George Allen took over in 1971 and coached Washington to 69 victories, five playoff appearances and the 1972 NFC championship in his seven years. Joe Gibbs, who led the Redskins from 1981 to 1992, ranks as the most successful coach in Redskins' history with a 140-65-0 record that produced eight playoff appearances, five NFC Eastern division championships and victories in Super Bowls XVII, XXII and XXVI. He was named NFL Coach of the Year in 1982 and 1983 and elected to the Pro Football Hall of Fame in 1996.

Denver Broncos linebacker John Mobley.

Chapter 13
Trivia

How much does your man really know?

We all know the best way to get information from a man is to quiz him—relentlessly. Really, though, the purpose of this trivia section is to provide insight into some obscure tidbits, details and data to further your quest for football facts.

But, IF a trivial competition comes up, at least you'll be armed. Check out the following Q and A for ammunition.

Q: If an official makes a grabbing motion in front of his face with one hand, what is he signaling?
A: *Facemasking penalty*

Q: With what team did legendary Bill Parcells have his first NFL head-coaching job?
A: *The New York Giants, winning two Super Bowls along the way*

Q: How many timeouts is a team allowed each half?
A: *Three*

Q: How many Super Bowls have the New Orleans Saints won?
A: *Trick question. None*

Q: How many yards is an offense penalized for illegal motion?
A: *Five*

Q: How many yards is an offense penalized for a delay of game?
A: *Five*

Q: How many yards is an offense penalized for holding?
A: *Ten*

Q: When measuring a first down, what part of the ball is used: the forward point or the backward point?
A: *The forward point*

Q: If an official extends both his arms straight above his head, what is he signaling?
A: *Touchdown (or a successful field goal or PAT)*

Q: What jersey number did Hall of Fame quarterback Terry Bradshaw wear: Number 4, Number 8, Number 12 or Number 16?
A: *Number 12*

Q: Which one of the following NFLers did not play at Notre Dame: Jerome Bettis, Tim Brown, Elvis Grbac, or Rick Mirer?

A: *Grbac, whose college career at Michigan ended in 1992.*

Q: Former Cincinnati Bengals running back Ickey Woods had a touchdown dance that became famous during his team's run to the AFC Championship in 1988. What was the dance called?

A: *The Ickey Shuffle*

Q: Name the former defensive lineman who is the lone Tampa Bay Buccaneers representative in the Pro Football Hall of Fame?

A: *Lee Roy Selmon, who made six trips to the Pro Bowl in a nine-year career.*

Q: Who won more games, including playoffs, as San Francisco 49ers coach: George Seifert or Bill Walsh?

A: *George Seifert.*

Q: Where did running back Barry Sanders play in college?

A: *Oklahoma State.*

Q: New York Jets quarterback Joe Namath guaranteed a victory in Super Bowl III and delivered. What team did they beat?

A: *The Baltimore Colts.*

Q: Where did former Dolphins quarterback Dan Marino play in college?

A: *University of Pittsburgh.*

Q: Name the Chicago Bears quarterback, who in 1995 set team single-season records for passing yards and touchdown passes?

A: *Erik Kramer.*

Q: Who has been the NFL Commissioner since 1989?

A: *Paul Tagliabue.*

Q: Where did former San Francisco quarterback Steve Young go to college?

A: *Brigham Young University, where he won the Davey O'Brien award.*

Q: Which position did Hall-of-Famer Don Maynard play: cornerback or wide receiver?

A: *Wide receiver. He was inducted into the Hall of Fame in 1987.*

Q: If a kickoff clears the opposing team's goal posts, what is the ruling?

A: *It's a touchback. There are no extra points awarded to the opposing team.*

Q: What is former quarterback Boomer Esianson's real first name?

A: *Norman*

Q: When was wide receiver Antonio Freeman's first season in the NFL?

A: *1995. He played for the Green Bay Packers primarily as a punt returner.*

Q: By what nickname is Arizona Cardinals quarterback Jake Plummer known?

A: *Jake the Snake*

Q: Name any one of the six players whose jersey numbers have been retired by the Philadelphia Eagles?

A: *Steve Van Buren #15, Tom Brookshier # 40, Pete Retzlaff # 44, Chuck Bednarik # 60,*

Al Wistert # 70, and Jerome Brown # 99

Q: Who is the only NFL player to be named Defensive Player of the Year and have a top 10 musical single in the same season (hint 1994)?
A: *"Primetime" Deion Sanders. The hit single was "Must be the Money."*

Q: Who proceeded Dennis Green as the Minnesota Vikings head coach?
A: *Jerry Burns; under whom the Vikings were 55-46 and made the playoffs three times from 1986 to 1991.*

Q: With what team did Hall of Fame linebacker Jack Ham play for his entire NFL career (1971-1982)?
A: *Pittsburgh Steelers, with whom Ham had 32 interceptions and was an eight time Pro Bowler.*

Q: About which Hall of Fame lineman was the book *Fatso* written?
A: *Art Donovan at 6'3" and 265 lbs., he was an offensive tackle who played 10 of his 12 pro seasons with the Baltimore Colts.*

Q: True or False? Former Buffalo head coach Marv Levy once coached the Kansas City Chiefs.
A: *True. Levy had a 31-42 record as Chiefs coach from 1978 to 1992.*

Q: True or False? Prior to the 1997 season, the Tampa Buccaneers had never appeared on *Monday Night Football.*
A: *False. They played three times on Monday night: a 23-0 loss to the Chicago Bears in 1980, a 23-17 defeat of the Miami Dolphins at home in 1982, and a 12-9 loss in over-time at the Green Bay Packers in 1983.*

Q: What was long time coach Ted Marchibroda during his NFL playing days; a center, guard, or quarterback?
A: *Quarterback. Marchibroda played in 1953, '55 and '56 with the Pittsburgh Steelers and '57 for the Chicago Bears. His only season as a starter was in 1956 with the Steelers.*

Q: Who was the last player to return a punt for a touchdown in a Super Bowl.
A: *Trick question. It has never been done.*

Q: How many NFL rushing titles did Walter Payton win in his Hall Of Fame career?
A: *The NFL's all-time leading rusher won only ONE rushing title in 1977 with 1,852 yards.*

Q: What is the difference between "Encroachment" and "Offsides?"
A: *Encroachment is called when a defensive player enters the neutral zone and makes contact with the opponent before the ball is snapped. A defensive player is offsides when any part of his body is beyond the line of scrimmage when the ball is snapped.*

Q: Troy Aikman was the Dallas Cowboys career leader in passing yards, but he doesn't yet own the team record for touchdown passes. Who does?
A: *Danny White, with 155.*

Q: Who was a defensive back for the Washington Redskins and the Minnesota Vikings, had 81 career interceptions, the league's all-time high in that category, amd was a Hall of Famer in 2000?
A: *Paul Krause*

Q: What head coach coined the term "Nickel Defense?"

A: *George Allen, head coach of the Los Angeles Rams and the Washington Redskins. He led the Redskins to the Super Bowl.*

Q: What two coaches have been the only ones to win a national collegiate championship and a Super Bowl title?

A: *Jimmy Johnson and Barry Switzer. Both men coached at Dallas, and led the Cowboys to Super Bowl victories.*

Q: What is retired Miami Dolphins quarterback Dan Marino's middle name?

A: *Constantine. Hall of Fame quarterback Johnny Unitas has the same middle name.*

Q: What quarterback was the first to have a pass intercepted and returned for a touchdown in each of the first three games of the season?

A: *John Elway became the first in 1984 against the Chargers, Jets, and Raiders, all losses.*

Q: What team drafted University of Louisville quarterback Johnny Unitas in 1955?

A: *The Steelers, who wound up cutting Unitas, allowing the Colts to pick him up on waivers in 1956.*

Q: True or False? NFL officials once blew horns to signal penalties?

A: *True. Horns were used to indicate infractions before the penalty flag was introduced in 1948.*

Q: What star quarterback first used the term "Hail Mary" to describe a late game heave to the end zone?

A: *Roger Staubach of the Dallas Cowboys.*

Q: Who was the number one overall pick in the 1998 draft?

A: *Peyton Manning, a quarterback from Tennessee, who was selected by the Indianapolis Colts.*

Q: Who is the New Orleans Saints all-time leader in passing yards and touchdown passes?

A: *Peyton's dad, Archie Manning, who threw for 21,734 yards and 115 touchdowns with the team from 1971 to 1982.*

Q: True or False? No Super Bowl ever has gone into overtime.

A: *True.*

Q: By what nickname was Hall of Fame running back Walter Payton known?

A: *Sweetness*

Q: Quarterback Jeff George finished his college career at Illinois, but he spent his freshman year at another Big Ten school. From which Hoosier State School did the Indianapolis native transfer to Illinois?

A: *George played for Purdue University before transferring to the University of Illinois.*

Q: Who is the only person to have played in the Super Bowl and the World Series?

A: *Dallas Cowboys cornerback Deion Sanders played in Super Bowls with the Cowboys and San Francisco 49ers, and in the World Series with the Atlanta Braves.*

Chapter 14
Glossary

Accept A Penalty
to agree that a penalty called against the other team should be enforced.

Accrued Season
when a player spends six or more regular-season games on a club's active or inactive list,meaning that he was on the injured reserve list or was physically unable to perform.

Adjustments
changes in the general game plan and other offensive and defensive strategies a team is using based on the observations and opinions of the members of the coaching staff on the field and in the press box (coaches in the press box usually join the rest of the team in the locker room during halftime).

Advance
to run forward with the football, or pass the ball, in order to give one's team better field position.

Agent
a person who represents players during contract negotiations. Many agents are attorneys; some are friends and relatives of the players they represent. Agents are banned from most college campuses.

Alignment
the way the defense lines up at its line of scrimmage before the ball is centered.

All Star Game
an exhibition game between two teams consisting of the best players in one or more leagues.

All-American
a college football player who has been determined by sportswriters to be the best among all college players at his position during a season.

All-pro
an NFL player who has been determined by sportswriters to be the best among all NFL players at his position during a season.

All-star
a player who has been determined to be the best at his or her position during one season of a league or at a certain level of competition.

And Long
with several yards to go for a first down.

Arena Football
a version of the game that is played in an indoor stadium on a smaller field than in other kinds of football and has some special rules. Most players play both offensive and defensive positions.

Artificial Turf
a surface on some football fields that is made from synthetic material in place of regular grass.

Assistant Coach
a coach on a football team who assists the head coach and may have various responsibilities for the team such as coaching the team's offensive or defensive unit or coaching players in individual positions, such as the linemen or wide receivers.

AstroTurf

a trademark for a type of artificial grass. A synthetic carpet-like playing field surface whose name derives from the Houston Astrodome, where the first of this kind of playing surface was installed.

At Home

on a team's home field.

Audible

a play change called at the line of scrimmage by the quarterback. He makes a switch in the play from the one he had just announced in the team huddle and alerts the other offensive players by calling a predetermined set of signals. Also called a check off.

Back Judge

an official who counts the number of players on the defense, who watches for interference infractions and other violations on passes far beyond the line of scrimmage, and who calls penalties like clipping near the spot on the field where punts and kickoffs are caught and returned.

Backfield

the area behind the offensive line where offensive backs line up before the start of plays.

Backpedal

to run or jog backward.

Backup

a second or third string player.

Backward Pass

any pass that is not a forward pass.

Balance Formation

equal number of offensive linemen on each side of the center.

Balanced Offense

team capable of moving the ball equally well by running or passing.

Ball Boys

attendants, usually young persons, who assist football officials in keeping footballs on both sidelines and putting new ones in play when needed.

Ball Control

1) describing a type of offensive strategy in which mostly rushing plays are attempted, with passes thrown only when necessary. Also called Conservative.
2) ball possession for a sustained period of time during the game.

Ball Carrier

a player running with the football.

Beat/Beat A Defender

to be able to get far enough away from the defender so that he has no chance of breaking up a pass.

Big Play

a play that results in a long gain or a touchdown, or a defensive play that results in a change of possession or a score.

Black Out

to require that a television station or network not broadcast a certain football game. Usually due to the seats not being sold out.

Blast

every team has the blast or dive run in its playback, as it's the simplest of carries. Usually led by a blocking fullback, the running back takes a quick handoff from the quarterback and hits a hole between an offensive guard and a tackle. On some teams, this run ends up between a guard and the center. The offense calls this run when it needs a yard or two for a first down. The runner lowers his head and hopes to move the pile before the middle linebacker tackles him.

Blocking

the term used when offensive players attempt to block, or push opposing players away from the quarterback or other ball carrier, using their bodies or limbs. Special teams players may also block on a kick return, and defensive players may block for a teammate who recovers a fumble or intercepts a pass.

Blocking Assignments

part of offensive play plans indicating which players on the defense are going to be blocked by each player on the offense.

Blocking Sled

a large platform with one or several large pads against which players, especially linemen, practice blocking. A coach often stands on top of the sled and gives directions, and the sled moves backward on rails when the players hit the pads.

Blow The Call

to make a mistake in calling or not calling a penalty.

Body Block

type of blocking in which a player turns sideways and throws one whole side of his body into the midsection or thighs of the defender.

Bomb

a pass pattern in which the quarterback throws the ball high into the air and far down the field to a receiver. If completed, this pass can result in a long gain and often a touchdown.

Bootleg

a running play in which the quarterback fakes a handoff to a running back, hides the ball against his hip and either runs with it around the end, pitches it out to another back or passes it. (same as quarterback keeper)

Boundary Line

the white border surrounding all four sides of the field, including the sidelines and the end line, signifying the area out of the field of play.

Bowl Bid

an invitation to play against another team in one of the college bowl games.

Bowl Game

a Division 1-A college football game played at the end of the season between two of the best college teams.

Break Up A Pass

to touch or bat a passed football so that it hits the ground before the receiver can catch it.

Breaking A Tackle

the ball carrier is hit by a defender, but avoids being tackled.

Broken Play

an offensive play that develops when the original plan becomes impossible, either because the defense anticipated the play or an offensive player failed his assignment. (also called a busted play)

Bullet Pass

a hard-thrown pass that travels in a straight line.

Bump And Run

a pass play in which defensive backs to slow down receivers. The defender bumps the receiver at the start of the play and attempts to keep his hands on him legally for five yards before running downfield with him.

Burned

when a defensive player does not carry out his assignment and his man makes a long run or catches a pass.

Button Hook

a pass pattern in which the receiver goes downfield and U-turns back sharply to receive the ball. Also known as a curl pattern.

Bye

When the one or two teams with the best regular-season records do not play during the first week, or round, of playoff games, but wait to play the teams who do play and win the first playoff games.

Bye Week

a week in which a football team does not have a game.

Cadence

the last in a series of numbers, words or sounds the quarterback calls at the line of scrimmage designating when the ball is snapped.

Call

selection of an offensive play.

Call A Penalty

to throw a penalty flag and signal for a stoppage of the game after the completion of the current play, if the play has already started when a violation has been spotted.

Call A Play

to announce to an offensive unit or a defensive unit which play the unit is to run on the next down.

Captains

a group of players on a football team who may be the best or the most senior players on the team. Each team has at least one captain for its offense, defense and special teams, though there may be several captains on a team. The captains have special responsibilities, such as representing their teams during the coin toss and officially accepting or declining penalties for their teams.

Career-Ending

describing an injury so severe that it prevents a player from ever playing football again.

Carry

the act of running with the ball. In statistical charts, a runner's rushing attempts are listed as carries.

Center

1) the offensive player who hikes or snaps the ball to the quarterback at the start of each play. The term center comes from the fact that this player is flanked on either side by a guard and a tackle. He's the middleman or center in a contingent of five offensive linemen or blockers. He handles the ball on every play and also snaps the ball to the punter and holder

Chain Gang

the six assistant officials along the sidelines who collectively handle the down indicator, yardage chain, drive start and forward stake indicator.

Chains

two poles connected by a chain that is exactly 10 yards long. The chains are used by officials to indicate the distance necessary for the ball to be advanced by the offense in order to get a first down, and also for measurements when it is not certain that the ball has been advanced more than 10 yards. The poles have bright reddish-orange trim (with black and white bars in the NFL) with a circular piece on top, and are at least five feet tall. The poles are connected to the ends of a small chain that is exactly 10 yards long.

Championship Game

a post-season football game, the winner of which is the champion of the league.

Change Of Field

between the first and second, and the third and fourth quarters, the teams reverse ends of the field and change goals to defend. The ball is put in play at the point corresponding exactly to the point at the other end of the field where the ball became dead at the end of the previous quarter, and in exactly the same way as if play had not been stopped.

Change Of Possession

when the team that was on defense goes on offense and vice versa.

Check Off

see Audible
a play change called at the line of scrimmage by the quarterback. He makes a switch in the play from the one he had just announced in the team huddle and alerts the other offensive players by calling a predetermined set of signals.

Chop Block

this play is used within three yards of the line of scrimmage to slow down the opposition's pass rush. A lineman blocks down low with his shoulders and arms, attempting to take the defender's legs from underneath him and stop his momentum. If this play occurs three yards or more beyond the line of scrimmage, the blocker is penalized 15 yards.

Chuck

the defense is allowed to give an eligible receiver one block, shove or push within five yards of the line of scrimmage.

Chucking

warding off an opponent who is in front of a defender by contacting him with a quick extension of arms, followed by the return of arm(s) to a flexed position, thereby breaking the original contact.

Claim On Waivers

to sign a player after he had been released by another team.

Cleats

small stubs or spikes on the soles of football shoes that help keep players from slipping by digging into the grass as they run on the football field.

Clinch

to be assured of ending the season in first place or with a playoff spot by being more games-up over the team in second place than there are games left in the season.

Clip

to block a player who does not have the ball by either hitting him below the waist while moving up from behind or throwing the body across the back of his legs.

Clipping

an illegal block that occurs when a player throws his body across the back of an opponents legs, or hits the opponent below the waist while moving up from behind.

Close Line Play

the area between the positions normally occupied by the offensive tackles, extending three yards on each side of the line of scrimmage.

Coaches

personnel on a football team who are responsible for instructing and training players and directing a team's play during a game.

Coaching Box

a six-foot-wide solid white border just outside both sidelines that runs between the two 32-yard lines, in which only a team's head coach and game officials or chain crew personnel are allowed during a game.

Coffin Corner

the area of the field close to the intersection of a sideline and the opposing team's goal line. Punters aim for this area to pin an opponent deep into his own territory.

Coin Toss

the procedure at the beginning of a football game by which the referee tosses a coin into the air in the middle of the field, and the captain of one of the teams has to predict which side of the coin (heads or tails) will be facing up when the coin lands on the ground. If the captain is right, his team wins the toss and gets the choice of receiving the opening kickoff or deciding which goal to defend.

Combination Blocking

a style of blocking in which two players are assigned to block one defensive player, each approaching the defender from a different side.

Comeback

a passing pattern which is used when the receiver is extremely fast. On the comeback the receiver runs hard downfield, between 12 and 20 yards, and then turns to face the football. The comeback route generally is run along the sideline. To work effectively, the quarterback throws the ball before the receiver turns, expecting to land the pass where the receiver will stop and turn.
(also called a timing pass)

Completion

a quarterback's pass that is successfully caught by a teammate.

Conference

an organization of football teams at roughly the same competitive level.

Conservative

describing a type of offensive strategy in which mostly rushing plays are attempted, with passes thrown only when necessary. Also called Ball Control.

Contain Defense

to play conservatively, so as to allow short yardage rather than a score.

Conversion

1) the extra point attempt scored after a touchdown by a kick, pass or run.
2) a first down earned on third or fourth down by having advanced the ball the necessary 10 yards.

Corner Blitz

a type of blitz in which a cornerback rushes in toward the quarterback.

Cornerback

a defender who lines up in the defensive backfield, close to the line of scrimmage in a corner of the defensive formation, responsible to cover offensive pass receivers. Also called a defensive back. There are usually two cornerbacks playing defense at a time.

Count

the signals that a quarterback shouts to the offense before the snap of the ball.

Counter

a running play desinged to go against the intended pursuit of the defense, that proceeds after a fake has been made to one running back heading in another direction.

Covered

closely guarded by a defensive back or another defensive player.

Covering

the defense's tactic in guarding an offensive pass receiver to prevent the offense from completing a pass. A defender may run alongside the receiver and seek to deflect or intercept the ball, but may not make contact with the receiver until the receiver touches the ball.

Crackback

eligible receivers who take or move to a position more than two yards outside the tackle may not block an opponent below the waist if they then move back inside to block.

Crackback Block

a legal block by a wide receiver within five yards of the line of scrimmage, as long as the opponent is not hit from behind or below the waist.

Crossbar

the horizontal part of the goal post.

Crossing Pattern

a pass pattern in which one receiver crosses the middle of the field a few yards in front of another receiver. This is effective because it's designed for the receiver to beat his defender by running across the field. The receiver can line up on the right side of the line of scrimmage, run straight for 10 yards, and then cut quickly to his left. When the receiver cuts, he attempts to lose the man veering him with either a head or shoulder fake or a quick stutter-step.

Curl

a pass pattern in which the receiver runs downfield and then curls back toward the line of scrimmage.

Cut

to release a player from a team due to lack of performance, or for other reasons such as salary cap or disciplinary problems.

Cut Back

a quick change of direction by the person carrying the ball, in an attempt to avoid the tackle.

Cut-Off Block

generally used on running plays, which are designed to allow a defensive player to come free, or untouched, across the line of scrimmage. After that happens, an offensive lineman deliberately gets in the way of this on-rushing defender. This block is sometimes called an angle block because the offensive lineman hits the defensive player from the side, or from an angle.

Dead Ball

1) describing a football that cannot be advanced because the play is over or has not yet started.
2) a ball not in play. The period between downs.

Decline A Penalty
accepting the result of the previous play even though the other team committed an infraction.

Deep
a pass that is thrown several yards downfield.

Deep Man
a punt or kickoff receiver, a pass receiver or a defensive back who is 30 to 40 yards behind his teammates.

Deep Threat
this is the wide receiver who can outrun people and run the deep pass patterns that result in big gains in yardage and, often, touchdowns. The presence of such a receiver allows an offensive team to "stretch" a defense, in that a man running deep can open areas for other receivers running shorter patterns "underneath." Not every team has a legitimate deep threat. However, those that do have many more offensive options in their arsenal.

Defense
the team that does not have possession of the ball at the beginning of the play and seeks to prevent the offense from advancing and also tries to gain possession of the ball for its own offensive unit

Defensive Back
a player on the defense whose main responsibility is to cover a receiver going out for a pass but who may also tackle a ballcarrier and rush the quarterback on blitzes.
There are usually four defensive backs.

Defensive Backfield
the defensive players who play behind the linebackers in the backfield. The players in the defensive backfield are also called defensive backs (cornerbacks and safeties)

Defensive Coordinator
the coach in charge of the defensive players. He decides what defensive schemes to run. The defensive coordinator meets with half the team on a typical practice day and prepares their defensive strategy by analyzing the offensive unit of an opposing team.

Defensive End
1) a player on the defense who lines up on one end of the defensive line.
2) the down linemen on the outside of each tackle in a four-three defensive alignment or on each side of the nose tackle in a three-four alignment.

Defensive Holding
a penalty called on an defensive player when he tries to restrict the movement of an offensive player by grabbing on to that player's body or uniform.

Defensive Line Coach
a coach who works exclusively with the defensive linemen. He trains players on individual technique, run stopping, gap control and pass rushing.

Defensive Lineman
two ends and one or two tackles depending on the particular defensive formation being used. Defensive linemen will rush the quarterback on passing plays and try to stop running plays at or near the line of scrimmage.

Defensive Offside
a penalty called on the defense when any part of a defensive player's body moves over the line of scrimmage before the ball is snapped and causes an offensive player directly opposite to react. This premature movement is more apt to occur when the intensity of the game rises, or a big offensive gain is at stake.

Defensive Pass Interference
penalty called when a defender interferes, by using physical contact, with an offensive receiver attempting to catch the ball.

Defensive Tackle
one of the two down linemen between the ends in a four-three defensive alignment. In a three-four, if one lines up between the ends, he is called a nose tackle.

Deflection

one circumstance that can happen when a quarterback throws the ball. A deflection is when a defensive player uses his hands or arms to knock down a pass before it reaches the receiver. This act usually occurs near the line of scrimmage when defensive linemen jump, arms raised, into a quarterback's visual passing lane. A successful deflection may lead to an interception or incompletion.

Delay

a running play that proceeds after a fake has been made to one running back heading in another direction. Sometimes two linemen will start to the right, in front of a back on what appears to be a sweep, but the quarterback will merely fake the handoff or backwards toss in that direction. Ultimately, after a second of delay, the ball will be slipped to the second back following the remaining linemen in the opposite or counter direction to the initial flow. (see counter)

Delay Of Game

a team's failure to be ready to start a game or down within the 40 seconds between lay. Any action that intentionally delays the start of the next down.

Depth Chart

a ranking of the players on a football team. At the top are the starters or first-string players, followed by the second, third and perhaps lower strings.

Dime Back

when the defense has six players in the secondary, the sixth player is called a dime back, because he's the second nickel back.

Disqualify

to prohibit a player from playing any more in a game.

Dive

a running play which is the equivalent of the sneak in terms of distance required and simplicity, only the ball is immediately handed to the closest running back for a forward plunge (or dive) over the tangle of linemen at the line of scrimmage and land beyond the first-down marker or in the end zone.

Division

a unit of a football league or conference consisting of a small group of its teams.

Division Champion

the team in each division with the most wins at the end of the regular season or that won in a tie-breaker.

Double Coverage

when two defenders are assigned to cover one receiver. This will often occur in man-to-man coverage to defend against the most dangerous receiver on the offensive team. However, complex zone coverage may also result in a type of double-team, as defenders "roll" or rotate the zone based on their read of the pass patterns being run. This approach is designed to stop certain types of passes as opposed to shutting down one particular individual receiving threat.

Double Foul

a foul by each team during the same down.

Double-Team

a style of blocking in which two players are assigned to block one defensive player, each approaching the defender from a different side.

Down

1) when a runner is contacted by a defensive player and any part of the runner's body, other than the feet or hands, touched the ground as a result of the contact. Or, if a runner falls and defender touches him while he's down, the player is "down" and all action stops. A runner is also "down" when his forward progress is stopped or he declares himself "down". A period of action that starts when the ball is put into play and ends when the ball is ruled dead (the play is complete). The offense gets four downs to advance the ball 10 yards. If it fails to do so, it must surrender the ball to the opponent, usually by punting on the fourth down.

Down And Out

a pass pattern where a receiver runs straight downfield, then turns sharply outside near the sideline.

Downfield

The direction the team with the ball takes on the field. Technically, the area three yards beyond the line of scrimmage.

Down Indicator

a four-foot high pole topped with four numbered flip cards: 1,2,3,4. The cards indicate the current down. The pole, located along the sidelines, marks the ball location at the start of each down.

Down Linemen

the defensive players who line up in a three-or-four point stance at the line of scrimmage opposite the offensive team's interior linemen.

Down Marker

a vertical post carried by one of the officials on the chain gang. The post has a sign on top, which displays the number of the current down to players and spectators.

Down Position

the three-point stance position in which offensive linemen must be during the quarterback count before the snap of the ball.

Downing

when the ball carrier touches his knee to the ground in his own end zone thereby signaling a touchback, and ending the play intentionally.

Draft

the formal procedure of a fixed number of rounds each year when pro teams pick players from the college ranks.

Draft Choice

a college player who has been selected by a pro club. The team that drafts him has the exclusive right for a limited time to sign him to a contract. No other team in the league can bid for his service.

Draw Play

a running play in which the quarterback retreats as though to pass, thus drawing in the defensive linemen, then hands the ball off to a back who runs through the gap left by on-charging defenders.

Drive

1) the movement by the offensive team downfield through a repeated series of plays. Also, the ability of the ball carrier to gain yardage despite defenders.
2) a series of consecutive offensive plays by one team.

Drive Block

straightforward blocking technique by which the offensive linemen drive the defenders backwards as best they can so that the back can advance after a simple handoff.

Drop Back

when the quarterback takes a few steps back from the line of scrimmage in an attempt to pass.

Eat Up The Clock

to keep the game clock running by having runners tackled in bounds so that the game will finish quickly with the team maintaining its lead and winning the game.

Eject

to disqualify a player from a game.

Eligible Receiver

the players who can legally catch passes. On the offensive team, they are the two ends on the scrimmage line and the players in the backfield who line up at least one yard behind the line of scrimmage. All offensive players become eligible after the ball touches an eligible receiver or a defensive player. All players on the defensive team are always eligible to intercept a pass.

Encroachment

when a defensive player enters the neutral zone before the ball is snapped and makes contact with the opposition. It's a five-yard penalty, and the offense repeats the down.

End Around

an offensive play where a tight end or wide receiver circles back behind the quarterback for a lateral or handoff.

End Lines

the two boundaries on a football field that are 10 yards beyond the goal lines.

End Zone

the 10-yard area at each end of the football field from the goal line to the end line and sideline to sideline where a touchdown can be scored.

Endorsement

when a professional football player or coach is paid to appear in a television commercial or other form of advertisement for a commercial product.

Equipment

items football players wear that are designed to protect specific parts of their bodies in collisions with other players, other players' equipment, and the ground.

Exhibition Game

games on a football team's schedule, usually played before the regular season begins, that are not considered official games. They are not counted in the standings, and the players' performances in the games are not included in individual or team statistics for the season.

Expansion Draft

the supplemental draft held to accommodate the formation of new teams in years when the NFL adds one or more franchises.

Expansion Team

a new team granted an NFL franchise. The team will be called an "expansion team" during its first season.

Expire

when the clock reaches 00:00.

Extra Point Attempt

after a touchdown, the scoring team is allowed an extra point try during one scrimmage down. The ball may be spotted anywhere between the hash marks, two or more yards from the goal line. A successful attempt, or conversion, scores one point for a kick through the goal posts or two points for running or passing the ball over the goal line.

Extra Points

a kick, worth one point, that's typically attempted after every touchdown. The ball is placed on either the two-yard line (NFL) or the three-yard line (college and high school) and is generally kicked from inside the 10-yard line after being snapped to the holder. It must sail between the uprights and above the crossbar of the goal posts to be considered good. Also known as a point after touchdown.

Face Mask

metal or hard plastic bars that are joined to the sides of a football helmet and curve around the open front roughly parallel with the player's mouth. Another bar may extend vertically from the forehead part of the helmet down to the horizontal bars. Also called a face guard.

Face Mask Foul

a penalty that arises when a player grabs the face mask of an opposing player's helmet during play.

Fair Catch

a play in which a punt returnee waves one hand in the air as the punt is coming down. This means that the returner will not run with the ball after catching it, and it also means that the members of the punting team must allow the returner to catch the ball. If the returner catches the ball after signaling a fair catch, the play is immediately over and the returner's team will take over on offense at the spot the ball is caught.

Fake (fake a handoff)

to pretend possession of the ball; to stimulate handing the ball to a player, but keep it or give it to another player; or deceive a defender by moving in one direction and then cutting sharply to another.

Fake Punt

a play in which an offense lines up on fourth down as though it's going to punt, but after the ball is snapped tries to run or pass the ball for a first down.

False Start

a penalty called when the offense moves before the snap of the ball, regardless of whether that player actually crosses the line of scrimmage.

Field Goal

a three-point play scored by the offensive team place kicking the ball from scrimmage above the opposing team's crossbar and between the uprights of the goal post.

Field Goal Range

a distance close enough to the goal line of an opponent so that a team has a good chance of kicking a field goal.

Field Judge

an official who calls penalties on forward passes and on punts and kickoffs and who, when present among the crew of officials, also indicates when the play clock should be started or stopped.

Field Position

the location of the ball on the field. When the offense has the ball near the opposition's goal line, it is said to have "good" field position.

First Down

to advance the ball the required 10 yards within four attempts to achieve a first down.

First String

describing players who are highest on a team's depth chart, or the teams starters.

First-Year Player

a player who spent the preceding season on an NFL practice squad, was injured and never played before, or played in another league such as The CFL or Arena, and isn't considered a rookie
by professional standards.

Five-Step Drop

when a quarterback takes five steps backward after the snap.

Flag

a small yellow piece of cloth that an official tosses into the air to indicate that he has seen a rules violation during a play.

Flag Football

A type of non-tackle football in which all players wear detachable pieces of fabric around their waists and a ballcarrier is ruled down when a player on the other team de-flags the ballcarrier.

Flagrant

an infraction that was clearly and deliberately committed.

Flak Jacket

pads around a player's abdomen that offer protection to parts of the body, the ribs in particular, that are not protected by the lower shoulder pads (also called flak jacket).

Flanker

a player who catches passes, also known in more general terms as a wide receiver. In an offensive formation, he usually lines up outside the tight end, off the line of scrimmage.

False Start

when an offensive lineman in a stance or set position moves prematurely prior to the snap of the ball. Five yard penalty, and replay of the down result.

Flat

the area of the field between the hash marks and the sideline and in close proximity to the line of scrimmage. A pass, generally to a running back, in this particular spot is described as a flat pass.

Flea-flicker

a deceptive offensive play designed to make the defense think it's going to be a running play. The quarterback hands the ball off to the back, who laterals or pitches back to the quarterback, who then passes the ball.

Fly

this is a 20- to 40-yard pass, generally to a receiver on the quarterback's throwing side. The receiver, who is aligned very wide and near the sidelines, runs as fast as he can down the sideline, hoping to lose the defensive man in the process. This play is designed to loosen up the defense, making it believe that the quarterback and the receiver have the ability to throw deep whenever they want to.

Forced Fumble

forcing the ball away from a receiver after he gains possession of the ball. Defensive backs have been known to use both hands to reach and pull the ball away from the receiver's grasp. Also known as stripping the ball.

Forklift

when a defensive lineman lifts an offensive lineman off the ground, moving him aside as he rushes the quarterback.

Formation

distinguishes the way the two teams line up at the line of scrimmage before a down begins. The words "formation" "offensive formation" and "set" are used for the offense.

Forward Pass

a pass thrown in the direction of the defensive goal line after leaving the passer's hands and before touching another player.

Forward Progress

the end of advancement by a ball carrier.

Foul

an infraction of the game rules and subject to a yardage penalty, and in some cases, a loss of down or disqualification.

Four Point Stance

the placing of two hands on the ground when lining up at the scrimmage line.

Four-Three, Three-Four Formation

two typical defensive formations reflecting the number of linemen and linebackers. The four-three describes four linemen (two tackles and two ends) and three linebackers while the three-four describes three linemen (one nose tackle and two ends) and four linebackers.

Franchise Player

a team designates only one of its players as a franchise player. This player must be paid a minimum of the average of the top five salaries at his position or 120 percent of his previous salary, whichever is greater. If the player declines this salary increase and wants even more money, the club can designate him as an exclusive rights player, and the player can negotiate with other teams for a better contract. However, his team can match the new club's offer or receive two first-round draft choices as compensation.

Free Agent

an eligible collegiate player who has not been drafted by the NFL or a pro player who has played out his contract or has been unconditionally released without another team in the league claiming him. He is free to negotiate and sign a contract with any team.

Free Ball

loose, live ball.

Free Kick

a kickoff or safety kick. It may be a place-kick, dropkick, or punt, except a punt may not be used on a kickoff following a touchdown, successful field goal, or to begin each half or overtime period. A tee cannot be used on a fair-catch or safety kick.

Free Play

a play in which the offense knows that a penalty, usually an offside penalty, is going to be called against the defense. The offense often tries a daring play like a long pass, with the realization that even if the pass is incomplete or intercepted, the penalty against the defense will result in the offense still having the ball farther upfield from the line of scrimmage.

Free Safety

a defensive player who lines up the deepest in the secondary. A free safety is the equivalent of baseball's center field. He defends the deep middle of the field and seldom has man-to-man responsibilities. The defensive backfield player between the cornerbacks who usually lines up on the opposite side of the ball from the offensive team's tight end but is free to roam to break up or intercept any forward pass thrown over the middle or deep into the side-lines.

Front Line

the players who line up at the line of scrimmage on both offense and defense.

Front Office

the management of a professional team.

Fullback
a running back who blocks for the runner, stays in the backfield to protect the quarterback, and occasionally swings out of the backfield to catch a pass.

Fumble
a ball in play that is dropped or knocked from ones hands.

Gadget Play
a play that involves unusual actions, such as a running back flipping the ball back to the quarterback after receiving a handoff.

Game Ball
a football that is traditionally awarded by a team to a player or players who performed especially well during the game or who were especially responsible for the team winning.

Game Clock
the clock on the scoreboard which keeps track of time remaining in each quarter.

Game Plan
a plan of action designed by the head coach and his assistants to use in a game.

Gang Tackling
two or more defensive men hitting the ball carrier and overpowering him.

Gap
the open space between players along the line of scrimmage when they are aligned.

General Manager
the team executive who directs the day-to-day team operations, including player trades and contracts.

Give
a handoff of the ball.

Giveaway
when a team turns the ball over to the other team.

Go For Two
to attempt a two-point conversion.

Go Long
to go far down the field to receive a pass.

Go Pattern Pass Play
a pass pattern in which the receiver runs as fast as possible straight down the field.

Goal Area
in Canadian football, the section at each end of the field that extends 20 yards out from the dead line to the goal line.

Goal Line
the line between the field of play and the end zone over which a team must move the ball to score a touchdown. The goal line is 10 yards in from the end line.

Goal Posts
two vertical posts connected by a crossbar, at each end of the field. The kicking team must kick the ball between the vertical posts and above the crossbar for a field goal or extra point conversion.

Goal To Go
describing an offensive series in which the offense starts the first down fewer than 10 yards from its opponent's goal line.

Goat
the player blamed for a team's loss.

Going To The Pass
attempting mostly passing plays.

Good Field Position
when a team has possession of the football in an area of the field from which they can be expected to score in the next few offensive series of plays.

Gridiron
a term used to describe the football field.

Ground Game
running plays.

Grounding
intentionally throwing the ball away when there is no defensive pressure on the passer.

Guard

a member of the offensive line. There are two guards on every play, and they line up either side of the offensive center. The guards protect the quarterback from an inside pass rush; they block defenders immediately over them and also swing out and run toward either end, looking to block any defender when the ball carrier runs wide.

Hail Mary

a passing play in which as many eligible receivers as possible run toward or into the other team's end zone, and the quarterback throws a very long pass downfield in hopes to connect with one of the receivers. The name of this play comes from the first words of a Catholic prayer, implying that this pass is so desperate it requires divine intervention.

Halfback

an offensive player who lines up in the backfield and is generally responsible for carrying the ball on run plays. Also known as a running back or tailback.

Halfback Pass

a play in which a running back receives a handoff, but throws a pass to a receiver before crossing the line of scrimmage.

Halftime

the intermission between the second and third quarters when the teams leave the field and go to the respective locker rooms. Times vary according to the NFL, college or high school levels.

Handoff

when the quarterback hands the football to another player on offense (typically a running back) who will try to advance the ball.
2) to give the football to another player on the same team, who then tries to advance the ball.

Hang Time

the amount of time that a punter's kick remains in the air. Normally, a longer hang time favors the punting team.

Hard Count

when a quarterback tries to make the defense jump offside by raising his voice at some point in the count but not on the actual snap signal.

Hash Marks

the two short lines intersecting each five-yard line. In the center of the field that signify 1 yard on the field. Before every play, the ball is spotted between the hash marks or on the hash marks, depending on where the ball carrier was tackled on the preceding play.

Head Coach

the leader of a football team's coaching staff. He has the final say on all the important decisions the team has to make during a game, such as offensive play selection, defensive and special-teams strategies, and the acceptance of penalties.

Head To Head

describing a situation of game or games between the two teams involved, such as the competition for a championship or playoff spot.

Helping The Runner

after the ball carrier crosses the line of scrimmage, an offensive lineman cannot push or pull him forward, helping him gain extra yardage. Ten-yard penalty and replay of the down results.

Hike

to pick up the football from the ground on the line of scrimmage and give it to the quarterback through the legs.

Hit

hard tackle.

Hold Out

to refuse to report to training camp, to practice or to play in any games for a professional football team until the team agrees to the player's contract demands.

Holder

the player who catches the snap from the center and places it down for the place-kicker to kick it. A holder is used on field goal and extra point attempts.

Holding

a most common penalty called against the offense when on a pass attempt. The offense receives a 10-yard penalty (and repeat of down) when any offensive player holds a defensive player by grabbing his jersey or locking his arm onto the defensive player's arm while that player is trying to approach the quarterback. This penalty is also known as defensive holding.

Hole

the space between any two or more linemen through which a running back may try to go on a rushing play.

Hole Number

the offensive coaching staff gives a number to each gap or space between the five offensive linemen and the tight end. The running backs then know which hole they should attempt to run though.

Homefield Advantage

teams playing before hometown fans traditionally win more often.

Hook

this is a common pass play designed mostly for a tight end, who releases downfield and then makes a small turn, coming back to face the quarterback and receive the ball. A hook is similar to a wide receiver running a curl, although it's a shorter pass of between 8 and 12 yards. The quarterback usually releases the ball before the tight end starts his turn. This is a timing route.

Huddle

when the 11 players on the field come together to discuss strategy between plays. On offense, the quarterback relays the plays in the huddle, which can be in the form of a semicircle or with teammates lined up in two rows of five facing the quarterback. On defense, the captain, generally a linebacker or secondary player, relays the coach's instructions for the proper alignment and how to defend the expected play.

Hurry Up

a type of offense in which the players do not go into a huddle after the conclusion of the previous play, but instead immediately line up in their positions. The quarterback usually lines up in the shotgun and then uses an audible to call the next play.

Hurry Up Offense

when several consecutive plays are run without a huddle between each one.

I Formation

an offensive formation that looks like an I because the two running backs line up directly behind the quarterback.

Illegal Formation

having fewer than seven offensive players on the line at the snap, or any offensive backfield players, other than the snap receiver, not being at least one yard behind the line of scrimmage at the snap.

Illegal Forward Pass

keeps the quarterback from crossing the line of scrimmage to throw the ball. This penalty often occurs when the quarterback runs forward, attempting to evade defensive players, and forgets where the line of scrimmage is. The offense is penalized 5 yards and loses a down.

Illegal Motion

more than one offensive backfield man moving, or the man in motion moving in a forward direction, during the final second before the ball is snapped.

Impetus

the action of a player that gives momentum to the ball.

In Bounds

in technical usage, the area of the football field between the hash marks from which the football must be put into play. Informally, anywhere on the football field inside of the sidelines and endlines.

In The Grasp

a rule that states, by judgment of the officials, a defensive player that has hold of a quarterback, limits the quarterback from further gain and immediately stops the play. The play is over, and the quarterback is considered tackled at that spot.

Incidental Contact

contact between a receiver and a defender that does not negatively affect or significantly impede the receiver.

Incomplete

a pass not caught before touching the ground or going out of bounds.

Independent

a football team that does not belong to a league or conference.

Ineligible Receiver

an offensive player who may not touch or catch a forward pass.Offensive linemen (center, guards, and tackles) are not eligible to receive passes unless a defensive player or an eligible receiver has already touched the ball.

Ineligible Receiver Downfield

linemen who are no longer blocking or have lost their man cannot run past the line of scrimmage when the quarterback is attempting to pass. Five-yard penalty and repeat of the down result.

Infraction

a penalty.

Injured Reserve

a designation of an injured NFL player meaning that although the player is unable to play in the team's games and he is temporarily removed from the active roster. He is still a member of the team and can play for it again when he has recovered from his injury.

Inside Linebacker

in a defense with four linebackers, one of the two linebackers who line up between the outside linebackers.

Intentional Grounding

occurs when a quarterback deliberately throws the ball out-of-bounds or into the ground, but it can be interpreted three different ways. The first two drastically penalize the offense.

No. 1: The quarterback is attempting to pass from his own end zone and, prior to being tackled, intentionally grounds the ball, throwing it out-of-bounds or into the ground. The defense is awarded a safety, worth two points, and the offense loses possession of the ball and has to kick the ball from its own 20-yard line.

No. 2: The quarterback is trapped more than 10 yards behind his own line of scrimmage and intentionally grounds the ball for fear of being tackled for a loss. This penalty is a loss of down, and the ball is placed at the spot of the foul, which in this case is where the quarterback was standing when he grounded the ball. Otherwise, the intentional grounding penalty calls for loss of down and 10 yards.

No. 3 The quarterback steps back from the center and immediately throws the ball into the ground, intentionally grounding it. This play is common when an offense wants to stop the clock because it either wants to preserve its time-outs or is out of time-outs. For this type of intentional grounding, the penalty is simply a loss of down.

Interception

1) a pass intended for an offensive receiver is caught by a defensive player in bounds before it touches the ground.

2) a pass that is caught by a defensive player, ending the offense's possession of the ball.

Interference

1) fair-catch interference: When a fair catch is called, no kicking team member may interfere with the receiver, the ball or the receiver's path to the ball.

2) run interference: It is legal for an offensive player to protect the ball carrier by lawfully blocking opposing players.

3) pass interference: It is illegal to hinder either a receiver's or defender's attempt to reach a pass or wave the hands so he can't see the ball.

Juke
a quick move by a ball carrier or pass receiver to escape a defender.

Junior Varsity
the unit of high school or college football team consisting of younger players who are not yet starters.

Keeper
the quarterback fakes a handoff, but keeps the ball and either runs around the opposite side from the back he had faked to or up the middle. (also called bootleg)

Key
1) the quarterback immediately knows which play the other team will attempt to run and to what direction.
2) read, anticipate or watch a teams' tendencies

Key On
to guard or focus on a certain player as a play develops.

Kick Return
when the receiving team takes possession of the kicked ball and attempts to run it back towards the kicking team's goal line.

Kick Returner
a player on a team receiving a kickoff stands at or near the goal line of the end zone.

Kicking Team
a special team squad that is responsible for kicking the ball.

Kickoff
the kick from a tee on the kicking team's 30-yard line (only in the NFL) at the start of each half and after a field goal or extra point attempt.

Knockout Tackle
the ultimate tackle that puts a wide receiver down for the count. Every safety in the league wants a knockout tackle because it's a sign of intimidation. Defensive backs believe in protecting their coverage space, and protecting it well. Cornerbacks want these hits, but many of them are satisfied with brining an offensive player down any way they can.

Late Hit
a personal foul penalty in which a defensive player makes contact with a ball carrier after an official has blown his whistle indicating the end of the play.

Lateral
1) to pass, pitch or toss the ball backwards from one player to another.
2) A lateral pass that touches the ground is a live ball.

Lead
to throw or pitch ahead of the receiver.

Lead Block
to run along just ahead of the runner and keep away potential tacklers.

Lead Blocker
a player on the offense who has the assignment of running ahead of the ball carrier, either through a hole or around an end of the line, to block the first defenders who get in a position to tackle the runner.

League
an organization of football teams at roughly the same competitive level.

Left Guard
the guard on the center's left side.

Left Tackle
the offensive tackle who lines up on the left side of the left guard.

Letter Of Intent
an official letter that indicates which college a high school student plans to attend and play football.

Limit Lines
lines outside of the sidelines and end lines that indicate how close persons other than players, coaches, other team personnel or game officials may be to the playing field during a game.

Line Judge
an official who is positioned on the sideline facing the current line of scrimmage and who calls penalties for illegal formations in the neutral zone.

Line Of Scrimmage

one of two imaginary lines, each of which passes through a tip of the ball and runs parallel to the goal lines. Opposing teams line up on these lines.

Line-to-Gain Indicator

a long, thin strip of brightly colored material that lies on the ground and points to the yard marker needed for a first down.

Linebacker

one of three or four defensive players who line up behind or between the down linemen, usually in an upright position and do everything on defense: rush the quarterback, stop the run, and cover receivers.

Linebacker Coach

a coach who works with linebackers, and depending on the style of defense, ranks a step below the coordinator. Defenses that exclusively utilize four linebackers need a coach who can teach all the variations necessary for this scheme to work. This coach must work on tackling, pass-rushing off the corner and particular pass coverage drops.

Linesman

an official who stands along the same sidelines as the primary chain operators and moves throughout the game so that he is always facing the current line of scrimmage. He calls penalties for any illegal formations in the neutral zone.

Live Ball

the ball is in play from the time a down begins with a legal snap or free kick until the down ends.

Long

a pass that is thrown several yards downfield.

Long Gainer

a play that results in a gain of 10 or more yards for the offense.

Long Snapper

a player who specializes in hiking the ball several yards through the air to a punter or a holder on a field goal attempt.

Look Off

when the quarterback looks in one direction, then suddenly turns and passes in the opposite.

Loose Ball

a live ball not in the possession of any player's during game action.

Man In Motion

a wide receiver, tight end, or running back who moves out of position in the formation and starts running across the field toward the quarterback before the snap of the ball.

Man-to-Man

each pass defender is assigned a specific receiver to cover.

Man-to-Man Coverage (or defense)

a coverage scheme in which one or sometimes two defensive players are assigned to cover each wide receiver, running back, or tight end who could go out for a pass.

Mark Off

to move the football back, for penalties against the offense, or forward, for defensive penalties, from where it ends up at the finish of a play.

Marker

symbols officials use during a game to indicate important field locations like the spot of a fumble. (also know as a penalty flag)

Measurement

when the chain operators bring the chains onto the field and use them to determine whether the football has been advanced 10 or more yards from the starting point of the current offensive series.

Middle Linebacker

in a defense with three linebackers, the linebacker who lines up opposite the center and between the outside linebackers.

Midfield

the middle of the field, marked by the 50-yard line.

Mini-Camp

two-to-five day training sessions for players during the off season.

Misdirected Play
the offense tricks the defense into committing itself to going in one direction, while the ball carrier runs the other.

Motion
when an offensive receiver or running back begins to move laterally behind the line of scrimmage. Once his teammates have assumed a ready stance and are considered set, he is in motion. This motion cannot be forward, and only one player is allowed to move at a time.

Mouthguard
an item made from clear or colored plastic that is molded to fit between a player's teeth and that the player keeps in the mouth while playing.

Muff
the touching of a loose ball by a player in an unsuccessful attempt to obtain possession.

MVP
most valuable player.

Neutral Zone
an imaginary zone between the line of scrimmage and the back end of the football on the ground before the start of the play, in which no offensive player besides the center can line up and which no defensive player can enter until the snap of the ball.

Nickel Back
the fifth man in the secondary. Since there are usually four, the extra is the nickel back.

Nickel Defense (Nickel Package)
a defensive alignment with five defensive backs.

No Huddle
a type of offense in which the players do not go into a huddle after the conclusion of the previous play, but instead immediately line up in their positions. The quarterback usually lines up in the shotgun and then uses an audible to call the next play.

Nose Guard
a defensive lineman in the three-four alignment who lines up nose to nose with the offensive team's center.

Nose Tackle
the player between the ends on the defensive line on a defense with three linemen, the lineman who lines up between the defensive ends and usually opposite the center.

Off Tackle Run
the oldest run around, a by-product of the old single wing offense of 90 years ago. It's a strong side run, meaning that the halfback heads toward the end of the line where the tight end, the extra blocker, lines up. The runner wants to take advantage of the hole supplied by the tackle, tight end, and his running mate, the fullback. He can take the ball either around the tight end or outside the tackle.

Off-Season
the period between the end of one football season and the start of preparation for another, in which there are no games or practices.

Offense
the unit of a team that has possession of the football. It tries to advance the ball toward the other team's goal line in order to score points.

Offensive Back
a player on the offense who lines up in the area behind the offensive linemen.

Offensive Backfield
the offensive players who start a play behind the offensive line. Usually consists of the quarterback and the running backs.

Offensive Coordinator
the coach in charge of the offensive players. He usually calls the plays and works directly with the quarterbacks. He's responsible for developing the offensive game and works with the head coach on how practice is organized.

Offensive End
one of two offensive players on the line who are eligible receivers. He lines up on the outside of a tackle either some distance away (split end) or close (tight end).

Offensive Formation
the manner in which the offensive players line up before the ball is centered.

Offensive Guard
one of the two offensive interior linemen who line up at each side of the center.

Offensive Holding
1) penalty.
2) a penalty called on an offensive player when he tries to restrict the movement of a defensive player by grabbing on to the defender's body or uniform.

Offensive Line Coach
a coach who works with the offensive linemen and has a solid understanding of the team's running game. The line coach and the offensive coordinator spend time discussing what running plays may work, depending on what the line coach views are his unit's strengths and weaknesses against the upcoming opponent.

Offensive Lineman
the center guards and tackles. The players align on the line of scrimmage and have full-time blocking responsibility. The are not eligible receivers.

Offensive Offsides
a penalty called when any part of an offensive player's body is beyond his line of scrimmage (or free kick line) before the ball is snapped or kicked.

Offensive Tackle
one of the two offensive interior linemen who line up next to and outside the guards.

Official
the men in striped shirts who officiate according to the rules of the game and call the penalties.

Offset I Formation
in the offset I formation, the running back remains deep, five to seven yards from the quarterback. When the running back is this deep, the majority of the time the team plans to run the ball. The fullback or blocking back can be as close as three yards to the line of scrimmage. The other back wants to be close to his target; the defender he must block. A good fullback needs only two yards before making blocking contact. Also, he's deep enough should the play require him to go in motion to either side and swing to the outside for a possible reception. The fullback can be set to the strong side or the weak side or the formation.

Offsetting
describes penalties that are committed by both teams on a play, in which case neither team is penalized, unless one is a major infraction and the other is minor.

Offsetting Goals
a violation by each team on the same play. Usually both penalties are nullified and the down is played over from the same spot.

Offsides
a player is offsides when any part of his body is beyond his line of scrimmage or the free kick line when the ball is snapped. When an offensive player lines up over the designated line of scrimmage, he may become guilty of this penalty when trying to gain an edge on blocking or by simply forgetting where he should be. Generally the lineman either places his hand over the line of scrimmage or tilts his upper body over the
line of scrimmage. Five yard penalty and repeat of the down results.

One On One
one offensive player competing against one defensive player.

Onrushing
describing a defensive player who is running or moving toward the quarterback or the ball carrier.

Onside Kick

a kickoff deliberately intended to go only the required 10 yards so the kicking team can try to recover the ball before the receiving team does.

Open The Hole

to block any defensive players who might be in the way of a running back going through a hole.

Open Week

a week in which a football team does not have a game scheduled to play.

Open-field Running

when a ball carrier is past the line of scrimmage and runs in a different direction downfield.

Opening

an area of the field with no or few defenders, toward which a ball carrier or a receiver might try to run.

Option Play

a play in which the quarterback runs with the ball around one of the ends of the line with a running back following closely behind. The quarterback can keep running across the line of scrimmage, can toss the ball back to the running back, or can attempt a pass.

Out

a pass pattern in which the receiver runs straight down the field for several yards and then turns to the right or left and runs toward the nearest sideline.

Out Of Bounds

when a player or the ball touches the ground outside of the boundary lines bordering the field.

Outside Linebacker

one of the two linebackers who line up on each side of the middle linebacker or the inside linebackers.

Outside Run

the ball carrier runs around the end toward one of the sidelines.

Overshift

alignment where there are more defensive players on one side to counter offensive formation strength.

Overtime

a quarter or quarters played after the regulation four quarters of a football game. This will take place at the end of the score-tied game. 2) if the score is tied at the end of regulation play, the game continues after a three-minute intermission until one team scores, or until 15 minutes of additional playing time elapses. If neither scores, the game ends in a tie (except in post-season playoff games when overtime periods continue until one team scores to break the tie). The first overtime begins with a coin toss and kickoff, and succeeding periods are treated the same as changing goals between first and second quarters in a regulation game. Overtime rules differ in college or high school.

Own Goal

the goal a team is guarding.

Pass

when the football is thrown forward to a receiver, or a play features such an action.

Pass Defense

a statistic that a defensive back achieves every time he deflects a pass or knocks the ball out of a receiver's hands. You can also say that the defensive back broke up a pass. A pass defense means an incompletion for the quarterback.

Pass Interference

a penalty called against the offense or defense when a player interferes with the opposing player's attempted catch by using physical contact while the ball is in the air.

Pass Pattern

a planned route for an eligible receiver on a pass play.

Pass Receiver

an eligible offensive player who runs downfield in an effort to catch a forward pass.

Pass Reception

when a receiver catches a pass.

Pass Rush
when the defense crosses the line of scrimmage in an effort to sack the quarterback, block a pass, or otherwise interfere with his passing attempt.

Pass-Protect
to block defenders away from a quarterback trying to throw a pass.

Passing Combination
a term used to describe a quarterback and pass receiver who work well together.

Passing Lane
a direct, unobstructed line between a quarterback and a receiver through which a pass can be thrown.

Passing Play
a play on which the offense seeks to complete a forward pass. Typically, the quarterback will take several steps back and look downfield to try and find an open receiver.

Passing Situation
when the conditions on a certain down require that the offense try to throw a pass to gain several yards.

Pattern
the path that receivers run in order to arrive at a prescribed location at the same time that the ball reaches that spot as delivered by the quarterback. The names of patterns often literally describe in what direction the receiver runs after starting up the field, as in "slant," "down and out" and "turn in." Similarly, a "post" pattern finds the receiver starting forward and then slanting toward the goal post, while a "flag" pattern sends him upfield and then toward the flag where the sideline and the goal line meet.

Payout
the money paid by the organizers of a college bowl game to the two colleges whose teams play in the game.

Penalty
the punishment assessed against the team committing an infraction of the rules. Depending on the seriousness, a penalty can cost the offending team anywhere from five to 15 yards and a loss of a down. For the most serious violations, a player can be ejected from the game.

Penalty Flag
a small yellow piece of cloth that an official tosses into the air to indicate that he has seen a rules violation during a play.

Penalty Yardage
the number of yards that are marked off against the offense or the defense for a specific penalty.

Personal Foul
an illegal act of aggression by an individual player against an opposing player or official; penalty 15 yards.

Pick
1) a type of blocking in which a player simply gets in the way between a ball carrier or receiver and a defender.
2) to move in front of a defender to impede his advancement or ward off an intended receiver.

Pick Off
to intercept a pass

Pigskin
a slang term for the football which originated from early balls that looked like a stuffed pig.

Pitch
the act of the quarterback tossing the ball to a running back, who is moving laterally away from him, toward either end of the line of scrimmage.

Pitchout
a play where the quarterback tosses the ball underhand to a back who is too far away to hand off to.

Place Kicker
the kick used to put the ball in play at the beginning of a half, after a touchdown or field goal or when attempting a field goal or a point after touchdown.

Place-kick

a kick made by a kicker when the ball is on the ground, including a kickoff, a field goal, or an extra point attempt. A kickoff is typically kicked from a plastic holder. A field goal attempt or extra point attempt is held in place by a teammate.

Play Action Pass

a passing play in which the quarterback, after getting the snap, fakes a handoff to a running back, then drops back and tries to throw to a receiver.

Play Clock

a clock, in addition to the official game clock, used in games to count the seconds after the game clock was stopped on the play. These seconds are the time an offense has before they must begin the next play.

Play Fake

a passing play in which the quarterback, after getting the snap, fakes a handoff to a running back, then drops back and tries to throw to a receiver.

Play-by-Play

a description and commentary of the action during a football game as it is happening.

Playbook

a team's manual detailing all the offensive and defensive plays, as well as team maneuvers and strategies.

Playoff Berth

the guaranteed right to play in a playoff game.

Playoff Game

a post-season football game for the best regular-season contenders. The winning team goes on to play in a semifinal or championship game.

Playoffs

the post season tournament which determines the winner in each conference and, ultimately, who will play in the Super Bowl.

Pocket

the protected area behind the line of scrimmage where offensive blockers form around the quarterback on a passing play.

Point After Touchdown

the try for one additional point following a touchdown during a scrimmage down with the spot of the snap from the specially marked two yard line. It is done by kicking the ball through the uprights, or running or passing it over the goal line.

Poll

survey of sportswriters or coaches that rank the best high school and college teams in the country.

Pooch

a short, high punt intended to stop short of the goal line.

Possession

1) when a player maintains control of the ball while clearly touching both feet, or any other part of his body other than his hand, to the ground inbounds. A team is also considered in possession of the ball whenever it has the ball on offense. A team's possession ends when it scores, turns over the ball, punts the ball, or when a game half ends.
2) when a team is on offense or returning a kick. When one player on the team is holding the football, the player can try to advance the ball forward toward the other team's goal line in order to score points.
3) legal control of the ball.

Possession Receiver

the term derives from this type of player so often making catches on third down, thus making a first down and keeping possession of the ball for his team. Sometimes this player is actually a
team's third wide receiver, who comes into the game in strategic situations that find defenders paying too much attention to wide receivers one and two.

Post

a forward pass that the quarterback throws down the center of the field as the intended receiver angles toward the goal post after running straight ahead.

Post-Possession Foul

a foul by the receiving team that occurs after a ball is legally kicked from scrimmage prior to the change of possession. The ball must cross the line of scrimmage and the receiving team must retain the kicked ball.

Post-Season

the part of a football league's season that takes place at the end of the regular season and features playoff, championship, or bowl games.

Practice Squad

players on NFL teams who participate in practices with the team but do not play in games. Each team can place five players on this squad and they are eligible only to practice. These players are paid a little more than $3,000 a week and are free agents.

Pregame Warm-Up

when players from both teams participate in calisthenics and drills on the field before the start of a football game.

Preliminary Indication

after a penalty flag has been thrown, the referee indicates just what the infraction is and the team to be called without announcing specifically who will be penalized and what results will be enforced.

Press Box

an area on top or in the middle of the stands of a football field or stadium where members of the media are located while they cover the game. This is also where some coaches and officials watch and analyze the game.

Press Coverage

when a wide receiver is challenged by a defensive back right at the line of scrimmage at the beginning of a pass play. Defenders may bump or "chuck" receivers only within the first five yards downfield from where the play originates.

Prevent

a type of defense in which the defensive backs and linebackers will be positioned deeper than normal to try to prevent the other team's offense from getting big plays.

Prevent Defense

when the defensive team plays loose and deep, with five or six men in the backfield. It will concede short yardage rather than a long gain.

Primary Receiver

the first choice receiver that the quarterback intends to pass to on a play.

Pro Set

an offensive formation with two running backs split several feet apart behind the quarterback.

Pro-bowler

a player who is selected by a vote of the fans, players, and coaching staffs to represent his conference in an all-star game that takes place the week after the Super Bowl. Any player selected to play in the Pro Bowl is considered among the leagues' elite. The Pro Bowl is held in Hawaii.

Prospect

a talented young football player whom teams want to recruit or draft.

Protected Free Agent

when a restricted free agent is offered a contract by a new team, the old team can match the new team's offer and the player remains with his original team. If that team does not match the new ones offer, the new team must compensate the one holding the player's contract with draft choices based on the player's salary

Pull

to step backward at the snap and then run around the nearer end of the offensive line to block for a ballcarrier also coming around the end. When an interior lineman runs laterally from his position at the snap to block for the runner.

Pulling Guard

the offensive guard moves quickly, from his position on the offensive line, in a lateral direction to lead the blocking of the play.

Pump Fake

1) when the quarterback makes an arm motion that looks like the start of a pass.
2) to draw back the throwing arm with the ball, move it forward as if to pass, but not release the ball.

Punt

a kick made when a player drops the ball and kicks it while it falls toward his foot. A punt is usually made on fourth down when the offense must surrender possession of the ball to the defense because it could not advance 10 yards. A punt cannot be recovered by the punting team unless the ball is touched by the receiving team.

Punter

a player on a football team who specializes in or whose assignment is punting the ball.

Pylons

small orange tubes made from a soft material that stick up from the eight points on the field where the sidelines intersect both goal lines and end lines.

Quarter

one of the four 15 or 12-minute periods dividing a football game.

Quarterback

an offensive back who calls plays in the huddle and begins every offensive play by getting the ball from the center. He has the choice of running with the ball, handing it off to another back, or passing it to a receiver.

Quarterback Coach

an assistant coach who monitors the physical and mental aspects of a quarterback's game. He works on the quarterback's footwork, pass-drop technique, and throwing motion. This coach also ensures the quarterback doesn't fall into bad mental or physical habits.

Quarterback Count

the signals that a quarterback shouts to the offense before the snap of the ball.

Quarterback Draw

a running play in which the quarterback drops back as if to pass but then suddenly runs forward with the ball.

Quarterback Drop

refers to the distance the quarterback retreats on any given pass play before setting himself and releasing the ball.

Quarterback Keeper

a running play in which the quarterback, either after dropping back as if to pass or right after getting the snap, runs around one of the ends of the line.

Quarterback Option

a play in which the quarterback runs with the ball around one of the ends of the line with a running back following closely behind. The quarterback can keep running across the line of scrimmage, can toss the ball back to the running back, or can attempt a pass.

Quarterback Sneak

the short-yardage play with the least amount of risk, in that the quarterback merely takes the snap and tries to burrow or leap forward for the needed gain. This is usually employed with less than a yard required for either a first down or touchdown.

Quick Kick

punt on any down prior to the fourth.

Quick Out

a pass pattern in which the receiver runs only a few yards forward and then suddenly turns toward the nearest sideline.

Reach Block

When an offensive lineman reaches for the next defender, meaning that he doesn't block the opponent directly in front of him, but moves for an opponent to either side. The reach block is common on run plays when the play calls for a guard to reach out and block an inside linebacker.

Read

to anticipate the play before it happens.

Receiver
an offensive player who is eligible to catch a pass. An eligible receiver can include a wide receiver, running back, or tight end.

Receiving Team
the special team which receives kickoffs or punts.

Reception
a forward pass caught by an eligible receiver.

Record
the number of games that a team has won, lost, or tied in a season or at some point in a season.

Recover
to gain possession of a fumbled ball.

Recover A Fumble
to pick up a fumbled ball or lie over it on the ground.

Recruit
to try to convince or attract a football player to play for a certain team.

Red Zone
the unofficial area from the 20 yard line to the opponent's goal line. Games are won and lost depending on how teams perform in this area. Offenses want to score touchdowns, and defenses strive to prevent them from doing so. Holding an opponent to a field goal in this area is considered a moral victory by the defense.

Redshirt
a college player who skips a year of eligibility due to injury or academic trouble. For example, a redshirt freshman is a player who is in his second year of school, but is playing his first season of football. Players have four years of eligibility and five years in which to use them, so they can be redshirted only once.

Referee
a chief or head football official, who announces all penalties and has the final decision on any calls made by the other officials. He also announces the infraction and penalties.

Refuse A Penalty
to not agree to enforce a penalty called against the other team. In other words, accepting the result of the previous play even though the other team committed an infraction during it.

Reserve
any player who is not on the first team.

Restraining Lines
lines outside of the sidelines and end lines that indicate how close persons other than players, coaches, team personnel or game officials may be to the playing field during a game.

Restricted Free Agent
a player who has completed three accrued seasons and now has an expired contract. Under the terms of the collective bargaining agreement, the club controls what he will be paid. Most teams attempt to sign this player to a long-term contract if he's deemed a valuable starter, preventing him from being an unrestricted free agent in his fourth season.

Return
the act of receiving a kick or punt and running toward the opponent's goal line with the intent of scoring or gaining significant yardage.

Return Man
a player who tries to receive kickoffs and punts and runs with the ball toward the kicking teams goal.

Reverse
a play in which the running back receives the handoff from the quarterback and then runs laterally behind the line of scrimmage before handing off to a receiver or flanker running toward him.

Rib Pads
pads around a player's abdomen that offer protection to parts of the body, the ribs in particular, not protected by the lower shoulder pads (also called flak jacket).

Right Guard
the guard on the center's right side.

Right Tackle

the offensive tackle who lines up on the right side of the right guard.

Road Game

a game played on the home field of an opponent.

Rodman

one of the assistant officials along the sidelines who tends the yardage chains, which is the 10-yard metal chain attached to the two rods and used to measure yardage for first downs.

Roll Out

instead of dropping back in the pocket on a passing play, the quarterback runs to his right or left while looking for a receiver.

Rookie

a player who's on a NFL roster for the first time. This can include a player who has played in another league, such as the CFL or the Arena League, is still considered a rookie by the NFL.

Roster

list of all the players eligible to play on a team in each regular season and post-season game.

Roster Reduction

each team is allowed to open training camp with 80 players on its roster. By mid-August, teams have to cut down to 60 players. The next week, each club must cut seven more players, leaving their roster to 53. The weekend before the start of the regular season, teams must announce their active rosters of 45 players. They are allowed to retain eight inactive players.

Roughing The Kicker

a 15-yard penalty called when a defensive player runs into a kicker and, in the judgment of the officials, uses deliberate and excessive force.

Roughing The Passer

this penalty was devised to protect the quarterback from injury. After the ball leaves the quarterback's hand, any defensive player must attempt to avoid contact with him. Because a defensive player's momentum may cause him to inadvertently run into the quarterback, he is allowed to take one step after he realizes the ball has been released. But, if he hits the quarterback on his second step, knowing that the ball is gone, the referee (the official standing near the quarterback) can call roughing. It's a 15-yard penalty against the defense and an automatic first down.

Round

when all the teams participating in a draft make one selection in the determined order.

Route

the direction downfield receivers run in order to arrive at a prescribed location at the same time the ball reaches that spot as delivered by the quarterback. The names of patterns often literally describe what direction the receiver runs after starting up the field, as in "slant," "down and out" and "turn in."

Run And Shoot

a type of offense with as many as four wide receivers, no tight ends, and only one running back in the backfield, and which usually features passing plays, since at least one of the receivers will probably get open for the quarterback to throw to.

Run Up The Score

to try to score as many points as possible in the remainder of a game when already having the lead.

Runback

yardage gained as a result of interception, return of punt, kickoff or missed field goal.

Running Back

an offensive player who lines up at least one yard behind the line of scrimmage. Includes fullback, halfback, setback, slotback, tailback and wing back. The name denotes the position of a player in the formation. The running back is any team's principle ball carrier

Running Game

the ability an offense has to execute running plays.

Running Into The Kicker

a 5-yard penalty called when a defensive player runs into a kicker after the ball is kicked.

Running Play

an offensive play that attempts to advance the ball by carrying it forward. Often, the quarterback will hand the ball off to a running back who takes the ball and runs with it

Running The Football

attempting mostly running plays.

Rush

to run with the ball on a play from scrimmage.

Rushing Play

a play in which a player on the offense tries to advance the football by running forward with it.

Sack

when the quarterback is tackled behind the line of scrimmage by any defensive player. The sack is the most prominent defensive statistic, one that the NFL has officially kept since 1982. (Tackles are considered an unofficial statistic because individual teams are responsible for recording them.)

Safety

one of the defensive backs who line up in the defensive backfield and serve as the last line of defense. There are typically two safeties in a defensive formation.

Safety (score)

a score, worth two points, that the defense earns by tackling an offensive player in possession of the ball in his own end zone. The defense is awarded two points and receives the kickoff from its opponent's 20-yard line

Safety Blitz

a sudden rush on the quarterback by a safety, one of the defensive backfield players.

Safety Kick

following a safety (score), the team scored upon free kicks from its own 20-yard line with no tee.

Salary Cap

the maximum amount of money that an NFL team can spend on the salaries of all its players.

Scalping

selling tickets to a football game for a higher price than their original or face value.

Schedule

a list of games arranged for the teams of a league to play on specific dates and at certain locations during a season.

Scheme

a slang term used to describe offensive and defensive formations and the overall strategy for using such formations.

Scholarship

the waiver of the full costs of tuition and room and board each year for a college student in return for the student's playing for the college's football team.

Scoreboard

the stadium board that gives information during a game such as the names of the teams, the score, quarter, time remaining in the quarter, down, yards to go for a first down, timeouts, and the team with the ball.

Scout

a team representative who researches college players and travels to other teams' football games and reports on the teams and certain players and collects information and tapes and charts future opponents.

Scout Team

a unit, typically composed of a football team's second or third string players, that plays the role of the next opponent during practices.

Scramble

when the quarterback runs, not by design, to avoid the tackle. If no receiver is open and the pass rushers are closing in, some quarterbacks have the wherewithal to run away from the pressure and gain yardage down the field.

Screen Pass

a passing play in which the pass is usually thrown to a running back who runs just a short distance out of the backfield to the left or right side. The defensive linemen are allowed to come through the offensive line and quarterback floats the ball over their heads to a running back, at or near the line of scrimmage.

Scrimmage

1) a type of football practice in which actual plays are run but the football is put back to the same spot after every play and no scoring or downs are recorded.
2) the action of two teams during a down which begins with a snap from center. Also, a practice game.

Script

to make a list of the plays to be attempted in sequence in a game or part of a game.

Seam

a direct, unobstructed imaginary line between a quarterback and a receiver through which a pass can be thrown.

Second-String

describing players who are behind the starters on a team's depth chart.

Secondary

the defensive backfield, including the cornerbacks and safeties and the area of the field patrolled by these players.

Secondary Coach

a coach who works with the defensive backs and must have a total understanding of pass offenses. He works on all aspects of pass coverage, from footwork and deep zone drops to how to prepare players for the particular receivers that they will face.

Semifinal Game

a game whose winning team advances to the Super Bowl (or championship game).

Shift

the action of two or more offensive players simultaneously changing the position of their feet and assuming a new set position for at least one second prior to the snap.

Shoot The Gaps

to have a defensive player in a position to cover any of the holes between the offensive linemen that a running back could come through.

Shotgun

the passing formation that finds the quarterback standing five yards behind the center prior to the snap instead of right behind him. In an obvious passing situation, this alignment gives the quarterback a chance to stand more erect and survey the defense to find a place in which to direct the attack.

Shoulder Pads

a one piece assembly of padding made from hard plastic and other materials with an opening in the middle that fits over the player's head and rests on his shoulders.

Shovel Pass

a forward pass that is thrown with an underhand motion to another player.

Show Blitz

to give signs that one or more players are going to blitz.

Shutout

a game that ends with one or both teams not having scored any points.

Side Block

when the entire offensive line slides down the line of scrimmage: a coordinated effort by the line to go either right or left. This technique is good when the quarterback prefers to roll or sprint right, running outside the tackle while attempting to throw the football.

Side Judge

an official who watches for penalties on passes and kicks and who also counts the number of defensive players.

Sidelines

two lines that extend the length of a football field and, with the end lines, set off the boundaries of the field.

Signals

1) a prearranged number, work, color or phrase the quarterback calls when the ball is to be snapped to start a scrimmage down.
2) the sign that an official makes with his hands, arms and body to signify a particular penalty.

Silent Count

when the quarterback does not shout signals before the snap of the ball, but rather the center hikes the ball whenever he thinks the quarterback is ready. Or, when the quarterback uses a gesture, such as lifting up and lowering one foot or leg, to signal the center to snap the ball.

Single-Wing Formation

an offensive formation devised by legendary coach Pop Warner after rules outlawed helping the ball carrier advance the ball by pulling or pushing him.

Single

in Canadian football, one point that is awarded to a team if, after this team kicks or punts a ball that enters the goal area, the receiving team does not return the ball past the goal line.

Single-Elimination

referring to playoff games whose winner will play in another game but whose loser will not or is eliminated.

Situation Substitution

when a defense takes some players off the field and puts players into the game who are better at defending against the type of play the defense thinks is coming from the offense.

Slant Pattern

a receiver runs out in a slanting angle to the place on the field where the pass is to be thrown.

Slotback

a running back who lines up in the area between the split end and the tackle, at least a yard behind the line.

Snap

the action in which the ball is hiked by the center to the quarterback, to the holder on a kick attempt, or to the punter. When the snap occurs, the ball is officially in play and action begins.

Snapper

the player (center) who snaps the ball to start a scrimmage down.

Spearing

a 15 yard penalty called on a player for using his helmet to hurt his opponent.

Special Teams

22 players who are on the field during kicks and punts. These units have "special" players who return punts and kicks, and also players who are experts at covering kicks and punts. Most teams have "special" units to block field goal and extra point attempts as well as punts.

Special Teams Coach

the coach who supervises the kickers, punters, kick return team, field goal protection team, punt block team, etc.

Specialist

in arena football, a quarterback, place-kicker, long snapper, wide receiver/ kick returner, or the player who replaces the quarterback on defense.

Speed Receiver

the wide receiver who can outrun people and run the deep pass patterns that result in big chunks of yardage and often touchdowns. The presence of such a receiver allows an offensive team to "stretch" a defense, in that a man running deep can open areas for other receivers running shorter patterns "underneath." This player is considered a deep threat, and offers more offensive options to his team.

Spike

to throw the football hard down onto the ground. This is often an act of celebration after an impressive or crucial play.

Spiral

the tight spin on the ball in flight after the quarterback releases it. The term "tight spiral" is often used to describe a solidly thrown football.

Split Back Formation

in the spit-back formation, the runners are aligned behind the two guards about five yards behind the line of scrimmage. Teams use this formation because its difficult for the defense to gauge whether the offense is running or passing. With split backs, the backfield is balanced and not aligned toward one side or the other, making it harder for the defense to anticipate the play. This formation may be a better passing formation because the backs can swing out of the backfield to either side as receivers.

Split Backfield

an offensive formation in which two halfbacks line up in back of, one on each side, of the quarterback.

Split End

1) a player who catches passes, also known in more general terms as a wide receiver. In an offensive formation, the split end usually lines up on the line of scrimmage.
2) in arena football, a player who lines up on the line of scrimmage, but no closer than five yards to players on one end of the line.

Spot

the placement of the ball on the field where the previous play ended or where it is moved because of a penalty.

Square-out

the receiver on this pattern runs 10 yards down the field and then cuts sharply toward the sideline, parallel to the line of scrimmage The square-out is a timing play because the quarterback must deliver the pass before the receiver reaches the sideline and steps out of bounds.

Squib Kick

a ball kicked downfield that is low and bouncing to make it more difficult to catch.

Standings

an official record that indicates how many games have been won, lost, or tied by each team in a football league.

Starter

a player who plays on a team's offensive or defensive unit at the beginning and throughout most of a game.

Stiff Arm

to push away a tackler with a straight arm. Only the ball carrier may use his hands to keep away potential tacklers.

Straight-Arm

to use one's outstretched arm to push away defensive players who are trying to make a tackle.

Streak

(see "fly.")

Strength Coach

a coach who specializes in weight training and conditioning. He makes sure that the players are strong and in shape throughout the season and often coordinates off-season training programs. A strength coach also works with team doctors to prepare and monitor rehabilitation exercises following player injuries.

Striking

to make contact with an opponent by swinging, clubbing, or propelling either arm or forearm.

Strip The Ball

to tear the ball away from the runner before or during a tackle.

Strong Safety

a defensive player who generally lines up deep in the secondary, but often aligns close to the line of scrimmage. In most defenses. this player lines up over the tight end and is responsible for both playing the pass the supporting the run. A strong safety usually is bigger and more physical than free safety and should be a great openfield tackler.

Strong Side

the side of the offensive formation where the tight end aligns. With a right-handed quarterback, the strong side is generally to his right side.

Stunt

a maneuver by two defensive linemen in which they alter their course to the quarterback, hoping to confuse the offensive linemen and maximize their strengths.

Substitution

each team is permitted 11 players on the field at one time. Unlimited substitution is permitted between plays, but no substitution is allowed once a play has begun.

Sudden Death

a type of overtime period in which the game is over as soon as one team scores any points; that team wins the game.

Super Bowl

the championship game between the winner of the AFC and the NFC. The game takes place in late January at a predetermined neutral site.

Suspend

to prohibit a player from playing for a certain period of time.

Sweep

a handoff or backwards toss to a running back who attempts to advance by first running wide toward the sidelines and then cutting up the field. This type of run is slower to develop than more standard straight-ahead plays, but can yield big gains if defenders are stacked to the middle or blocked to the inside by the receivers. A speedy back who can "turn the corner" is most often deployed.

3) a fairly common run in every team's play-

book. It begins with two or more offensive linemen leaving their stances and running toward the outside of the line of scrimmage. The ball carrier takes a handoff from the quarterback and runs parallel to the line of scrimmage waiting for his blockers to lead the way around the end. This run is designed to attack the defensive end, outside linebacker, and cornerback on a specific side.

Swing

this is a simple throw to a running back who runs out of the backfield toward the sideline. The pass is thrown when the running back turns and heads upfield. This is generally a touch pass, meaning that the quarterback doesn't necessarily throw it as hard as he does a deep square-out. He wants to be able to float it over a linebacker and make it easy for the running back to catch.

Tackle

the use of hands or arms to hold, pull or knock down a runner so any part of his body other than his feet or hands touches the ground.

Tackle

an offensive tackle is a lineman who lines up outside the offensive guards. A defensive tackle is a lineman who line up inside the defensive ends. On offense, there are two tackles and on defense, there are one or two tackles.

Tailback

one of the running backs whose position in a formation is farthest back from the line of scrimmage, and whose primary role is to carry the ball.

Takeaway

when a team forces its opponent to turn over the ball.

Tee

a plastic holder on which the ball may be placed for kickoff.

Territory

the 50 yards extending from the end zone that is defended by one team.

Third-String
players behind the second-string players on a team's depth chart.

Three And Out
three downs and a punt

Three Point Stance
crouching position with one leg slightly in front of the other, supported by one arm with the fingers of the hand or the knuckles touching the ground and the other arm bent over the knee of the leg that's farther back. This is the starting position for most lineman before the play. The two feet and the hand on the ground make the three points.

Throw Away
to pass the football out of bounds or to a spot on the field where no defensive player can intercept it.

Tight End
an offensive player who lines up on the end of the line of scrimmage and has responsibilities which alternate between receiving passes and blocking. Also known ad a pass receiver.

Time-out
when the game clock is stopped by the request of one of the teams or the officials. This gives the team a chance to regroup and plan its strategy. Each team is allotted three time outs per half.

Touchback
when a kick returner catches the ball in his own end zone and elects not to run it back out of the end zone, he signifies the election of a touchback by touching one knee down on the field. The next play automatically starts on the receiving team's 20-yard line. A touchback also occurs automatically when a kicker kicks the ball past the receiving team's end zone. The team gaining possession of the ball begins the next play from its 20-yard line.

Touchdown
when any part of the ball, legally in possession of a player inbounds, breaks the plane of the opponent's goal line, provided it is not a touchback. A touchdown is worth 6 points.

Trading Period
generally begins in mid-February and ends on the Tuesday following the sixth regular-season game, which is usually in early October.

Training Camp
1) a period before the beginning of a professional football season in which players and coaches gather in one location and prepare for the season. this also includes player practice, and tryouts for prospective players to make the squad.

Transition Player
this player's club must pay him the average of the prior season's top ten salaries of players at the same position or 120 percent of the player's previous year's salary, whichever is greater. A transition player can seek a contract from another team, but his current team has seven days to match the offer. A team can have no more than two transition players in the same season, as long as it doesn't also have a designated franchise player.

Trap Block
this block, depending on the play's design, can come from a guard or a tackle. Teams run this play to either side, and it's important that the center protects the back side of this land, negating any pursuit by the defense. The trap block is also called an indulge block because you want to draw the defender upfield and then go out and trap him. Good passing teams tend to be good trapping teams because defenders usually charge hard upfield, hoping to reach the quarterback.

Trap Play

1) a quick-hitting handoff up the middle during which the linemen at the point of attack trap the defensive linemen into thinking they are going to be unblocked. What happens in an instant is that the blocks come from players on an angle, as the offensive linemen execute a switch in the traditional blocking pattern. Often, the a defender's own momentum against the flow of the play will take him out of any position in which the ball carrier could possibly be tackled.

2) when the offensive line deliberately allows a defensive player to cross the line of scrimmage untouched and then blocks him with a guard or tackle from the opposite side or where he's not expecting it. The intent is to create a running lane in the area that the defender vacated.

Trapping

when a receiver uses the ground to help him catch a pass that is thrown on a low trajectory. For an official not to rule a reception a trap, the receiver must make sure that either his hands or his arms are between the ball and the ground when he makes a legal catch. Often, this play occurs so quickly that only instant replay shows that the receiver was not in possession of the ball (he trapped it along the ground) when making the catch.

Trash Talking

when a player degrades or baits players on the other team. This is done not just as a challenge, but for subtle psychological reasons, especially to get the players on the other team angry and make them concentrate less on actually playing the game.

Trenches

area near the scrimmage line where the linemen down (defense) and interior (offense) meet.

Triple Option

the quarterback can either pass, run or pitch to another back for a run.

Turnover

to enable the other team to get possession of the football, as through an interception, fumble, or failure to convert on a fourth down.

Two Minute Drill

an offensive strategy in which a team tries to get as much yardage in as little time as possible, mostly through passing plays that end with the receiver going out of bounds, thereby stopping the game clock.

Two Minute Warning

in professional football, a time-out that is called by the officials near the end of each half when there are two minutes left on the game clock.

Two Point Conversion

after scoring a touchdown, the offensive team can opt for two points instead of the extra point. The team lines up on the two-yard line and must advance the ball over the goal line, yet again. If they succeed, they gain two points on top of the six-point touchdown.

Two Point Stance

an upright position, as opposed to a crouched three (one hand on the ground) or four-point (both hands on the ground) stance.

Two Way

a football player who regularly plays both an offensive and a defensive position. Usually in Arena and high school football.

Umpire

an official who stands four to five yards behind the defensive line at the beginning of every play, counts the number of offensive players, and watches for offsides penalties and for ineligible receivers coming downfield.

Under Center

immediately behind the center. The usual position of the quarterback receiving the snap on scrimmage downs.

Under Pressure

with oncoming defensive players getting near.

Underdog

a team that is not believed to have much chance of beating another team in a game.

Underneath
a short pass thrown to a receiver who tries to stay between the quarterback and any defenders.

Unnecessary Roughness
a 15-yard personal foul penalty that is called when a player uses excessive force on another player.

Unrestricted Free Agent
a player who has completed four or more accrued seasons and now has an expired contract. He can be signed without his previous team receiving compensation.

Unsportsmanlike Conduct
any act contrary to the generally understood principles of sportsmanship which results in a 15-yard penalty.

Up Men
the members of the receiving team who position themselves upfield from the kick returner in order to block.

Up Pattern
a pass pattern in which the receiver runs as fast as possible straight down the field.

Up Position
a slightly crouched stance not requiring that a hand touch the ground.

Up The Middle
toward and through the offensive line.

Uprights
the two vertical posts on a goal post that rise 30 feet above the crossbar.

Upset
to defeat unexpectedly.

Varsity
the unit of a high school or college football team that consists of the oldest and the best players and is the unit that competes during the team's regularly scheduled games.

Veer
a quick hitting run in which the ball is handed to either running back, whose routes are determined by the slant or charge of the defensive linemen. The term veer comes from the back veering away from the defense.

Veteran
a player who has played at least one season in the NFL.

Waive
to release a player and offer him to each of the other teams in a league, anyone of which can claim and sign the player.

Waiver
the procedure by which a player's contract or NFL rights are made available by his current team to other teams in the league. During the procedure, the 30 other teams either file a claim to obtain the player or waive the opportunity to do so, thus the term waiver. The claiming period is typically 10 days during the off-season, but from early July through December, it lasts only 24 hours. If a player is claimed by two or more teams in this period, priority is based on the inverse won-lost standing of the teams. The team with the worst record has priority. If no team selects this player, he's free to sign with any team, including his previous employer. If no one signs him, he is unemployed.

Waivers
Contract of a player to be released is offered to the other teams at his present salary and with no compensation to the releasing team.

Walk-Off
to pick up the football from where it ended at the finish of a play and move it either forward, for penalties against the defense, or backward, for penalties against the offense, the appropriate number of yards for the specific penalty called.

Walk-On
a college player not recruited to play football or granted a football scholarship, but nonetheless makes the team.

Walk-Through
a rehearsal of the motions players will go through during the various plays expected to be run in a game.

Warm The Bench
to remain on the sidelines and not get to play in a game.

Weak Side
the side of the offense opposite the side on which the tight end lines up.

Wedge
a formation used by some of the blockers of a receiving team on a kickoff in which the players move forward in front of the returner while standing close together.

West Coast Offense
a type of offense that relies on timing passing plays that are generally short and underneath.

Wide Receiver
a receiver who lines up outside the offensive tackle. An offensive configuration can use from one to three wide receivers, who are responsible for catching the majority of passes on offense.

Wideout
a wide receiver.

Wild Card
a team that does not win its division, but has a good enough win/loss record to win a spot in the post-season playoffs. Three wild card teams from each conference (regardless of division) earn the right to compete in post-season play.

Wingback
a running back who lines up close behind, but just to the outside, of a tight end.

Wishbone
offensive formation with all four backfield men, the quarterback, fullback, and two half-backs, lined up resembling a chicken wish-bone.

Work The Clock
to use the clock to one's advantage, such as taking timeouts, throwing the ball out of bounds or using the hurry-up offense.

Wounded Duck
a football that hasn't been thrown with the right passing motion, making it wobble and possibly go end over end, not traveling very far.

X Pole
sideline marker that shows where a team's ball possession originated and is moved only when ball change possession. It is tended by an assistant official.

Y Pitch
the quarterback takes the snap and fakes a handoff to the first back who is heading laterally to the other back, who has begun to move to directly toward the line of scrimmage. He then he tosses (pitches) the ball toward the inside. Pitch plays can be designed to go in either direction.

Yard Lines
marks along the length of the field to keep track of each team's progress on the field.

Yardage Chain
a 10-yard length of chain connected by a five-foot-high rod at the other end. The chain is used to determine if the offensive team has gained the 10 yards necessary for a first down. It is tended along the sidelines by two assistant officials (rodmen).

Zebras
nickname given to the officials because of the black and white striped shirts they wear.

Zeroing In On A Receiver
the quarterback is focused on throwing to one specific receiver. The quarterback watches the receiver while he's running his route and then releases the ball when he's open.

Zone Block

each lineman protects a specific area or zone. Even if the defensive player leaves this area, the blocker must stay in his zone because the play or ball may be coming in that direction and the quarterback wants to see that area uncluttered. Blocking in a zone is generally designed to key on a specific defensive player who is disrupting the offensive game plan.

Zone Coverage

coverage in which the secondary and linebackers drop away from the line of scrimmage into specific areas when defending a pass play. Zone means that the players are defending areas, not specific offensive players. (also zone defense)

Zone Defense

a type of defensive strategy that required the defenders to cover specific areas of the field rather than specific players.

Chapter 15
Medical/Injury Glossary

AC Joint
Acromioclavicular joint; joint of the shoulder where acromion process of the scapula and the distal end of the clavicle meet; most shoulder separations occur at this point.

Abduct
Movement of any extremity away from the midline of the body. This action is achieved by an abductor muscle.

Abrasion
Any injury which rubs off the surface of the skin.

Abscess
An infection which produces pus; can be the result of a blister, callus, penetrating wound or laceration.

Adduct
Movement of an extremity toward the midline of the body. This action is achieved by an adductor muscle.

Achilles' Tendon
The tendon at the back of the heel.

Adhesion
Abnormal adherence of collagen fibers to surrounding structures during immobilization following trauma or as a complication of surgery which restricts normal elasticity of the structures involved.

Aerobic
Exercise in which energy needed is supplied by oxygen inspired and is required for sustained periods of vigorous exercise with a continually high pulse rate.

Anabolic Steroids
Steroids that promote tissue growth by creating protein in an attempt to enhance muscle growth. The main anabolic steroid is testosterone (male sex hormone).

Anaerobic
Exercise without use of oxygen as an energy source; short bursts of vigorous exercises.

Anaphylactic Shock
Shock that is caused by an allergic reaction.

Anterior Compartment Syndrome
Condition in which swelling within the anterior compartment of the lower leg jeopardizes the viability of muscles, nerves and arteries that serve the foot. In severe cases, emergency surgery is necessary to relieve the swelling and pressure.

Anterior Cruciate Ligament (ACL)
A primary stabilizing ligament within the center of the knee joint that prevents hyperextension and excessive rotation of the joint. A complete tear of the ACL necessitating reconstruction could require up to 12 months of rehabilitation.

Anterior Talofibular Ligament
A ligament of the ankle that connects the fibula (lateral ankle bone) to the talus. This ligament is oft times subject to sprain.

Anti-Inflammatory
Any agent which prevents inflammation, such as aspirin or ibuprofen.

Anteriogram
A film demonstrating arteries after injection of a dye.

Arthrogram
X-ray technique for joints using air and/or dye injected into the affected area; useful in diagnosing meniscus tears of the knee and rotator cuff tears of the shoulder.

Arthroscope
An instrument used to visualize the interior of a joint cavity.

Arthroscopy
A surgical examination of the internal structures of a joint by means for viewing through an arthroscope. An arthroscopic procedure can be used to remove or repair damaged tissue or as a diagnostic procedure in order to inspect the extent of any damage or confirm a diagnosis.

Articular Cartilage
Cartilage lining the opposing surfaces of bones.

Aspiration
The withdrawal of fluid from a body cavity by means of a suction or siphonage apparatus, such as a syringe.

Atrophy
To shrivel or shrink from disuse, as in muscular atrophy.

Avascular Necrosis
Death of a part due to lack of circulation.

Avulsion
The tearing away, forcibly, of a part or structure.

Baker's Cyst
Localized swelling of a bursa sac in the posterior knee as a result of fluid that has escaped from the knee capsule. A Baker's cyst indicates that there is a trauma inside the knee joint that leads to excessive fluid production.

Bone Scan
An imaging procedure in which a radioactive-labeled substance is injected into the body to determine the status of a bony injury. If the radioactive substance is taken up the bone at the injury site, the injury will show as a "hot spot" on the scan image. The bone scan is particularly useful in the diagnosis of stress fractures.

Brachial Plexus
Network of nerves originating from the cervical vertebrae and running down to the shoulder, arm, hand, and fingers.

Bruise
A discoloration of the skin due to an extravasation of blood into the underlying tissues.

Burner
Common term for brachial plexus trauma in the neck. Usually results in burning or tingling sensation into the shoulder or arm when the neck is forced beyond the normal range of motion.

Bursa
A fluid-filled sac that is located in areas where friction is likely to occur, then minimizes the friction; for example between a tendon and bone. Capsule - An enclosing structure which surrounds the joint and contains ligaments which stabilize that joint.

Cartilage
Smooth, slippery substance preventing two ends of bones from rubbing together and grating.

CAT Scan
Use of a computer to produce a cross sectional view of the anatomical part being investigated from X-ray data.

Cellulitis
Inflammation of cellular or connective tissue.

Cervical Vertebrae
Group of seven vertebrae located in the neck.

Charley Horse
A contusion or bruise to any muscle resulting in intramuscular bleeding. No other injury should be called a charley horse.

Chondral Fracture
Fracture to the chondral (cartilaginous) surfaces of bone.

Chondromalacia
A roughening of the cartilage surface. Best known for the roughening of the underside of the kneecap.

Clavical
The collar bone; the bone connecting the breastbone with the shoulder blade.

Colles' Fracture
A fracture of the distal end of the radium with the lower end being displaced backward.

Concentric Muscle Contraction
A shortening of the muscle as it develops tension and contracts to move a resistance.

Concussion
Jarring injury of the brain resulting in dysfunction. It can be graded as mild, moderate or severe depending on loss of consciousness, amnesia and loss of equilibrium.

Contusion
An injury to a muscle and tissues caused by a blow from a blunt object.

Cortical Steroids
Used to suppress joint inflammation.

Cortisone
An anti- inflammatory medication.

Costochondral
Cartilage that separates the bones within the rib cage.

Cryokinetics
Treatment with cold and movement.

Cryotherapy
A treatment with the use of cold.

Cyst
Abnormal sac containing liquid or semi-solid matter.

Debridement
The removal of foreign material and dead or damaged tissue.

Degenerative Joint Disease
Changes in the joint surfaces as a result of repetitive trauma.

Deltoid Ligament
Ligament that connects the tibia to bones of the medial aspect of the foot and is primarily responsible for stability of the ankle on the medial side. Is sprained less frequently than other ankle ligaments.

Deltoid Muscle
Muscles at top of the arm, just below the shoulder, responsible for shoulder motions to the front, side and back.

Disc, Intervertebral
A flat, rounded plate between each vertebrae of the spine. The disc consists of a thick fiber ring which surrounds a soft gel-like interior. It functions as a cushion and shock absorber for the spinal column.

Dislocation
Complete displacement of joint surfaces.

Eccentric Muscle Contraction
An overall lengthening of the muscle as it develops tension and contracts to control motion performed by an outside force; oft times referred to a "negative" contraction in weight training.

Eccymosis
Bleeding into the surface tissue below the skin, resulting in a "black and blue" effect.

Edema
Accumulation of fluid in organs and tissues of the body; swelling.

Effusion
Accumulation of fluid, in various spaces in the body, or the knee itself. Commonly, the knee has an effusion after an injury.

Electrical Galvanic Stimulation (EGS)
An electrical therapeutic modality that sends a current to the body at select voltages and frequencies in order to stimulate pain receptors, disperse edema, or neutralize muscle spasms among other functional applications.

Electromyogram (EMG)
Test to determine nerve function.

Epicondylitis
Inflammation in the elbow due to overuse.

Ethyl Chloride
"Cold spray," a chemical coolant sprayed onto an injury site to produce a local, mild anesthesia.

Fascia
A connective tissue sheath consisting of fibrous tissue and fat which unites the skin to the underlying tissues.

Fat Percentage
The amount of body weight that is adipose, fat tissue. Fat percentages can be calculated by underwater weighing, measuring select skinfold thickness, or by analyzing electrical impedance.

Femur
Thigh bone; longest bone in the body.

Fibula
Smaller of the two bones in the lower leg; runs from knee to the ankle along the outside of the lower leg.

Flexibility
The ability of muscle to relax and yield to stretch forces.

Flexibility Exercise
General term used to describe exercise performed by a player to passively or actively elongate soft tissue without the assistance of an athletic trainer.

Fracture
Breach in continuity of a bone. Types of fractures include simple, compound, comminuted, greenstick, incomplete, impacted, longitudinal, oblique, stress, or transverse.

Gamekeeper's Thumb
Tear of the ulnar collateral ligament of the metacar-pophalangeal joint of the thumb.

Glycogen
Form in which foods are stored in the body as energy.

Grade One Injury
A mild injury in which ligament, tendon, or other musculoskeletal tissue may have been stretched or contused, but not torn or otherwise disrupted.

Grade Two Injury
A moderate injury when musculoskeletal tissue has been partially, but not totally, torn which causes appreciable limitation in function of the injured tissue.

Grade Three Injury
A severe injury in which tissue has been significantly, and in some cases totally, torn or otherwise disrupted causing a virtual total loss of function.

Hamstring
Category of muscle that runs from the buttocks to the knee along the back of the thigh. It functions to flex the knee, and is oft times injured as a result of improper conditioning or lack of muscle flexibility.

Heat Cramps
Painful muscle spasms of the arms or legs caused by excessive body heat and depletion of fluids and electrolytes.

Heat Exhaustion
Mild form of shock due to dehydration because of excessive sweating when exposed to heat and humidity.

Heat Stroke
Condition of rapidly rising internal body temperature that overwhelms the body's mechanisms for release of heat and could result in death if not cared for appropriately.

Heel Cup
Orthotic device that is inserted into the shoe and worn under the heel to give support to the Achilles tendon and help absorb impacts at the heel.

Hematoma
Tumor-like mass produced by an accumulation of coagulated blood in a cavity.

Hip Pointer
Contusion to the iliac crest.

Hot Pack
Chemical pack that rests in water, approximately 160 degrees, and retains its heat for 15-20 minutes when placed in a towel for general therapeutic application.

Humerus
Bone of the upper arm that runs from the shoulder to the elbow.

Hydrotherapy
Treatment using water.

Hyperextension
Extreme extension of a limb or body part.

Illiotibial Band
A thick, wide fascial layer that runs from the iliac crest to the knee joint and is occasionally inflamed as a result of excessive running.

Impingment Syndrome
Pinching together of the supraspinatus muscle and other soft tissue inthe shoulder, which is common in throwing.

Inflammation
The body's natural response to injury in which the injury site might display various degrees of pain, sweating, heat, redness, and/or loss of function.

Internal Rotation
Rotation of a joint or extremity medially, to the inside.

Lateral Collateral Ligament (LCL)
Ligamament of knee attaching lateral femoral condyle to the fibula head. It provides lateral stability to the knee.

Lesion
Wound, injury or tumor.

Ligament
Band of fibrous tissue that connects bone to bone or bone to cartilage and supports and strengthens joints.

Lumbar Vertebrae
Five vertebrae of the lower back that articulate with the sacrum to form the lumbosacral joint.

Malleolus
Rounded projection on either side of the ankle joint.

Magnetic Resonance Imaging (MRI)
Imaging procedure in which a radio frequency pulse causes certain electrical elements of the injured tissue to react to this pulse and through this process a computer display and permanent film establish a visual image. MRI does not require radiation and is very useful in the diagnosis of soft tissue, disc, and meniscus injuries.

Medial Collateral Ligament (MCL)
Ligament of knee attaching to medial femoral condyle and to medial tibia. It provides medial stability to the knee.

Medial Retinaculum
The band of connective tissue that attaches to the medial structures of the knee joint, including the patella and patellar tendon.

Meniscectomy
An intra-articular surgical procedure of the knee by which all or part of the damaged meniscus is removed.

Meniscus
Crescent shaped cartilage, usually pertaining to the knee joint; also known as "cartilage." There are two menisci in the knee, medial and lateral. These work to absorb weight within the knee and provide stability.

Metacarpals
Five long bones of the hand, running from the wrist to the fingers.

Metatarsals
Five long bones of the foot, running from the ankle to the toes.

Myosistis
Inflammation of a muscle.

Necrotic
Relating to death of a portion of tissue.

Neoprene
Lightweight rubber used in joint and muscle sleeves designed to provide support and/or insulation and heat retention to the area.

Neuritis
Inflammation of a nerve.

Orthotic
Any device applied to or around the body in the care of physical impairment or disability, commonly used to control foot mechanics.

Parasthesia
Sensation of numbness or tingling, indicating nerve irritation.

Patella
The kneecap. The patella functions to protect the distal end of the femur as well as increase the mechanical advantage and force generating capacities of the quadriceps muscle group.

Patella Tendinitis
Inflammation of the patella ligament; also known as "jumpers knee."

Patellofemoral Joint
Articulation of the kneecap and femur. Inflammation of this joint can occur through: 1) acute injury to the patella, 2) overuse from excessive running particularly if there is an associated knee weakness, 3) chronic wear and tear of the knee, 4) as a result of poor foot mechanics. Patellofemoral irritation can lead to chondromalancia, which in its most chronic condition, could require surgery.

Peroneal Muscles
Group of muscles of the lateral lower leg that are responsible for everting the knee. Tendons of these three muscles are vital to the stability of the ankle and foot.

Phalanx
Any bone of the fingers or toes; plural is phalanges.

Phlebitis
Inflammation of a vein.

Plantar
Pertaining to the sole of the foot.

Plantar Fascia
The tight band of muscle beneath the arch of the foot.

Plica
Fold of tissue in the joint capsule and a common result of knee injury.

Posterior Cruciate Ligament (PCL)
A primary stabilizing ligament of the knee that provides significant stability and prevents displacement of the tibia backward within the knee joint. A complete tear of this ligament necessitating reconstruction could require up to 12 months of rehabilitation.

Quadricep Muscles "Quads"
A group of four muscles of the front thigh that run from the hip and form a common tendon at the patella; they are responsible for knee extension.

Radiography
Taking of X-rays.

Radius
Forearm bone on the thumb side.

Reconstruction
Surgical rebuilding of a joint using natural, artificial or transplanted materials.

Referred Pain
Pain felt in an undamaged area of body away from the actual injury.

Retraction
The moving of tissue to expose a part or structure of the body.

Rotator Cuff
Comprised of four muscles in the shoulder area that can be irritated by overuse. The muscles are the supraspinatus (most commonly injured), infra-spinatus, teres minor, and subscapularis.

Rotator Cuff Impingement Syndrome
A microtrauma or overuse injury caused by stress, and the four stages are: 1) Tendentious with temporary thickening of the bursa and rotator cuff; 2) Fiber dissociation in the tendon with permanent thickening of the bursa and scar formation; 3) A partial rotator cuff tear of less than 1 cm.; and 4) A complete tear of 1 cm. or more.

Sacrum
Group of five fused vertebrae located just below the lumbar vertebrae of the low back.

Scapula
Shoulder blade.

Sciatica
Irritation of the sciatic nerve resulting in pain or tingling running down the inside of the leg.

Sciatic Nerve
Major nerve that carries impulses for muscular action and sensations between the low back and thigh and lower leg; it is the longest nerve in the body.

Shin Splint
A catch-all syndrome describing pain in the shin that is not a fracture or tumor and cannot be defined otherwise.

Sorbothane
An energy absorbing polyurethane utilized in some foot orthotics to absorb shock forces of the foot.

Spasm (Theory)
Muscle soreness induced by exercise; is the result of reduced muscle blood flow, which results in pain.

Spleen
Large, solid organ responsible for the normal production and destruction of blood cells.

Spondylitis
Inflammation of one or more vertebrae.

Spondylolisthesis
Forward displacement of one vertebrae over another below it due to a developmental defect in the vertebrae.

Spondylosis
Abnormal vertebral fixation or immobility.

Sprain
Injury resulting from a stretch or twist of the joint and causes various degrees of stretch or tear of a ligament or other soft tissue at the joint.

Sternum
The breast bone.

Steroids
Any one of a large number of hormone-like substances. See Anabolic steroids and cortical steroids.

Stinger
Common term for plexus trauma in the neck.

Strain
Injury resulting from a pull or torsion to the muscle or tendon that causes various degrees of stretch or tear to the muscle or tendon tissue.

Stress Fracture
A hair-line type of break in a bone caused by overuse.

Stress X-ray
A continual X-ray taken when a portion of the body is stressed to its maximum in order to determine joint stability. This is a test utilized in some ankle injuries.

Stretching
Any therapeutic maneuver designed to elongate shortened soft tissue structures and thereby increase flexibility.

Subluxation
Partial dislocation of a joint. The term usually implies that the joint can return to its normal position without formal reduction.

Talus
The ankle bone that articulates with the tibia and fibula to form the ankle joint.

Target Heart Rate
A pre-determined pulse to be obtained during exercise when circulation is working at full efficient capacities.

Tarsals
Group of seven bones of the foot consisting of the calnavicular, talus, cuboid and three cuneiform bones.

Temporomandibular Joint (TMJ)
The articulation of the jaw and skull; considered by some to be vital in resolution of injuries throughout the body.

Tendinitis
Inflammation of the tendon and/or tendon sheath, caused by chronic overuse or sudden injury.

Tendon
Tissue that connects muscle to bone.

Tennis Elbow
General term for lateral elbow pain.

Thoracic
Group of twelve vertebrae located in the thorax and articulate with the twelve ribs.
Thoracic Outlet Compression Syndrome
A neuro-vascular disorder of the upper extremity common in throwing.

Tibia
Larger of the two bones of the lower leg and is the weight-bearing bone of the shin.

Tomograph
A special type of X-ray apparatus that demonstrates an organ or tissue at a particular depth.

Trachea
The windpipe.

Trascutaneous Electrical Nerve Stimulator (TENS)
An electrical modality that sends a mild current through pads at the injury site which stimulates the brain to release the natural analgesic, endorphin.

Transverse Process
Small lateral projection off the right side and left side of each vertebrae that functions as an attachment site for muscles and ligaments of the spine.

Trapezius
Flat triangular muscle covering the posterior surface of the neck and shoulder.

Triceps
Muscle of the back of the upper arm, primarily responsible for extending the elbow.

Turf Toe
Sprain of the metatarsophalangeal (MTP) joint of the great toe.

Ulna
Forearm bone that runs from the tip of the elbow to the little finger side of the wrist.

Ulnar Nerve
Nerve in elbow commonly irritated from excessive throwing.

Ultrasound
An electrical modality that transmits a sound wave through an applicator into the skin to the soft tissue in order to heat the local area for relaxing the injured tissue and/or disperse edema.

Valgus
Angulation outward and away from the midline of the body.

Varus
Angulation inward and toward the midline of the body.

Vasoconstriction
Decrease of local blood flow.

Vasodilation
Increase of local blood flow.

"Wind Knocked Out"
Syndrome describing a contraction of the abdominal nerve truck, the solar plexus, as a result of an abdominal contusion.

Wrist
The junction between the two forearm bones (radius and ulna) and the eight wrist bones (trapezium, trapezoid, capitate, hamate, pisiform, triquetral, lunate and scaphoid).

Zygoma
The cheekbone.

Internet football resources

Pro Football Resource

CBS Sportsline	www.cbssportsline.com
CNN/SI	www.cnnsi.com/football
ESPN	www.espn.go.com
Excite Football	www.sports.excite.com/nfl
Fox Sports	www.foxsports.com
Monday Night Football	www.abcmnf.com
MSNBC	www.msnbc.com
Nando Football	www.sportserver.com
NFL.com	www.nfl.com
Rivals.com	www.rivals.com
Sporting News	www.sportingnews.com
SuperBowl.com	www.SuperBowl.com
USA Today	www.usatoday.com/sports
Washington Post	www.washingtonpost.com
Yahoo Football	www.sports.yahoo.com
Inside Corner	www.insidecorner.com

Fantasy Football Information

Fanball.com	www.fanball.com
Krause Fantasy Sports	www.krause.com
RotoNews	www.rotonews.com
Sporting News	www.sportingnews.com/fantasy
STATS, Inc.	www.stats.com
theHuddle.com	www.thehuddle.com
USA Today Fantasy Sports	www.usatoday.com/sports/fantasy
Sandbox Fantasy Football	www.sandbox.net
Small World Football	www.fantasy.football.smallworld.com
Sporting News	www.games.sportingnews.com
Yahoo Fantasy Football	www.football.fantasysports.yahoo.com

The official web sites of each NFL teams

Arizona Cardinals	www.azcardinals.com/
Atlanta Falcons	www.atlantafalcons.com/
Baltimore Ravens	www.baltimoreravens.com/
Buffalo Bills	www.buffalobills.com/
Carolina Panthers	www.panthers.com/
Chicago Bears	www.chicagobears.com/
Cincinnati Bengals	www.bengals.com/
Cleveland Browns	www.clevelandbrowns.com/
Dallas Cowboys	www.dallascowboys.com
Denver Broncos	www.denverbroncos.com/
Detroit Lions	www.detroitlions.com/
Green Bay Packers	www.packers.com/
Houston Texans	www.houstontexans.com
Indianapolis Colts	www.colts.com

Jacksonville Jaguars	www.jaguars.com/
Kansas City Chiefs	www.kcchiefs.com/
Miami Dolphins	www.dolphinsendzone.com/
Minnesota Vikings	www.vikings.com/
New England Patriots	www.patriots.com
New Orleans Saints	www.neworleanssaints.com/
New York Giants	www.giants.com/
New York Jets	www.newyorkjets.com/
Oakland Raiders	www.raiders.com/
Philadelphia Eagles	www.philadelphiaeagles.com
Pittsburgh Steelers	www.steelershome.com/
San Diego Chargers	www.chargers.com/
San Francisco 49ers	www.sf49ers.com/
Seattle Seahawks	www.seahawks.com/
St. Louis Rams	www.stlouisrams.com/
Tampa Bay Buccaneers	www.buccaneers.com/
Tennessee Titans	www.titansonline.com/
Washington Redskins	www.redskins.com/
NFL PlayersAthletesDirect	www.athetesdirect.com
NFL.com Players	www.nfl.com/players
NFL Players	www.sportingnews.com/nfl/players
Sporting News Player Bios	www.sportsline.com/u/football/nfl/players
CBS Sportsline Player Profiles	www.cbs.sportsline.com
Players Inc.	www.nflplayers.com
The Sporting News	www.sportingnews.com
Yahoo! Sports	www.sports.yahoo.com
NFL.COM	www.nfl.com
Chicks on Football	www.chicksonfootball.com
Football Insight	www.footballinsight.com
Girls Talk Sports	www.girlstalksports.com
Gridiron Grumblings	www.gridirongrumblings.com
Love Football	www.lovefootball.com
Motorola/NFL	www.motorola.com
My Pigskin	www.mypigskin.com
National Spectators Association	www.nsa.com
NFL Alumni Headquarters	www.nflalumni.org
NFL Digest	www.nfldigest.rivals.com
The NFL Referee Web Site	www.members.tripod.com/refereestats
NFLfans	www.nflfans.rivals.com
NFLTalk.com	www.nfltalk.com
Playcenter.com	www.playcenter.com
Playfootball.com	www.playfootball.com
Pro Football Hall of Fame	www.profootballhof.com
Pro Football Insider	www.nfl.profootballinsider.net
Professional Football Researchers Association	www.geocities.com/Colosseum/sideline/5960
Saks Sports	www.saks-sports.com
Sports Central - NFL	www.sports-central.org
The Sports Network	www.sportsnetwork.com
TwoMinuteWarning.com	www.twominutewarning.com
Wide Right	www.wideright.com

Index

Notes

....
....
....
....
....
....
....
....
....
....
....
....
....
....
....
....
....
....
....
....
....
....
....
....
....
....
....
....

Notes

....
....
....
....
....
....
....
....
....
....
....
....
....
....
....
....
....
....
....
....
....
....
....
....
....
....
....
....
....
....

Notes

....
....
....
....
....
....
....
....
....
....
....
....
....
....
....
....
....
....
....
....
....
....
....
....
....
....
....
....
....
....
....

Notes

....

....

....

....

....

....

....

....

....

....

....

....

....

....

....

....

....

....

....

....

....

....

....

....

....

....

....

....

....

....